John Donne

SELECT POEMS

John Donne

SELECT POEMS

[Edited with Complete Introduction, Biography, Author's Background, Complete Text, Study Questions, Select Criticism and Bibliography]

Mansi Sachdeva
B.A. English (Hons), Delhi University;
M.A., M. Phil. (English), IGNOU

ANMOL PUBLICATIONS PVT. LTD.
NEW DELHI - 110 002 (INDIA)

ANMOL PUBLICATIONS PVT. LTD.

H.O.: 4374/4B, Ansari Road, Darya Ganj,
New Delhi-110 002 (India)
Ph.: 23278000, 23261597

B.O.: No. 1015, Ist Main Road, BSK IIIrd Stage
IIIrd Phase, IIIrd Block
Bangalore - 560 085 (India)
Visit us at: www.anmolpublications.com

Select Poems

First Published, 2009

PRINTED IN INDIA

Printed at Mehra Offset Press, Delhi.

Contents

Preface

John Donne (1572 - 1631) was one of the major representatives of metaphysical poetry. He was also a Jacobean poet and preacher. Most of his works were known for realistic as well as sensual style. His major works mainly comprise of sonnets, love poetry, religious poems, Latin translations, epigrams, elegies, sermons, satires and songs.

Donne has experienced persecution, as he was from Roman Catholic family. Later, he converted to Anglican Church. John Donne was highly educated and had great poetic talent, yet he spent major part of his life in poverty. In the year 1615, he was appointed as an Anglican priest and later in 1621 he became Dean of St. Paul's. John Donne has always been regarded as the chief representative of metaphysical conceit. A few popular works of John Donne are Death Be Not Proud, Ecstasy, Love's Usury, Song: Go and Catch a Falling Star and To His Mistress Going To Bed.

Author

Chapter 1

Biography: John Donne

The life of Donne—especially that part of it which concerns the student of his poetry—as well as the canon and text of his poems presents problems which are only in process of solutionsome of them probably never will be solved. A full but concise statement of all that we know regarding his *Lehr-* and *Wander-jahre* is necessary both for the sake of what it contains, and because of the clearness with which it defines the questions that await further investigation.

John Donne (the name was pronounced so as to rime with "done" and was frequently spelt "Dun" or "Dunne") was the eldest son of a London ironmonger—probably of Welsh extraction—and of Elizabeth, the third (not, as hitherto believed, the only1) daughter of John Heywood, the famous dramatist of queen Mary's reign, by his wife Elizabeth Rastell. This Elizabeth was herself the daughter of John Rastell and Elizabeth the sister of Sir Thomas More. Donne thus, on his mother's side at any rate, came of a line of distinguished and devoted adherents of the old faith. He himself was bred in that faith, and, despite his conversion and later polemical writing and preaching, his most intimate religious poems indicate very clearly that he never ceased to feel the influence of his Catholic upbringing.

According to Walton and Anthony à Wood, Donne proceeded to Oxford in 1584 at the early age of eleven. Here, he formed a friendship with Henry Wotton, a friendship which counted for something in Donne's later life. From Oxford, he passed to Cambridge, where, Walton tells us, he studied diligently till the age of seventeen, but, neither here nor at

Oxford, endeavored after a degree on account of the "averseness of his friends to some parts of the oath that is always tendered at those times." Nevertheless, in 1610 he was entered in the Oxford registers as already an M.A. of Cambridge. Of these college years, no contemporary documentary evidence is extant.

Our first scrap of such evidence dates from 1592, the year of the first unmistakable reference to Shakespeare as a London actor and playwright. On the 6th of May in that year, Donne was entered at Lincoln's inn, having been already, the document testifies, admitted at Thavies's inn. Of his life between that year and his marriage in 1601, we have very few particulars, but these appear to indicate a life spent in England; a life similar to that led by many young members of the inns of court as Donne describes them, Of study and play made strange hermaphrodites; a life, too, of gradually broadening activity, a life, too, of gradually broadening activity, which led him to the doorway of a public and political career.

In Donne's case, both the study and the play of these years were more than ordinarily intense. The record of the latter is his songs and elegies and earliest satires, the greater number of which were written, Donne told Johnson, before his twenty-fifth year. That he did not neglect law entirely for poetry, we know from his own statement, and this is corroborated by the poems themselves, in which legal metaphors abound. But the years 1593 and 1594 were also given to a serious and careful survey "of the body of divinity as it was then controverted betwixt the Reformed and the Roman Church." "About his twentieth year," Walton says, that is, apparently, in his twenty-first, he showed, to the then dean of Gloucester, all the works of Bellarmine, "marked with many weighty observations under his own hand." Bellarmine's *Disputationes,* indeed, were not published until 1593, and Rudde, who is the dean in question, ceased to hold that office in 1594, which gives but a short time for the study of such an important issue.

But it is quite possible that Bellarmine's work, in which Donne found the best defence of the Roman cause, may have fallen into his hands at the end, not (as Walton implies) at the beginning, of a course of theological and controversial reading. To a mind that worked with the rapidity of Donne's, the analysis and digestion of an elaborate argument would not prove a lengthy task. Nor was his active adherence to the Anglican church precipitate. All that we can say with confidence is that when he entered the service of Sir Thomas Egerton, in 1597, he cannot have been a professed Romanist, and, in 1601, he disclaimed indignantly "love of a corrupt religion." Donne's first approach to a public career was made by service as a volunteer in two combined military and naval expeditions. In 1595, Henry Wotton returned from a prolonged residence in Germany and Italy, to become at once an adherent of Essex, whom he had already served by his correspondence while abroad.

The letters in verse and prose which passed between Donne and Wotton during the next few years (some of them yet unpublished) show that the intimacy begun at Oxford was renewed with ardour; and it is a fair conjecture, though only a conjecture, that it was Wotton's influence which brought Donne into contact with Essex, and induced him to join his friend as a volunteer in the expedition to Cadiz in 1596, and to the Azores in 1597. One of the letters referred to was written from Plymouth when the fleet, on the second of these expeditions, was driven back by press of weather; and Donne's verse epistles to Christopher Brooke, a Cambridge friend, *The Storm* and *The Calm,* describe, with extraordinary vividness and characteristic extravagance of "wit," the experiences of his voyage. They were the first of his poems, apparently, to attract attention outside the circle of his friends. Another verse epistle, dated 20 July, 1598, to Wotton, refers to their common adventure:

Here's no more newes than vertue,

he cries, writing "At Court,"

I may as well
Tell you Cales2or St. Michaels tales for newes, as tell
That vice doth heere habitually dwell.

On the second of these expeditions, Donne and Wotton were accompanied by another young volunteer, Thomas, eldest son of Sir Thomas Egerton, lord keeper of the great seal. By this young man, who was among those knighted for gallantry after the expedition, Donne was recommended to the lord keeper towards the close of 1597, and for four years was secretary to that influential statesman. The door which was thus opened to Donne leading to preferment, it might be even to wealth and station, was abruptly closed by his own rash action, a runaway marriage with Anne More, daughter of Sir George More of Losely and niece of the lord keeper's second wife. It may be that, in Donne's complex nature, love was blended with ambitious hopes of securing his position and strengthening his claims on Sir Thomas Egerton. If so, he was grievously disappointed. At the instance of Sir George More, he and his friends Christopher and Samuel Brooke, who assisted at the marriage, were thrown into prison; and, although Donne was soon released, and his father-in-law by degrees and perforce reconciled to the marriage, the poet's hopes of preferment were blasted by his dismissal from the service of the lord keeper.

This sketch of Donne's earlier years would be incomplete without a reference to the problem of his residence abroad, a residence the effect of which on his work is palpable. Through Walton, we have Donne's own authority for the statement that he visited Italy with the intention of proceeding to the east to view the Holy Sepulchre; that, prevented from doing so, he passed over into Spain; that he "made many useful observations of those countries, their laws and manners of government, and returned perfect in their languages." Walton assigns this episode to the years following the "Islands expedition"; but this is manifestly erroneous, for, during these years, Donne was actively employed as Egerton's secretary.

It is almost equally difficult to find a place for it in the years from 1592 to 1596, when he was studying law, theology and life in London. It is noteworthy that the earliest portrait of Donne, dated 1591, shows him in military dress and bears a Spanish motto. Again, in one of the three earlier satires, which Harleian MS. 5110 assigns to 1593, Donne describes his library as already lined with, Giddie fantastique poets of each land, and, long afterwards, he declared that it contained more Spanish authors than of any other nation, "and that in any profession from the mistress of my youth, Poetry, to the wife of mine age, Divinity." The books in a man's library would not, to-day, be a safe index to his travels, but, in the sixteenth and seventeenth centuries, it was not usual for a young man to have a considerable collection of foreign books unless, like Drummond and Milton, he had himself brought them home.

It is difficult to avoid the conclusion that the time which Donne spent abroad must have been in the last years of his earlier education, when he was still a Catholic and under Catholic direction. If this were so, it would explain his silence about the exact circumstances of a voyage probably undertaken without the permission of the government, and, possibly, with the intention on the part of his guardians that he should enter a seminary, despite the law of 1585, or take service under a foreign ruler.3With more light on this point, we might be able to see in the singularly emancipated moral tone of Donne's mind and its complete openness on religious questions during the early years in London something of a reaction in his nature against a bent which others would have imposed upon it. Lastly, an early date fits best the evidence in the poems of foreign influence, which is not to be found specially in Donne's "wit," but in the spirit of Italian literature and life reflected in the frank sensuality of some, the virulent satire of others, of his elegies and songs. The spirit of the renascence in Latin countries, and a wide acquaintance with Spanish casuists and other religious writers, are the most palpable indications of foreign influence in Donne's work. His direct indebtedness to any particular poet, Italian or Spanish, has not been established. Of all Elizabethan poets, he is, for good or evil, the most independent.

From 1601 to 1615, Donne's life was one of dependence on, and humiliating adulation of, actual or possible patrons. He lived at Pyrford on the charity of his wife's cousin Francis Wooley; at Mitcham or in the Strand, on his wife's allowance from her father; at the town house of Sir Robert Drury, whose patronage he had gained by writing on the death of Elizabeth

Drury, a girl of sixteen whom he had never seen, the most elaborate and exalted of his *Funerall Elegies*. He twice went abroad, on the second occasion accompanying Sir Robert Drury to France and Spa. He assisted Thomas Morton, afterwards dean of Gloucester and bishop of Durham, in his controversies with Roman Catholics, for, though by no means yet a devoted adherent of the Anglican church, he heartily detested the Jesuits.

He wrote courtly letters in verse and prose to the countess of Bedford and other great ladies, or elegies on the death of their friends and relatives. He found one patron in the person of lord Hay, later earl of Doncaster, and he courted another in the king's favourite, Robert Carr, earl of Somerset, for whose marriage with the divorced countess of Essex he wrote a splendid epithalamium. Of his writings of this period, some are in the brilliant, but often coarse, satiric vein of his earlier satires and satiric elegies; one, *BIA[char]ANATO[char]*, is an erudite, subtle and strangely mooded excursus into the field of casuistry; and one, *Pseudo-Martyr*, published in 1610, is a more restrained and official contribution to the controversies of the day, a defence of the oath of allegiance, Donne's first public appearance on the Anglican side, in which, however, he does not wander far from the single point at issue, and writes, not to convert Catholics, but to persuade them that they may take the oath.

Such were Donne's "steps to the altar." As early as 1607, Morton, on being appointed dean of Gloucester, had urged upon his collaborator the advisability of taking orders. But Donne did not feel that the author of the popular and widely circulated *Satyres* and *Elegies*, the *Paradoxes* and *Problems* and *The Progresse of the Soule*, could become a "priest to the temple" without some scandal to the friends and admirers of the brilliant and irregular "Jack Donne," not yet quite buried in the sage and serious husband and father, the controversialist and the courtly friend of Mrs. Herbert and lady Bedford. *Ignatius his Conclave* was written about this very year, the witty verses prefixed to *Coryats Crudities* in 1611, and he was yet to write the *Epithalamium* for Somerset. It is easier to respect, than to wonder at, such a decision, whether in 1607 or 1610. Moreover, it is doubtful, as Gosse has insisted, if, in his heart of hearts, Donne, by 1607 or 1610, was a convinced Anglican. As late as 1617, when he had been nearly three years in orders, he could write:

Show me, dear Christ, Thy Spouse so bright and clear.
What? Is it she who on the other shore
Goes richly painted? or who robb'd and tore
Laments and mourns in Germany and here?
Sleeps she a thousand, then peeps up one year?

This is not the language of one who is walking in the *Via Media* with the intellectually untroubled confidence of Herbert.

When Donne at length became a priest in Anglican orders, it was as one convinced that, for him, every other path to preferment was closed, not to be opened even by the influence of Somerset. The king had resolved that Donne should enter the church, and, on 25 January, 1615, he was ordained by bishop King of London. The period of privation and suitor ship was over. In 1616, he became divinity reader at Lincoln's inn, where many of his sermons were preached. In 1619 and 1620, he was in Germany as chaplain to his friend the earl of Doncaster, and preached before the unfortunate queen of Bohemia one of the noblest and most illuminating of his sermons. In 1621, king James appointed him dean of St. Paul's, where his fame as a preacher attracted large audiences and rose to its height about the beginning of Charles's reign. For a moment he fell under suspicion with the pedantic and imperious Laud. But the cloud soon passed and, had Donne lived, he would have been made a bishop.

But, often ailing, he was stricken down at his daughter's house in the late summer of 1630. The strange and characteristic monument which stands in St. Paul's was prepared by his own directions while he lay ill. Some of the most intense and striking of his hymns were written at the same time. Once, he rose from his bed to preach the sermon entitled *Death's Duel*. Six weeks later, on 31 March, 1631, he died.

However blended the motives may have been which

carried Donne into holy orders, he gave to the ministry a single-hearted and strenuous devotion. Whatever doubts may, at times, have agitated his secret thoughts, or found expression in an unpublished sonnet, they left no reflection in his sermons. He adopted and defended the doctrines of the church of England, and the policy in church and state of her rulers, in their entirety and without demur. His was a nature in which the will commanded, but was always able to enlist in the service of its final choice a swift and subtle intellect, an intense and vivid imagination and a vast store of varied erudition. And, while he made amends for his Catholic upbringing, and for a middle period of mental detachment, by the orthodoxy of his Anglicanism, the memory of the licence of his earlier life and wit was forgotten in his later asceticism and in the spiritual exaltation of the *Sermons*, the *Devotions* and the *Divine Poems*.

Chapter 2

A Brief Chronology of Donne's Life and his Works

TIMELINE

1572	Born in Bread Street, London
1576	Father dies suddenly
1583	Enters at Hart Hall, University of Oxford - He studies there for three years
1586	Spends three years at the University of Cambridge, takes no degree because he refuses to take the Oath of Supremacy
1591	Admitted to study law as a member of Thavies Inn
1593	Donne's brother Henry dies of a fever in prison, Donne begins to question his faith.
1596	Joins the naval expedition that Robert Devereux, 2nd Earl of Essex, led against Cádiz, Spain
1598	Returns to England and appointed private secretary to Sir Thomas Egerton, Lord Keeper of the Great Seal
1601	Secretly marries Lady Egerton's niece, seventeen-year-old Anne More. Her father, Sir George More has Donne thrown to Fleet Prison for some weeks
1607	*Divine Poems* published

1610	*Pseudo-Martyr* and *A Funerall Elegie* published
1611	*An Anatomy of the World* and *Ignatius his Conclave* published
1612	*Of the Progress of the Soul* published
1614	Cambridge confers the degree of Doctor of Divinity on Donne
1615	Donne reluctantly enters the ministry and is later appointed Royal Chaplain
1616	Appointed Reader in Divinity at Lincoln's Inn
1617	Anne Donne dies 15 August
1618	*Holy Sonnets* published
1618	Journeys as chaplain with Viscount Doncaster in his embassy to the German princes
1620	Returns to London
1621	Appointed Dean of Saint Paul's
1624	Appointed vicar of St Dunstan's-in-the-West
1631	Dies in London 31 March

Chapter 3

John Donne: A Metaphysical Poet

METAPHYSICAL POETRY, in the full sense of the term, is a poetry which, like that of the *Divina Commedia,* the *De Natura Rerum,* perhaps Goethe's *Faust,* has been inspired by a philosophical conception of the universe and the role assigned to the human spirit in the great drama of existence. These poems were written because a definite interpretation of the riddle, the atoms of Epicurus rushing through infinite empty space, the theology of the schoolmen as elaborated in the catechetical disquisitions of St.

Thomas, Spinoza's vision of life *sub specie aeternitatis,* beyond good and evil, laid hold on the mind and the imagination of a great poet, unified and illumined his comprehension of life, intensified and heightened his personal consciousness of joy and sorrow, of hope and fear, by broadening their significance, revealing to him in the history of his own soul a brief abstract of the drama of human destiny. 'Poetry is the first and last of all knowledge—it is as immortal as the heart of man.' Its themes are the simplest experiences of the surface of life, sorrow and joy, love and battle, the peace of the country, the bustle and stir of towns, but equally the boldest conceptions, the profoundest intuitions, the subtlest and most complex classifications and 'discourse of reason', if into these too the poet can 'carry sensation', make of them passionate experiences communicable in vivid and moving imagery, in rich and varied harmonies.

It is no such great metaphysical poetry as that of Lucretius and Dante that the present essay deals with, which this volume seeks to illustrate. Of the poets from whom it culls, Donne is familiar with the definitions and distinctions of Mediaeval Scholasticism; Cowley's bright and alert, if not profound mind, is attracted by the achievements of science and the systematic materialism of Hobbes. Donne, moreover, is metaphysical not only in virtue of his scholasticism, but by his deep reflective interest in the experiences of which his poetry is the expression, the new psychological curiosity with which he writes of love and religion. The divine poets who follow Donne have each the inherited metaphysic, if one may so call it, of the Church to which he is attached, Catholic or Anglican. But none of the poets has for his main theme a metaphysic like that of Epicurus or St. Thomas passionately apprehended and imaginatively expounded. Donne, the most thoughtful and imaginative of them all, is more aware of disintegration than of comprehensive harmony, of the clash between the older physics and metaphysics on the one hand and the new science of Copernicus and Galileo and Vesalius and Bacon on the other:

The new philosophy calls all in doubt,
The element of fire is quite put out;
The sun is lost and the earth, and no man's wit
Can well direct him where to look for it.
And freely men confess that this world's spent,
When in the planets and the firmament
They seek so many new; they see that this
Is crumbled out again to his atomies.
Have not all souls thought
For many ages that our body is wrought
Of air and fire and other elements?
And now they think of new ingredients;
And one soul thinks one, and another way
Another thinks, and 'tis an even lay.

The greatest English poet, indeed, of the century was, or believed himself to be, a philosophical or theological poet of the same order as Dante. *Paradise Lost* was written to be a justification of 'the ways of God to men', resting on a theological system as definite and almost as carefully articulated in the *De Doctrina Christiana* as that which Dante had accepted from the *Summa* of Aquinas. And the poet embodied his argument in a dramatic poem as vividly and intensely conceived, as magnificently and harmoniously set forth, as the *Divina Commedia.* But in truth Milton was no philosopher. The subtleties of theological definition and inference eluded his rationalistic, practical, though idealistic, mind. He proved nothing.

The definitely stated argument of the poem is an obvious begging of the question. What he did was to create, or give a new definiteness and sensible power to, a great myth which, through his poem, continued for a century or more to dominate the mind and imagination of pious protestants without many of them suspecting the heresies which lurked beneath the imposing and dazzling poem in which was retold the Bible story of the fall and redemption of man.

Metaphysical in this large way, Donne and his followers to Cowley are not, yet the word describes better what is the peculiar quality of their poetry than any other, e.g. fantastic, for poetry may be fantastic in so many different ways, witness Skelton and the Elizabethans, and Hood and Browning. It lays stress on the right things—the survival, one might say the recantation, of the metaphysical strain, the *concetti metafisici ed ideali* as Testi calls them in contrast to the simpler imagery of classical poetry, of mediaeval Italian poetry; the more intellectual, less verbal, character of their wit compared with the conceits of the Elizabethans; the finer psychology of which their conceits are often the expression; their learned imagery; the argumentative, subtle evolution of their lyrics; above all the peculiar blend of passion and thought, feeling and ratiocination which is their greatest achievement. Passionate thinking is always apt to become metaphysical, probing and investigating the experience from which it takes its rise. All these qualities are in the poetry of Donne, and Donne is the great master of English poetry in the seventeenth century.

The Italian influence which Wyatt and Surrey brought into English poetry at the Renaissance gave it a more serious, a more thoughtful colour. They caught, especially Wyatt in some of the finest of his sonnets and songs, that spirit of 'high seriousness' which Chaucer with all his admiration of Italian poetry had failed to apprehend. English mediaeval poetry is often gravely pious, haunted by the fear of death and the judgment, melancholy over the 'Falls of Princes'; it is never serious and thoughtful in the introspective, reflective, dignified manner which it became in Wyatt and Sackville, and our 'sage and serious' Spenser, and in the songs of the first group of Elizabethan courtly poets, Sidney and Raleigh and Dyer. One has but to recall 'My lute, awake! perform the last', 'Forget not yet the tried intent', 'My mind to me a kingdom is', and to contrast them in mind with the songs which Henry VIII and Cornish were still composing and singing when Wyatt began to write, in order to realise what Italy and the Renaissance did to deepen the strain of English lyric poetry as that had flowed under French influence from the thirteenth to the sixteenth centuries. But French influence, the influence of Ronsard and his fellows, renewed itself in the seventies, and the great body of Elizabethan song is as gay and careless and impersonal as the earlier lyric had been, though richer in colour and more varied in rhythm. Then came Donne and Jonson (the schoolman and the classical scholar, one might say, emphasizing for the moment single aspects of their work), and new qualities of spirit and form were given to lyrical poetry, and not to lyrical poetry alone.

In dealing with poets who lived and wrote before the eighteenth century we are always confronted with the difficulty of recovering the personal, the biographical element, which, if sometimes disturbing and disconcerting, is yet essential to a complete understanding of their work. Men were not different from what they are now, and if there be hardly a lyric of Goethe's or Shelley's that do not owe something to the accidents of their lives, one may feel sure it was in varying degrees the same with poets three hundred years ago. Poems are not written by influences or movements or sources, but come from the living hearts of men. Fortunately, in the case of Donne, one of the most individual of poets, it is possible to some extent to reproduce the circumstances, the inner experiences from which his intensely personal poetry flowed.

He was in the first place a Catholic. Our history text-books make so little of the English Catholics that one is apt to forget they existed and were, for themselves at any rate, not a political problem, but real and suffering individuals. 'I had my first breeding and conversation', says Donne, 'with men of a suppressed and afflicted religion, accustomed to the despite of death and hungry of an imagined martyrdom.' In these circumstances, we gather, he was carefully and religiously educated, and after some years at Oxford and Cambridge was taken or sent abroad, perhaps with a view to entering foreign service, more probably with a view to the priesthood, and visited Italy and Spain.

And then, one conjecture, a reaction took place, the rebellion of a full-blooded, highly intellectual temperament against a superimposed bent. He entered the Inns of Court in 1592, at the age of nineteen, and flung himself into the life of a student and the life of a young man about town, Jack Donne, 'not dissolute but very neat, a great visitor of ladies, a great frequenter of plays, a great writer of conceited verses'. 'Neither was it possible that a vulgar soul should dwell in such promising features.' He joined the band of reckless and raffish young men who sailed with Essex to Cadiz and the Islands. He was taken into the service of Sir Thomas Egerton. Ambition began to vie with the love of pleasure, when a hasty marriage closed a promising career, and left him bound in shallows and in miseries, to spend years in the suitor ship of the great, and to find at last, not altogether willingly, a haven in the Anglican priesthood, and reveal himself as the first great orator that Church produced.

The record of these early years is contained in Donne's satires—harsh, witty, lucid, full of a young man's scorn of fools and low callings, and a young thinker's consciousness of the problems of religion in an age of divided faiths, and of justice in a corrupt world—and in his Love Songs and Sonnets and Elegies. The satires were more generally known; the love poems the more influential in courtly and literary circles.

Donne's genius, temperament, and learning gave to his love poems certain qualities which immediately arrested attention and have given them ever since a power at once fascinating and disconcerting despite the faults of phrasing and harmony which, for a century after Dryden, obscured, and to some still outweigh, their poetic worth. The first of these is a depth and range of feeling unknown to the majority of Elizabethan sonneteers and song-writers. Over all the Elizabethan sonnets, in greater or less measure, hangs the suggestion of translation or imitation.

Watson, Sidney, Daniel, Spenser, Drayton, Lodge, all of them, with rarer or more frequent touches of individuality, are pipers of Petrarch's woes, sighing in the strain of Ronsard or more often of Desportes. Shakespeare, indeed, in his great sequence, and Drayton in at any rate one sonnet, sounded a deeper note, revealed a fuller sense of the complexities and contradictions of passionate devotion. But Donne's treatment of love is entirely unconventional except when he chooses to dally half ironically with the convention of Petrarchian adoration. His songs are the expression in unconventional, witty language of all the moods of a lover that experience and imagination have taught him to understand—sensuality aerated by a brilliant wit; fascination and scornful anger inextricably blended:

When by thy scorn, O murdress, I am dead
And that thou think'st thee free
From all solicitations from me,
Then shall my ghost come to thy bed;
the passionate joy of mutual and contented love:
All other things to their destruction draw,
Only our love hath no decay;
This no to-morrow hath nor yesterday,
Running it never runs from us away,
But truly keeps his first, last, everlasting day;

The sorrow of parting which is the shadow of such joy; the gentler pathos of temporary separation in married life:

Let not thy divining heart
Forethink me any ill,
Destiny may take thy part,
And may thy fears fulfil;

But think that we
Are but turn'd aside to sleep;
They who one another keep
Alive ne'er parted be;
the mystical heights and the mystical depths of love:
Study me then you who shall lovers be
At the next world, that is, at the next Spring:
For I am every dead thing
In whom love wrought new Alchemy.

If Donne had expressed this wide range of intense feeling as perfectly as he has done at times poignantly and startlingly; if he had given to his poems the same impression of entire artistic sincerity that Shakespeare conveys in the greater of his sonnets and Drayton once achieved; if to his many other gifts had been added a deeper and more controlling sense of beauty, he would have been, as he nearly is, the greatest of love poets. But there is a second quality of his poetry which made it the fashion of an age, but has been inimical to its general acceptance ever since, and that is its metaphysical wit. 'He affects the metaphysics', says Dryden, 'not only in his satires but in his amorous verses where nature only should reign; and perplexes the minds of the fair sex with nice speculations of philosophy when he should engage their hearts and entertain them with the softnesses of love.' 'Amorous verses', 'the fair sex', and 'the softnesses of love' are the vulgarities of a less poetic and passionate age than Donne's, but metaphysics he does affect.

But a metaphysical strand, *concetti metafisici ed ideali,* had run through the mediaeval love-poetry of which the Elizabethan sonnets are a descendant. It had attained its fullest development in the poems of Dante and his school, had been subordinated to rhetoric and subtleties of expression rather than thought in Petrarch, and had lost itself in the pseudo-metaphysical extravagances of Tebaldeo Cariteo, and Serafino. Donne was no conscious reviver of the metaphysics of Dante, but to the game of elaborating fantastic conceits and hyperboles which was the fashion throughout Europe, he brought not only a full-blooded temperament and acute mind, but a vast and growing store of the same scholastic learning, the same Catholic theology, as controlled Dante's thought, jostling already with the new learning of Copernicus and Paracelsus. The result is startling and disconcerting,—the comparison of parted lovers to the legs of a pair of compasses, the deification of his mistress by the discovery that she is only to be defined by negatives or that she can read the thoughts of his heart, a thing 'beyond an angel's art'; and a thousand other subtleties of quintessence and nothingness, the mixture of souls and the significance of numbers, to say nothing of the aerial bodies of angels, the phoenix and the mandrake's root, Alchemy and Astrology, legal contracts and *non obstantes,* 'late schoolboys and sour prentices', 'the king's real and his stamped face'. But the effect aimed at and secured is not entirely fantastic and erudite. The motive inspiring Donne's images is in part the same as that which led Shakespeare from the picturesque, natural and mythological, images of *A Midsummer-Night's Dream* and *The Merchant of Venice* to the homely but startling phrases and metaphors of *Hamlet* and *Macbeth,* the 'blanket of the dark', the fat weed

that rots itself in ease on Lethe wharf,' the rank sweat of an enseamed bed'. It is the same desire for vivid and dramatic expression. The great master at a later period of dramatic as well as erudite pulpit oratory coins in his poems many a startling, jarring, arresting phrase:

For God's sake hold your tongue and let me love:
Who ever comes to shroud me do not harm
Nor question much
That subtle wreath of hair, which crowns my arm:
I taught my silks their rustling to forbear,
Even my opprest shoes dumb and silent were.
I long to talk with some old lover's ghost
Who died before the God of love was born;
Twice or thrice had I loved thee
Before I knew thy face or name,
So in a voice, so in a shapeless flame,
Angels affect us oft and worshipped be;
And whilst our souls negotiate there

We like sepulchral statues lay;
All day the same our postures were
And we said nothing all the day.
My face and brest of haircloth, and my head
With care's harsh, sudden hoariness o'er-spread.

These vivid, simple, realistic touches are too quickly merged in learned and fantastic elaborations, and the final effect of every poem of Donne's is a bizarre and blended one; but if the greatest poetry rises clear of the bizarre, the fantastic, yet very great poetry may be bizarre if it be the expression of a strangely blended temperament, an intense emotion, a vivid imagination.

What is true of Donne's imagery is true of the other disconcerting element in his poetry, its harsh and rugged verse. It is an outcome of the same double motive, the desire to startle and the desire to approximate poetic to direct, unconventional, colloquial speech. Poetry is always a balance, sometimes a compromise, between what has to be said and the prescribed pattern to which the saying of it is adjusted. In poetry such as Spenser's, the musical flow, the melody and harmony of line and stanza, is dominant, and the meaning is adjusted to it at the not infrequent cost of diffuseness—if a delightful diffuseness—and even some weakness of phrasing logically and rhetorically considered.

In Shakespeare's tragedies the thought and feeling tend to break through the prescribed pattern till blank verse becomes almost rhythmical prose, the rapid overflow of the lines admitting hardly the semblance of pause. This is the kind of effect Donne is always aiming at, alike in his satires and lyrics, bending and cracking the metrical pattern to the rhetoric of direct and vehement utterance. The result is often, and to eighteenth-century ears attuned to the clear and defined, if limited, harmony of Waller and Dryden and Pope was, rugged and harsh. But here again, to those who have ears that care to hear, the effect is not finally inharmonious. Donne's verse has a powerful and haunting harmony of its own. For Donne is not simply, no poet could be, willing to force his accent, to strain and crack a prescribed pattern; he is striving to find a rhythm that will express the passionate fullness of his mind, the fluxes and refluxes of his moods; and the felicities of verse are as frequent and startling as those of phrasing. He is one of the first masters, perhaps *the* first, of the elaborate stanza or paragraph in which the discords of individual lines or phrases are resolved in the complex and rhetorically effective harmony of the whole group of lines:

If yet I have not all thy love,
Deare, I shall never have it all,
I cannot breathe one other sigh, to move,
Nor can entreat one other tear to fall,
And all my treasure, which should purchase thee,
Sighs, tears, and oaths, and letters I have spent.
Yet no more can be due to me,
Than at the bargain made was meant,
If then thy gift of love was partial,
That some to me, some shuld to others fall,
Deare, I shall never have thee all.
But I am none; nor will my sunne renew.
You lovers for whose sake the lesser sunne
At this time to the Goat is run
To fetch new lust and give it you,
Enjoy your summer all;
Since she enjoys her long night's festival,
Let me prepare towards her, and let me call
This hour her Vigil and her Eve, since this
Both the years and the days deep midnight is.

The wrenching of accent which Jonson complained of is not entirely due to carelessness or indifference. It has often both a rhetorical and a harmonious justification. Donne plays with rhythmical effects as with conceits and words and often in much the same way. Mr. Fletcher Melton's interesting analysis of his verse has not, I think, established his main thesis, which like so many 'research' scholars he over-emphasizes, that the whole mystery of Donne's art lies in his use of the same sound now in *arsis*, now in *thesis;* but his examples show that this is one of many devices by which Donne secures two effects, the troubling of the regular fall of the verse stresses by the intrusion of rhetorical stress on syllables which the metrical pattern leaves unstressed, and, secondly, an echoing and re-echoing of similar sounds parallel to his fondness for resemblances in thoughts and things apparently the most remote from one another. There is, that is to say, in his verse the same blend as in his diction of the colloquial and the bizarre. He writes as one who *will* say what he has to say without regard to conventions of poetic diction or smooth verse, but what he has to say is subtle and surprising, and so are the metrical effects with which it is presented. There is nothing of unconscious or merely careless harshness in such an effect as this:

Poor soul, in this thy flesh what dost thou know?
Thou know'st thyself so little that thou knowst not
How thou didst die, nor how thou wast begot.
Thou neither know'st how thou at first camest in,
Nor how thou took'st the poison of man's sin;
Nor dost thou though thou know'st that thou art so
By what way thou art made immortal know.

In Donne's pronunciation, as in southern English to-day, 'thou', 'how', 'soul', 'know', 'though', and 'so' were not far removed from each other in sound and the reiterated notes ring through the lines like a tolling bell. Mr. Melton has collected, and any careful reader may discover for himself, many similar subtleties of poetical rhetoric; for Donne is perhaps our first great master of poetic rhetoric, of poetry used, as Dryden and Pope were to use it, for effects of oratory rather than of song, and the advance which Dryden achieved was secured by subordinating to oratory the more passionate and imaginative qualities which troubled the balance and movement of Donne's packed but imaginative rhetoric.

It was not indeed in lyrical verse that Dryden followed and developed Donne, but in his eulogistic, elegiac, satirical, and epistolary verse. The progress of Dryden's eulogistic style is traceable from his earliest metaphysical extravagances through lines such as those addressed to the Duchess of York, where Waller is his model, to the verses on the death of Oldham in which a more natural and classical strain has entirely superseded his earlier extravagances and elegancies. In truth Donne's metaphysical eulogies and elegies and epistles are a hard nut to crack for his most sympathetic admirers. And yet they have undeniable qualities.

The metaphysics are developed in a more serious, a less paradoxical, strain than in some of the songs and elegies. In his letters he is an excellent, if far from a perfect, talker in verse; and the personality which they reveal is a singularly charming one, grave, loyal, melancholy, and witty. If some of the elegiac pieces are packed with tasteless and extravagant hyperboles, the *Anniversaries* (especially the second) remains, despite all its faults, one of the greatest poems on death in the language, the fullest record in our literature of the disintegrating collision in a sensitive mind of the old tradition and the new learning. Some of the invocational passages in *Of the Progresse of the Soule* are among the finest examples of his subtle and passionate thinking as well as of his most elaborate verse rhetoric.

But the most intense and personal of Donne's poems, after the love songs and elegies, are his later religious sonnets and songs; and their influence on subsequent poetry was even more obvious and potent. They are as personal and as tormented as his earlier 'love-song weeds', for his spiritual Aeneid was a troubled one. To date his conversion to Anglicanism is not easy. In his satires there is a veiled Roman tone. By 1602 he disclaims to Egerton 'all love of a corrupt religion', but in the autumn of the previous year he had been meditating a satire on Queen Elizabeth as one of the world's great heretics.

His was not a conversion but reconciliation, an acquiescence in the faith of his country, the established religion of his legal sovereign, and the act cost him some pangs. 'A convert from Popery to Protestantism,' said Dr. Jonson, 'gives up so much of what he has held as sacred as anything that he retains, there is so much laceration of mind in such a conversion, that it can hardly be sincere and lasting.' Something of that laceration of mind is discernible in Donne's religious verse:

Show me dear Christ that spouse so bright and clear.

But the conflict between the old and the reformed faiths

was not the only, nor perhaps the principal trouble for Donne's enlightened mind ready to recognize in all the Churches 'virtual beams of one sun', 'connatural pieces of one circle'. A harder fight was that between the secular, the 'man of the world' temper of his mind and the claims of a pious and ascetic calling. It was not the errors of his youth, as the good Walton supposed, which constituted the great stumbling block, though he never ignores these:

O might those sighs and tears return again
Into my breast and eyes, which I have spent,
That I might in this holy discontent
Mourn with some fruit, as I have mourned in vain.

It was rather the temperament of one who, at a time when a public career was more open to unassisted talent, might have proved an active and useful, if ambitious, civil servant, or professional man, at war with the claims of a religious life which his upbringing had taught him was incompatible with worldly ambition. George Herbert, a much more contented Anglican than Donne ever became, knew something of the same struggle before he bent his neck to the collar.

The two notes then of Donne's religious poems are the Catholic and the personal. He is the first of our Anglo-Catholic poets, and he is our first intensely personal religious poet, expressing always not the mind simply of the Christian as such, but the conflicts and longings of one troubled soul, one subtle and fantastic mind. For Donne's technique—his phrasing and conceits, the metaphysics of mediaeval Christianity, his packed verse with its bold, irregular fingering and echoing vowel sounds—remains what it had been from the outset. The echoing sounds in lines such as these cannot be quite casual:

O might those sighs and tears return again
Into my breast and eyes, which I have spent,
That I might in this holy discontent
Mourn with some fruit, as I have mourned in vain;
In mine Idolat'ry what showers of rain
Mine eyes did waste? What griefs my heart did rent?
That sufferance was my sin; now I repent
Cause I did suffer I must suffer pain.

In the remaining six lines the same sound never recurs. A metaphysical, a philosophical poet, to the degree to which even his contemporary Fulke Greville might be called such, Donne was not. The thought in his poetry is not his primary concern but the feeling. No scheme of thought, no interpretation of life became for him a complete and illuminating experience. The central theme of his poetry is ever his own intense personal moods, as a lover, a friend, an analyst of his own experiences worldly and religious. His philosophy cannot unify these experiences.

It represents the reaction of his restless and acute mind on the intense experience of the moment, a reading of it in the light now of one, now of another philosophical or theological dogma or thesis caught from his multifarious reading, developed with audacious paradox or more serious intention, as an expression, an illumination of that mood to himself and to his reader. Whether one choose to call him a metaphysical or a fantastic poet, the stress must be laid on the word 'poet'. Whether verse or prose be his medium, Donne is always a poet, a creature of feeling and imagination, seeking expression in vivid phrase and complex harmonies, whose acute and subtle intellect was the servant, if sometimes the unruly servant, of passion and imagination.

II

Donne's influence was felt in his own day by two strangely different classes of men, both attached by close ties to the Court. For the Court, the corrupt, ambitious, intriguing, dissolute but picturesque and dazzling court of the old pagan Elizabeth, the pedantic and drunken James, the dignified and melancholy and politically blinded Charles, was the centre round which all Donne's secular interests revolved. He can speak of it as bitterly and sardonically as Shakespeare in *Hamlet:*

Here's no more newes, then vertue, I may as well
Tell you Cales or St. Michael's tale for newes, as tell
That vice doth here habitually dwell.
But now 'tis incongruity to smile,

Therefore I end; and bid farewell a while,
At Court, though From Court were the better style.

He knows its corruptions as well as Milton and commends Lady Bedford as Milton might have commended Alice Egerton. All the same, to be shut out from the Court, in the city or the country, is to inhabit a desert, or sepulchre, for *there:*

The Princes favour is defused o'er all,
From which all Fortunes, Names, and Natures fall.
And all is warmth and light and good desire.

It was among the younger generation of Courtiers that Donne found the warmest admirers of his paradoxical and sensual audacities as a love-poet, as it was the divines who looked to Laud and the Court for Anglican doctrine and discipline who revered his memory, enshrined by the pious Izaak Walton, as of a divine poet and preacher. The 'metaphysicals' were all on the King's side. Even Andrew Marvell was neither Puritan nor Republican. 'Men ought to have trusted God', was his final judgement on the Rebellion, 'they ought to have trusted the King with the whole matter'. They were on the side of the King, for they were on the side of the humanities; and the Puritan rebellion, whatever the indirect constitutional results, was in itself and at the moment a fanatical upheaval, successful because it also threw up the John Zizka of his age; its triumph was the triumph of Cromwell's sword:

And for the last effect
Still keep the sword erect.
Besides the force it has to fright
The spirits of the shady night,
The same arts that did gain
A power must it maintain.

To call these poets the 'school of Donne' or 'metaphysical' poets may easily mislead if one takes either phrase in too full a sense. It is not only that they show little of Donne's subtlety of mind, immoderate thirst of human learning', but they want, what gives its interest to this subtle and fantastic misapplication of learning,—the complexity of mood, the range of personal feeling which lends such fullness of life to Donne's strange and troubled poetry. His followers, amorous and courtly, or pious and ecclesiastical, move in a more rarefied atmosphere; their poetry is much more truly 'abstract' than Donne's, the witty and fantastic elaboration of one or two common moods, of compliment, passion, devotion, penitence. It is very rarely that one can detect a deep personal note in the delightful love-songs with which the whole period abounds from Carew to Dryden. The collected work of none of them would give such an impression of a real history behind it, a history of many experiences and moods, as Donne's Songs and Sonnets and the Elegies, and, as one must still believe, the sonnets of Shakespeare record.

Like the Elizabethan sonneteers they all dress and redress the same theme in much the same manner, though the manner is not quite the Elizabethan, nor the theme. Song has superseded the sonnet, and the passion of which they sing has lost most of the Petrarchian, chivalrous strain, and become in a very definite meaning of the words, 'simple and sensuous'. And if the religious poets are rather more individual and personal, the personal note is less intense, troubled and complex than in Donne's Divine Poems; the individual is more merged in the Christian, Catholic or Anglican.

Donne and Jonson are probably in the main responsible for the unconventional purity and naturalness of their diction, for these had both 'shaken hands with' Spenserian archaism and strangeness, with the 'rhetoric' of the sonneteers and poems like *Venus and Adonis;* and their style is untouched by any foreshadowing of Miltonic diction or the jargon of a later poetic vocabulary.

The metaphysicals are the masters of the 'neutral style', of diction equally appropriate, according as it may be used, to prose and verse. If purity and naturalness of style is a grace, they deserved well of the English language, for few poets have used it with a more complete acceptance of the established tradition of diction and idiom. There are no poets till we come perhaps to Cowper, and he has not quite escaped from jargon, or Shelley, and his imagination operates in a more ethereal atmosphere, whose style is so entirely that of an English gentleman of the best type, natural, simple, occasionally careless, but never diverging into vulgar colloquialism, as after the Restoration, or into conventional, tawdry splendour, as in the century of Akenside and Erasmus Darwin. Set a poem by George Herbert beside Gray at his best, e.g.

Sweet day so cool, so calm, so bright,
The bridal of the earth and sky,
The dew shall weep thy fall to-night,
For thou must die; & c.

set that beside even a good verse from Gray, and one realizes the charm of simplicity, of perfect purity of diction:

Still is the toiling hand of Care;
The panting herds repose:
Yet harks how through the peopled air
The busy murmur glows!
The insect-youth are on the wing,
Eager to taste the honied spring,
And float amid the liquid noon:
Some lightly o'er the current skim,
Some show their gaily-gilded trim
Quick-glancing to the sun.

'The language of the age is never the language of poetry', Gray declares, and certainly some of our great poets have created for themselves a diction which was never current, but it is equally true that some of the best English poetry has been written in a style which differs from the best spoken language only as the language of feeling will naturally diverge from the language of our less exalted moods. It was in the seventeenth-century poets that Wordsworth found the best corrective to the jargon of the later eighteenth-century poetry, descriptive and reflective, which he admired in his youth and imitated in his early poems; for as Coleridge pointed out, the style of the 'metaphysicals' 'is the reverse of that which distinguishes too many of our most recent versifiers; the one conveying the most fantastic thoughts in the most correct language, the other in the most fantastic language conveying the most trivial thoughts'.

But even the fantastic thoughts, the conceits of these courtly love poets and devout singers are not to be dismissed so lightly as a later, and still audible, criticism imagined. They played with thoughts, Sir Walter Scott complained, as the Elizabethans had played with words. But to play with thoughts it is necessary to think. 'To write on their plan', says Dr. Jonson, 'it was at least necessary to read and think. No man could be born a metaphysical poet, nor assume the dignity of a writer, by descriptions copied from descriptions, by imitations borrowed from imitations, by traditional imagery and hereditary similes, by readiness of rhyme and volubility of syllables.' Consider a poem, *The Repulse,* by a comparatively minor poet, Thomas Stanley. That is not a mere conceit. It is a new and felicitous rendering of a real and thrilling experience, the discovery that you might have fared worse in love than not to be loved, you might have been loved and then abandoned. Carew's *Ask me no more* is a coruscation of hyperboles, but

Now you have freely given me leave to love, What will you do? is a fresh and effective appeal to the heart of a woman. And this is what the metaphysicals are often doing in their unwearied play with conceits, delightfully naughty, extravagant, fantastic, and frigid—they succeed in stumbling upon some conceit which reveals a fresh intuition into the heart, or states an old plea with new and prevailing force. And the divine poets express with the same blend of argument and imagination the deep and complex current of religious feeling which were flowing in England throughout the century, institutional, theological, mystical, while in the metaphysical subtleties of conceit they found something that is more than conceit, symbols in which to express or adumbrate their apprehensions of the infinite.

The direct indebtedness of the courtly poets to Ben Jonson is probably, as Professor Gregory Smith has recently argued, small. But not only Herrick, metaphysical poets like Carew and Stanley and others owe much both of their turn of conceit and their care for form to Jonson's own models, the Latin lyrists, Anacreon, the Greek Anthology, neo-Latin or Humanist poetry so rich in neat and pretty conceits. Some of them, as Crashaw and Stanley, and not only these, were familiar with

Italian and Spanish poętry, Marino and Garcilasso and their elegantly elaborated confections. But their great master is Donne. If he taught them many heresies, he instilled into them at any rate the pure doctrine of the need of passion for a lover and a poet. What the young courtiers and university wits admired and reproduced in different degrees and fashions were his sensual audacity and the peculiar type of evolution which his poems accentuated, the strain of passionate paradoxical reasoning which knits the first line to the last and is perhaps a more intimate characteristic than even the far-fetched, fantastic comparisons. This intellectual, argumentative evolution had been of course a feature of the sonnet which might fancifully be called, with its double quatrain and sestet, the poetical analogy of the syllogism. But the movement of the sonnet is slow and meditative, a single thought expanded and articulated through the triple division, and the longer, decasyllabic line is the appropriate medium:

Then hate me when thou wilt; if ever, now;
Now while the world is bent my deeds to cross,
Join with the spite of Fortune, make me bow,
And do not drop in for an after-loss;
Ah, do not when my heart hath scaped this sorrow,
Come in the rearward of a conquer'd woe,
Give not a windy night a rainy morrow,
To linger out a purpos'd overthrow.
If thou wilt leave me, do not leave me last
When other petty griefs have done their spite,
But in the onset come; so shall I taste
At first the very worst of Fortune's might;
And other strains of woe which now seem woe,
Compared with loss of thee will not seem so.

What Donne had done was to quicken this movement, to intensify the strain of passionate ratiocination, passionate, paradoxical argument, and to carry it over from the sonnet to the song with its shorter lines, more winged and soaring movement, although the deeper strain of feeling which Donne shares with Shakespeare, and with Drayton at his best, made him partial to the longer line, at least as an element in his stanzas, and to longer and more intricate stanzas. Lightening the feeling and the thought, the courtly poets simplified the verse, attaining some of their most wonderful effects in the common ballad measure [4, 3] or the longer [4, 4] measure in couplets or alternate rhymes. But the form and content are intimately associated. It is the elaboration of the paradoxical argument, the weight which the rhetoric lays on those syllables which fall under the metrical stress, that gives to these verses, or seems to give, their peculiar *élan:*

My love is of a birth as rare
As 'tis for object strange and high;
It was begotten by Despair
Upon Impossibility.

The audacious hyperboles and paradoxical turns of thought give breath to and take wings from the soaring rhythm.

It is needless here to dwell at length on the several poets from whom I have selected examples of love-song and complimentary verses. Their range is not wide—love, compliment, elegy, occasionally devotion. Herrick had to leave the court to learn the delights of nature and country superstitions. Lord Herbert of Cherbury, philosopher and coxcomb, was just the person to dilate on the Platonic theme of soul and body in the realm of love on which Donne occasionally descanted in half ironical fashion, Habington with tedious thin-blooded seriousness, Cleveland and others with naughty irreverence.

But Lord Herbert's *Ode,* which has been, like most of his poems, very badly edited, seems to me the finest thing inspired by Donne's *Ecstasy* and more characteristic of the romantic taste of the court of Charles. But the poetic ornament of that Court is Thomas Carew. This young careless liver was a careful artist with a deeper vein of thought and feeling in his temperament than a first reading suggests. His masque reveals the influence of Bruno. In Carew's poems and Vandyke's pictures the artistic taste of Charles's court is vividly reflected, a dignified voluptuousness, an exquisite elegance, if in some of the higher qualities of man and artist Carew is as inferior to Wyatt or Spenser as Vandyke is to Holbein. His *Ecstasy* is the most daring and poetically the happiest of the imitations of Donne's clever if outrageous elegies; Cartwright's *Song of Dalliance* its nearest rival. His letter to Aurelian Townshend on the death of the King of Sweden breathes the very enchanted air of Charles's court while the storm was brewing as yet unsuspected.

The text of Richard Lovelace's *Lucasta* (1649) is frequently corrupt, and the majority of the poems are careless and extravagant, but the few good things are the finest expression of honour and chivalry in all the Cavalier poetry of the century, the only poems which suggest what 'Cavalier' came to mean when glorified by defeat. His *Grasshopper* has suffered a hard fate by textual corruption and from dismemberment in recent anthologies. Only the fantastic touch about 'green ice' ranks it as 'metaphysical', for it is in fact an experiment in the manner of the Horatian ode, not the heroic ode, but the lighter Epicurean, meditative strain of 'Solvitur acris hiems' and 'Vides ut alta stet nive candidum', description yielding abruptly to reflection.

A slightly better text or a little more care on the poet's part would have made it perfect. The gayest of the group is Sir John Suckling, the writer of what should be called *vers de société,* a more careless but more fanciful Prior. His beautiful *Ballad on a Wedding* is a little outside the scope of this volume. Thomas Stanley, classical scholar, philosopher, translator, seems to me one of the happiest of recent recoveries, elegant, graceful, felicitous, and if at times a little flat and colourless, not always flat like the Catholic puritan William Habington. But the strongest personality of all is Andrew Marvell. Apart from Milton he is the most interesting personality between Donne and Dryden, and at his very best a finer poet than either. Most of his descriptive poems lie a little outside my beat, though I have claimed *The Garden* as metaphysical, Annihilating all that's made To a green thought in a green shade,and I might have claimed *The Nymph and the Faun* had space permitted. But his few love poems and his few devotional pieces are perfect exponents of all the 'metaphysical' qualities—passionate, paradoxical argument, touched with humour and learned imagery:

As lines, so loves oblique, may well
Themselves in every angle greet:
But ours so truly parallel,
Though infinite, can never meet;

and above all the sudden soar of passion in bold and felicitous image, in clangorous lines:

But at my back I always hear
Time's wingèd chariot hurrying near,
And yonder all before us lay
Deserts of vast eternity.
Thy beauty shall no more be found;
Nor in thy marble vault shall sound
My echoing songthen worms shall try
That long preserv'd virginity;
And your quaint honour turn to dust;
And into ashes all my lust.
The grave's a fine and private place,
But none I think do there embrace.

These lines seem to me the very roof and crown of the metaphysical love lyric, at once fantastic and passionate. Donne is weightier, more complex, more suggestive of subtle and profound reaches of feeling, but he has not one single passage of the same length that combines all the distinctive qualities of the kind, in thought, in phrasing, in feeling, in music; and Rochester's most passionate lines are essentially simpler, less metaphysical.

When wearied with a world of woe,might have been written by Burns with some differences. The best things of Donne and Marvell could only have been composed—except, as an imitative *tour de force,* like Watson's

Bid me no more to other eyes—in the seventeenth century. But in that century there were so many poets who could sing, at least occasionally, in the same strain. Of all those whom Professor Saintsbury's ardent and catholic but discriminating taste has collected there is none who has not written too much indifferent verse, but none who has not written one or two songs showing the same fine blend of passion and paradox and music. The 'metaphysicals' of the seventeenth century combined two things, both soon to pass away, the fantastic dialectics of mediaeval love poetry and the 'simple, sensuous' strain which they caught from the classics—soul and body lightly yoked and glad to run and soar together in the winged chariot of Pegasus. Modern love poetry has too often sacrificed both to sentiment.

III

English religious poetry after the Reformation was a long time in revealing a distinctive note of its own. Here as elsewhere, Protestant poetry took the shape mainly of Biblical paraphrases or dull moralizings less impressive and sombre than the *Poema Morale* of an earlier century. Sylvester's translation of Du Bartas's *Weeks and Days* eclipsed all previous efforts and appealed to Elizabethan taste by its conceits and aureate diction. Catholic poets, on the other hand, like Robert Southwell, learned from the Italians to write on religious themes in the antithetic, 'conceited', 'passionating' style of the love poets of the day.

His Tears of St. Peter, if it is not demonstrably indebted to Tansillo's Le Lagrime di San Pietro, is composed in the same hectic strain and with a superabundance of the conceits and antitheses of that and other Italian religious poems of the sixteenth century:

Launch forth, my soul, into a main of tears,
Full-fraught with grief, the traffic of thy mind;
Torn sails will serve, thoughts rent with guilty fears;
Give care the stern, use sighs in lieu of wind:
Remorse thy pilot; thy misdeeds thy card;
Torment thy haven, shipwreck thy best reward.

His best poem, *The Burning Babe,* to have written which Jonson 'would have been content to destroy many of his', has the warmth and glow which we shall find again in the poetry of a Roman convert like Crashaw. It is in Donne's poems, *The Crosse, The Annuntiation and Passion, The Litanie,* that the Catholic tradition which survived in the Anglican Church becomes articulate in poetry; and in his sonnets and hymns that English religious poetry becomes for the first time intensely personal, the record of the experiences and aspirations, not of the Christian as such merely, but of one troubled and tormented soul. But the Catholic tradition in Donne was Roman rather than Anglican, or Anglican with something of a conscious effort; and Donne's passionate outpourings of penitence and longing lack one note of religious poetry which is audible in the songs of many less complex souls and less great poets, the note of attainment, of joy and peace. The waters have gone over him, the waters of fear and anguish, and it is only in his last hymns that he seems to descry across the agitation of the waves by which he is overwhelmed a light of hope and confidence:

Swear by thyself that at my death thy Son
Shall shine as he shines now and heretofore;
And having done that thou hast done,
I fear no more.

The poet in whom the English Church of Hooker and Laud, the Church of the *via media* in doctrine and ritual, found a voice of its own, was George Herbert, the son of Donne's friend Magdalen Herbert, and the younger brother of Lord Herbert of Cherbury.

His volume *The Temple, Sacred Poems and Private Ejaculations, By Mr. George Herbert,* was printed at Cambridge in the year that a disorderly collection of the amorous, satirical, courtly and pious poems of the famous Dean of St. Paul's, who died in 1631, was shot from the press in London as *Poems, by J. D., with Elegies on the Author's Death.* As J. D. the authors continued to figure on the title-page of each successive edition till that of 1669; nor were the additions made from time to time of a kind to diminish the complex, ambiguous impression which the volume must have produced on the minds of the admirers of the ascetic and eloquent Dean.

There is no such record of a complex character and troubled progress in the poetry of Herbert. It was not, indeed, altogether without a struggle that Herbert bowed his neck to the collar, abandoned the ambitions and vanities of youth to become the pious rector of Bemerton. He knew, like Donne, in what light the ministry was regarded by the young courtiers whose days were spent

In dressing, mistressing and compliment.

His ambitions had been courtly. He loved fine clothes. As Orator at Cambridge he showed himself an adept in learned and elegant flattery, and he hoped 'that, as his predecessors, he might in time attain the place of a Secretary of State'. When he resolved, after the death of 'his most obliging and powerful friends', to take Orders, he 'did acquaint a court-friend' with his resolution, 'who persuaded him to alter it, as too mean an employment, and too much below his birth, and the excellent abilities and endowments of his mind'.

All this is clearly enough reflected in Herbert's poems, and I have endeavoured in my selection to emphasize the note of conflict, of personal experience, which troubles and gives life to poetry that might otherwise be too entirely doctrinal and didactic. But there is no evidence in Herbert's most agitated verses of the deeper scars, the profounder remorse which gives such a passionate, anguished *timbre* to the harsh but resonant harmonies of his older friend's *Divine Poems:*

Despair behind, and death before doth cast
Such terror, and my feeble flesh doth waste
By sin in it, which it t'wards hell doth weigh.

Herbert knows the feeling of alienation from God; but he knows also that of reconcilement, the joy and peace of religion:

You must sit down, says Love, and taste my meat:
So I did sit and eat.

Herbert is too in full harmony with the Church of his country, could say, with Sir Thomas Browne, 'There is no Church whose every part so squares unto my Conscience; whose Articles, Constitutions and Customs, seem so consonant unto reason, and as it were framed to my particular Devotion, as this whereof I hold my Belief, the Church of England':

Beauty in thee takes up her place,
And dates her letters from thy face,
When she doth write.
A fine aspect in fit array,

Neither too mean, nor yet too gay,
Shows who is best.
But, dearest Mother, (what those misse)
The mean, thy praise and glory is,
And long may be.
Blessed be God, whose love it was
To double moat thee with his grace,
And none but thee.

It was from Donne that Herbert learned the 'metaphysical' manner. He has none of Donne's daring applications of scholastic doctrines. Herbert's interest in theology is not metaphysical but practical and devotional, the doctrines of his Church—the Incarnation, Passion, Resurrection, Trinity, Baptism—as these are reflected in the festivals, fabric, and order of the Church and are capable of appeal to the heart. But Herbert's central theme is the psychology of his religious experiences.

He transferred to religious poetry the subtler analysis and record of moods which had been Donne's great contribution to love poetry. The metaphysical taste in conceit, too, ingenious, erudite, and indiscriminate, not confining itself to the conventionally picturesque and poetic, appealed to his acute, if not profound mind, and to the Christian temper which rejected nothing as common and unclean. He would speak of sacred things in the simplest language and with the aid of the homeliest comparisons:

Both heav'n and earth
Paid me my wages in a world of mirth.

Prayer is:

Heaven in ordinary, man well drest,
The milky way, the bird of Paradise.

Divine grace in the Sacramental Elements:

Knoweth the ready way,
And hath the privy key
Op'ning the soul's most subtle rooms;
While those, to spirits refin'd, at door attend
Dispatches from their friend.

Night is God's 'ebony box' in which:

Thou dost inclose us till the day
Put our amendment in our way,
And give new wheels to our disorder'd clocks.
Christ left his grave-clothes that we might, when grief
Draws tears or blood, not want a handkerchief.

These are the 'mean' similes which in Dr. Jonson's view were fatal to poetic effect even in Shakespeare. We have learned not to be so fastidious, yet when they are not purified by the passionate heat of the poet's dramatic imagination the effect is a little stuffy, for the analogies and symbols are more fanciful or traditional than natural and imaginative. Herbert's nature is generally 'metaphysical',—'the busy orange-tree', the rose that purges, the 'sweet spring' which is 'a box where sweets compacted lie'. It is at rare moments that feeling and natural image are imaginatively and completely merged in one another:

And now in age I bud again,
After so many deaths I live and write;
I once more smell the dew and rain,
And relish versingO my only light,
It cannot be
That I am he
On whom thy tempests fell all night.

But if not a greatly imaginative, Herbert is a sincere and sensitive poet, and an accomplished artist elaborating his argumentative strain or little allegories and conceits with felicitous completeness, and managing his variously patterned stanzas—even the symbolic wings and altars and priestly bells, the three or seven-lined stanzas of his poems on the Trinity and Sunday—with a finished and delicate harmony. *The Temple* breathes the spirit of the Anglican Church at its best, primitive and modest; and also of one troubled and delicate soul seeking and finding peace.

Herbert's influence is discernible in the religious verse of all the minor Anglican poets of the century, but his two greatest followers were poets of a temper different from his own. Henry Vaughan had written verses of the fashionable kind—I have included one mild if elegant love-poem—before the influence of Herbert converted his pen to the service of Heaven; but all his *poetry* is religious. In *Silex Scintillans* he often imitates his predecessor in name and choice of theme, but his best work is of another kind. The difference between Herbert and Vaughan, at his best, is the difference on which Coleridge and Wordsworth dilated between fancy and imagination, between the sensitive and happy discovery of analogies and the imaginative apprehension of emotional identity in diverse experiences, which is the poet's counterpart to the scientific discovery of a common law controlling the most divergent phenomena. Herbert's 'sweet day, so cool, so calm, so bright' is a delightful play of tender fancy. Vaughan's greatest verses reveal a profounder intuition, as when Night is:

God's silent, searching flight;
When my Lord's head is fill'd with dew, and all
His locks are wet with the clear drops of night;
His still, soft call;
His knocking-time; the soul's dumb watch
When spirits their fair kindred catch.

Vaughan is a less effective preacher, a far less neat and finished artist than Herbert. His temper is more that of the mystic. The sense of guilt which troubles Donne, of sin which is the great alienator of man's soul from God in Herbert's poems, is less acute with Vaughan, or is merged in a wider consciousness of separation, a veil between the human soul and that Heaven which is its true home. His soul is ever questing, back to the days of his own youth, or to the youth of the world, or to the days of Christ's sojourn on earth, when God and man were in more intimate contact:

In Abraham's tent the winged guests
—O how familiar then was heaven!—
Eat, drink, discourse, sit down and rest,
Until the cool and shady even;

or else he yearns for the final reconciliation beyond the grave:

Where no rude shade or night
Shall dare approach us; we shall there no more
Watch stars or pore
Through melancholy clouds, and say,

'Would it were Day!'
One everlasting Sabbath there shall run
Without succession, and without a sun.

To this mystical mood Nature reveals herself, not as a museum of spiritual analogies, a garden of religious simples, but as a creature simpler than man, yet, in virtue of its simplicity and innocence, in closer harmony with God. 'Etenim res creatae exserto capite observantes exspectant revelationem filiorum Dei.' At brief moments Vaughan writes of nature and childhood as Wordsworth and Blake were to write, but generally with the addition of some little pietistic tag which betrays his century. It is indeed only in short passages that Vaughan achieves adequate imaginative vision and utterance, but the spirit of these passages is diffused through his religious verse, more quietistic, less practical, in spirit than Herbert's.

Vaughan's quietist and mystical, Herbert's restrained and ordered, temper and poetry are equally remote from the radiant spirit of Richard Crashaw. Herbert's conceits are quaint or homely analogies, Vaughan's are the blots of a fashion on a style naturally pure and simple. Crashaw's long odes give the impression at first reading of soaring rockets scattering balls of coloured fire, the 'happy fireworks' to which he compares St. Teresa's writings.

His conceits are more after the confectionery manner of the Italians than the scholastic or homely manner of the followers of Donne. Neither spiritual conflict controlled and directed by Christian inhibitions and aspirations, nor mystical yearning for a closer communion with the divine, is the burden of his religious song, but love, tenderness, and joy. In Crashaw's poetry, as in the later poetry of the Dutch Vondel, a note is heard which is struck for the first time in the seventeenth century, the accent of the convert to Romanism, the joy of the troubled soul who has found rest and a full expansion of heart in the rediscovery of a faith and ritual and order which give entire satisfaction to the imagination and affections. And that is not quite all. The Catholic poet is set free from the painful diagnosis of his own emotions and spiritual condition which so preoccupies the Anglican Herbert:

How should I praise thee, Lord! How should my rhymes
Gladly engrave thy name in steel,
If what my soul doth feel sometimes
My soul might ever feel!
Although there were some forty heav'ns or more,
Sometimes I peer above them all;
Sometimes I hardly reach a score,
Sometimes to hell I fall.

The Catholic poet loses this anxious sense of his own moods in the consciousness of the *opus operatum* calling on him only for faith and thankfulness and adoration. It is this *opus operatum* in one or other of its aspects or symbols, the Cross, the name of Christ, the Incarnation, the Eucharist, the life of the saint or death of the martyr, which is the theme of all Crashaw's ardent and coloured, sensuous and conceited odes, composed in irregular rhythms which rise and fall like a sparkling fountain. All other moods are merged in faith and love:

Faith can believe
As fast as love new laws can give.
Faith is my force. Faith strength affords
To keep pace with those powerful words.
And words more sure, more sweet than they
Love could not think, truth could not say.

Crashaw's poetry has a limited compass of moods, but it has two of the supreme qualities of great lyric poetry, poetry such as that of Shelley and Swinburne, ardour and music. Of the other poets from whose work I have selected not much need be said. Quarles hardly belongs to the 'metaphysical' tradition. In his paraphrases of Scripture he continues the Elizabethan fashion of Drayton and the later Giles Fletcher, but in the *Emblemes* [1635, 1639 1643] he is a religious lyrist of real if unequal power, with the taste for quaint and homely analogy of Herbert.

I have felt no disposition to cut and carve the sincere and ardent poems selected to represent his sense of alienation and reconcilement. To include Milton's *Hymn* in an anthology of metaphysical poems will seem less warrantable, for Milton is not enamoured of the quaint, the homely, or the too ratiocinative evolution, though he was also an erudite poet. Yet it would be to fail in literary perspective not to recognize that in this poem Milton wrote in a manner he was not to use again, that his models here are Italian rather than classical (the poem may owe something to Tasso's *Canzone sopra la Cappella del Presepio*), that the verses are a sequence of poetical and delightful conceits, some of which, as that of the blushing earth and the snow, or the Glimmering Orbs 'that' glow, Until their Lord himself bespake, and bid them go, are not very remote from the blushing dagger on which Boileau commented. Milton's style was to become more uniformly classical, but with the conceits departed alas! also the tenderness of spirit that gives to this early poem an ineffable charm.

Milton's young friend Andrew Marvell imbibed no more of Milton's classical inspiration than his graceless nephews and pupils, the Phillipses. In his religious as in his amorous and descriptive verses he is a 'metaphysical' dallying with poetic conceits in pure and natural English. But the temper of these few poems is of the finest that the Puritan movement begot, as devoted to the 'restrictive virtues' as Milton's, with less of polemical narrowness and arrogance; the temper of one in the world yet not of the world, recognizing and loyal to a scale of values that is not the world's:

Earth cannot show so brave a sight
As when a single soul does fence
The batteries of alluring sense,
And heaven views it with delight.

In no poetry more than the religious did the English genius in the seventeenth century declare its strong individuality, its power of reacting on the traditions and fashions which, in the Elizabethan age, had flowed in upon it from the Latin countries of Europe. There are individual poets who have risen to greater heights of religious and mystical feeling—some of the mediaeval hymn-writers, Dante, perhaps John of the Cross—but no country or century has produced a more individual or varied devout poetry, resting on the fundamental religious experience of alienation from and reconciliation to God, complicated by ecclesiastical and individual varieties of temperament and interpretation, than the country and century of Giles Fletcher and John Donne, Herbert and Vaughan, and Traherne and Crashaw, of John Milton, to say nothing of great poet-preachers like Donne and Taylor, or the allegory of Bunyan and the musings of Sir Thomas Brown.

IV

When Dryden and his generation passed judgement, not merely on the conceits, but on the form of the earlier poetry, what they had in view was especially their use of the decasyllabic couplet in eulogistic, elegiac, and satiric and narrative verses. 'All of them were thus far of Eugenius his opinion that the sweetness of English verse was never understood or practised by our fathers... and every one was willing to acknowledge how much our poesy is improved by the happiness of some writers yet living, who first taught us to mould our thoughts into easy and significant words, to retrench the superfluities of expression, and to make our rhyme so properly a part of the verse, that it should never mislead the sense, but itself be led and governed by it.' 'Donne alone', Dryden tells the Earl of Dorset, 'of all our countrymen had your talentbut was not happy enough to arrive at your versification; and were he translated into numbers and English, he would yet be wanting in the dignity of expression.'

Sweetness and strength of versification, dignity of expression—these were the qualities which Dryden and his generation believed they had conferred upon English poetry. 'There was before the time of Dryden no poetical diction, no system of words at once refined from the grossness of domestic use, and free from the harshness of terms appropriated to particular arts.... Those happy combinations of words which distinguish poetry from prose had been rarely attempted; we had few elegances or flowers of speech, the roses had not yet been plucked from the brambles, or different colours had not been joined to enliven one another.' Jonson is amplifying and emphasizing Dryden's 'dignity of expression', and it is well to remember that Scott at the beginning of the next century is still of the same opinion.

It is also worth remembering, in order to see a critical period of our poetical history in a true perspective, that Milton fully shared Dryden's opinion of the poetry of his time, though he had a different conception of how poetic diction and verse should be reformed. He, too, one may gather from his practice and from occasional references, disapproved the want of selection in the 'metaphysicals'' diction, and created for himself a poetic idiom far removed from current speech. His fine and highly trained ear disliked the frequent harshness of their versification, their indifference to the well-ordered melody of vowel and consonant, the grating, 'scrannel pipe' concatenations which he notes so scornfully in the verse of Bishop Hall:

> *'Teach each hollow grove to sound his love*
> *Wearying echo with one changeless word.*

And so he well might, and all his auditory besides, with his "teach each"' (*An Apology for Smectymnuus*). But the flowers which Milton cultivated are not those of Dryden, nor were his ear satisfied with the ring of the couplet. He must have disliked as much as Dryden the breathless, headlong overflow of *Pharonnida* (if he ever read it), the harsh and abrupt crossing of the rhythmical by the rhetorical pattern of Donne's *Satires,* but he knew that the secret of harmonious verse lay in this subtle crossing and blending of the patterns, 'apt numbers, fit quantity of syllables, and the sense variously drawn out from one verse into another'. Spenser was Milton's poetic father, and his poetic diction and elaborately varied harmony are a development of Spenser's art by one who has absorbed more completely the spirit, understood more perfectly the art, of Virgil and the Greeks, who has taken Virgil and Homer for his teachers rather than Ariosto and Tasso. Dryden's reform was due to no such adherence to an older and more purely poetic tradition though he knew and admired the ancients. His development was on the line of Donne and the metaphysicals, their assimilation of poetic idiom and rhythm to that of the spoken language, but the talk of which Dryden's poetry is an idealization is more choice and select, less natural and fanciful, and rises more frequently to the level of oratory. Like other reforms, Dryden's was in great measure a change of fashion. Men's minds and ears were disposed to welcome a new tone and tune, a new accent, neither that of high song, passionate thoughts

To their own music chanted, nor of easy, careless, but often delightful talk and song blended, which is the tone of the metaphysical lyric, but the accent of the orator, the political orator of a constitutional country.

It was in satire, the Satires of Hall, Marston, and Donne—especially the last—that the 'unscrewing' of the decasyllabic couplet began, in part as a deliberate effort to reproduce the colloquial ease of Horace's, the harshness of Persius's satiric style and verse. The fashion quickly spread to narrative, eulogistic, elegiac, and reflective poetry, and like other fashions—*vers libre* for example—was welcomed by many who found in it an easier *gradus ad Parnassum,* a useful discovery when every one had at times to pen a compliment to friend or patron.

After Spenser Elizabethan narrative poetry suffered almost without exception from the 'uncontented care to write better than one could', the sacrifice of story and character to the elaboration of sentimental and descriptive rhetoric. Shakespeare's *Venus and Aldonis* and *Rape of Lucrece* are no exception to this failure to secure that perfect balance of narrative, dramatic and poetic interest, which makes Chaucer's tales unsurpassed models in their kind.

The 'metaphysical' fashion changed merely the character of the rhetoric, shifting the weight from diction and verse to wit, to [Greek]. One can study the result in Davenant's *Gondibert* and Cowley's *Davideis,* where the dramatic thread of story is almost lost to sight in the embroidery of comment and 'witty' simile:

Oswald in wars was worthily renowned;
Though gay in Courts, coarsely in Camps could live;
Judg'd danger soon, and first was in it found;
Could toil to gain what he with ease did give.

Yet toils and dangers through ambition lov'd;
Which does in war the name of Virtue own;
But quits that name when from the war remov'd,
As Rivers theirs when from their Channels gone.

The most readable—if with somewhat of a wrestle—is Chamberlayne's *Pharonnida.* The story is compounded of the tedious elements of Greek romance—shepherds and courts and loves and rapes and wars—and no one can take the smallest interest in the characters. The verse is breathless and the style obscure, as that of Mr. Doughty is, because the writer uses the English language as if he had found it lying about and was free of it without regard to any tradition of idiom or structure. Still Chamberlayne does realise the scenes which he describes and decorates with all the arabesques of a fantastic and bewildering yet poetic wit:

The Spring did, when
The princess first did with her pleasure grace
This house of pleasure, with soft arms embrace
The Earth—his lovely mistress—clad in all
The painted robes the morning's dew let fall
Upon her virgin bosom; the soft breath
Of Zephyrus sung calm anthems at the death
Of palsy-shaken Winter, whose large grave,
The earth, whilst they in fruitful tears did lave,
Their pious grief turned into smiles, they throw
Over the hearse a veil of flowers; the low
And pregnant valleys swelled with fruit, whilst Heaven
Smiled on each blessing its fair hand had given.

But the peculiar territory of the metaphysical poets, outside love-song and devout verse, was eulogy and elegy. They were pedants but also courtiers abounding in compliments to royal and noble patrons and friends and fellow poets. Here again Donne is the great exemplar of erudite and transcendental, subtle and seraphic compliments to noble and benevolent countesses. One may doubt whether the thing ought to be done at all, but there can be no doubt that Donne does it well, and no one was better aware of the fact than Dryden, whose eulogies, whether in verse or in prose, as the dedication of the *State of Innocence* to Mary of Modena, are in the same seraphic vein and indeed contain lines that are boldly 'lifted' from Donne. They are not vivid by the accumulation of concrete details, though there are some not easily to be surpassed, as Ben Jonson's favourite lines:

No need of lanterns, and in one place lay
Feathers and dust, to-day and yesterday.

But the most vivid impressions are secured not by objective detail, but by the suggestion of their effect upon the mind. The nervous effect of storm and calm is conveyed by Donne's conceits and hyperboles in a way that is not only vivid but intense.

One cannot say much for the metaphysical eulogies of Donne's imitators. Even Professor Saintsbury has omitted many of them from his collection of the other poems by their authors, as Godolphin's lines on Donne and on Sandys's version of the Psalms, which are by no means the worst of their kind. He has, on the other hand, included one, Cleveland's on Edward King, some lines of which might be quoted to illustrate the extravagances of the fashion:

I like not tears in tune, nor do I prize
His artificial grief who scans his eyes.
Mine weep down pious beads, but why should I
Confine them to the Muses' rosary?
I um no poet here; my pen's the spout
Where the rain-water of mine eyes run out
In pity of that name, whose fate we see
Thus copied out in grief's hydrography.
The Muses are not mermaids, though upon
His death the ocean might turn Helicon.
When we have filled the roundlets of our eyes
We'll issue 't forth and vent such elegies
As that our tears shall seem the Irish Seas,
We floating islands, living Hebrides.

The last word recalls the great poem which appeared along with it:

Where ere thy bones are hurl'd,
Whether beyond the stormy Hebrides,

Where thou perhaps under the whelming tide
Visit'st the bottom of the monstrous world.

Cleveland is not much worse than Joseph Beaumont on the same subject, and neither is quite so offensive as Francis Beaumont in his lines on the death of Mrs. Markham:

As unthrifts grieve in straw for their pawned beds,
As women weep for their lost maidenheads
(When both are without hope of remedy),
Such an untimely grief have I for thee.

It would be difficult to imagine anything in worse taste, yet, from the frequency with which the poem recurs in manuscript collections, it was apparently admired as a flight of 'wit'. There are better elegies than these, as Herrick's and Earle's and Stanley's on Beaumont and Fletcher, Cleveland's (if it be his) on Jonson, Carew's noble lines on Donne, but in proportion as they become readable they cease to be metaphysical. Donne's *a priori* transcendentalism few or none were able to recapture.

Their attempts to rise meet the fate of Icarus. The lesser metaphysical poets are most happy and most poetical when their theme is not this or that individual but death in general. Love and death are the foci round which they moved in eccentric cycles and epicycles. Their mood is not the sombre mediaeval horror of 'Earth upon earth', nor the blended horror and fascination of Donne's elegies, or the more magnificent prose of his sermons. They dwell less in the Charnel House. Their strain is one of pensive reflection on the fleetingness of life, relieved by Christian resignation and hope:

Like as the damask rose you see,
Or like the blossom on the tree,
Or like the dainty flower in May,
Or like the morning of the day,
Or like the sun, or like the shade,
Or like the gourd which Jonas had—
Even such is manwhose thread is spun,
Drawn out and cut and so is done.
If none can scape Death's dreadful dart,
If rich and poor his beck obey,

If strong, if wise, if all do smart,
Then I to scape shall have no way.
O grant me grace, O God, that I
My life may mend since I must die.

In Abraham Cowley 'metaphysical' poetry produced its last considerable representative, and a careful study of his poetry reveals clearly what was the fate which overtook it. His wit is far less bizarre and extravagant than much in Donne, to say nothing of Cleveland and Benlowes. But the central heat has died down. Less extravagant, his wit is also less passionate and imaginative. The long wrestle between reason and the imagination has ended in the victory of reason, good sense. The subtleties of the schoolmen have for Cowley none of the significance and interest they possessed for Donne:

So did this noble Empire wast,
Sunk by degrees from glories past,
And in the School-men's hands it perished quite at last.
Then nought but words it grew,
And those all barbarous too.
It perish't and it vanisht there,
The life and soul breath'd out, became but empty air.

The influence of the new philosophy simplified with such dogmatic simplicity by Hobbes has touched him,—atoms and determinism, witness the ode *To Mr. Hobbes* and the half-playful, charming *Destinie;* and though that philosophy might appeal to the imagination, the intellectual imagination, by its apparent simplicity and coherency, it could make no such appeal to the spiritual nature as the older, which had its roots in the heart and conscience, which had endeavoured to construct a view of things which should include, which indeed made central, the requirements and values of the human soul. Cowley is not wanting in feeling any more than in fancy, witness his poem *On the Death of Mr. William Hervey,* and he was a Christian, but neither his affections nor his devotion expressed themselves imaginatively as these feelings did in Donne's most sombre or bizarre verses or those of his spiritual followers; his wit is not the reflection of a sombre or bizarre, a passionately colored or mystically tinted conception of life and love and death.

The fashion of 'metaphysical' wit remains in Cowley's poems when the spirit that gave it colour and music is gone. Yet Cowley's poetry is not merely frigid and fantastic. The mind and temper which his delightful essays, and the poems which accompany them, express has its own real charm—a mind of shy sensitiveness and clear good sense. It was by a natural affinity that Cowley's poetry appealed to Cowper. But wit which is not passionate and imaginative must appeal in some other way, and in Dryden it began to do so by growing eloquent.The interest shifted from thought to form, the expression not the novelty of the thought, wit polished and refined as an instrument of satire and compliment and declamation on themes of common interest. Dryden and Pope brought our witty poetry to a brilliant close. They are the last great poets of an age of intense intellectual activity and controversy, theological, metaphysical, and political. 'The present age is a little too warlike', Atterbury thought, for blank verse and a great poem. With the peace of the Augustans the mood changed, and poetry, ceasing to be witty, became sentimental; but great poetry is always metaphysical, born of men's passionate thinking about life and love and death.

I have closed my selections from seventeenth-century poetry not with Cowley or Dryden, but with Butler as a reminder of the full significance of the word 'metaphysical', which has a wider connotation than poetry. The century was metaphysical, and the great civil war was a metaphysical war. So many constitutional developments have been the ultimate consequence of the movement which the war began that it has obscured to our eyes the issue as it appeared to the combatants. To them the main issue was not constitutional. Pym and Parliament were more indifferent to the constitution than Charles and Clarendon. Cromwell's army was not inspired by any passion for the constitution; it fought to found the Kingdom of the Saints. Butler's *Hudibras* is a savage record of what the human spirit had suffered under the tyranny of metaphysical saints.

My selection, like every selection, is a compromise between what one would like to give and what space permits.

Inevitably, too, I have omitted one or two poems which on second thoughts I might prefer to some of those included. I regret especially that 'wonderful piece of word-craft', *Musics Duel.* Such as it is, my selection owes more than I can easily define to the suggestions, encouragement, advice—even when we occasionally differed in opinion—and patient scrutiny of the general editor, Mr. David Nichol Smith.

Chapter 4

History of Donne's Poems

The history of his poems is involved in the difficulties and obscurities of his biography. Only three were published in his life time, *The Anatomy of the World* (1611, 1612); the satirical lines *Upon Mr. Thomas Coryat's Crudities* (1611); and the *Elegie on Prince Henry* (1613). In 1614, when about to cross the Rubicon, Donne thought of hurriedly collecting and publishing his poems before the doing so could be deemed an actual scandal to his office. He had, apparently, no autograph copies, at least of many of them, but was driven to apply to his friends, and especially to Sir Henry Goodere, the Warwickshire friend to whom the larger number of his letters is addressed. "This made me ask to borrow that old book of you." The edition in question never appeared, but when, in 1633, the first collection was issued posthumously, the source was very probably this same "old book" (though Goodere had died before Donne), for, along with the poems, were printed eight letters addressed to Goodere and one to the common friend of Goodere and Donne, the countess of Bedford. In this edition, the poems were arranged in a rather chaotic sequence of groups.

The volume opened with *The Progresse of the Soule* and closed with the paraphrased *Lamentations of Jeremy* and the *Satyres,* the latter edited with a good many cautious dashes. There are obvious errors in the printing, but the text of such poems as this edition contains is more correct than in any subsequent one. In 1635, a second edition was issued, in which many fresh poems were added, and the grouping of the poems was carried out more systematically, the arrangement being adopted which has been generally adhered to since, and is useful for reference—*Songs and Sonets, Epigrams, Elegies, Epithalamiums, Satyres, Letters to Severall Personages, Funerall Elegies, The Progresse of the Soule, Divine Poems.* The editions which followed that of 1635 added individual poems from various sources, sometimes rightly, sometimes wrongly; and made alterations from time to time in the text, conjecturally, or with the help of MS. copies, which are sometimes emendations, more often further corruptions. Modern editors have followed in their wake, printing more carefully, correcting many errors, but creating not a few fresh ones. The canon of Donne's poems is far from being settled. Modern editions contain poems which are demonstrably not his, while there are genuine poems still unpublished. The text of many of his finest poems is disfigured by errors and misprints.

The order of the groups in the edition of 1635 corresponds, roughly, to the order of composition. Donne's earliest works were love songs or sonnets (using the word in the wider, freer sense of the Elizabethans) and elegies (after the manner of the Latin poets), through many of which runs a vein of pungent and personal satire, and regular verse satires. Of these last the editions since 1669 contain seven. We have, however, the explicit testimony of Sir William Drummond that Donne wrote only five. It is clear, from MSS. such as Harleian 5110 and others which have survived in whole or in part, that the first five, or some of them, were copied and circulated by themselves. These alone were included in the edition of 1633. The so-called sixth, which was added in 1635, if it be Donne's, is much more in the manner of the satirical elegies than of the regular satires; while the seventh, addressed *To Sir Nicholas Smith,* which was first inserted in the edition of 1669, an edition the text of which abounds in conjectural emendations, differs radically in style and tone from all the others, and there can be little doubt that it is the work of Sir John Roe, to whom it is assigned in more than one MS.

Chapter 5

Donne as a Satirist

Donne's satires have features in common with the other imitations of Juvenal, Persius and Horace which were produced in the last decade of the sixteenth century, notably a heightened emphasis of style and a corresponding vehemence and harshness of versification. But, in verse and style and thought, Donne's satires are superior to either Hall's "dashing, smirking, fluent imitations of the ancients" or Marston's tedious and tumid absurdities. The verse of these poets is much less irregular than Donne's. It approximates more closely to the balanced couplet movement of Drayton's *Heroicall Epistles*. Hall's couplets are neat and pointed, Marston's more irregular and *enjambed*. But Donne's satiric verse shows something like a consistent effort to eschew a couplet structure, and to give to his verse the freedom and swiftness of movement to which, when he wrote, even dramatic blank verse had hardly yet attained. He uses all the devices—the main pause in the middle of the line, weak and light endings (he even divides one word between two lines)—by which Shakespeare secured the abrupt, rapid effects of the verse of *Macbeth* and the later playsGracchus loves all [*i.e.* religions as one,and thinks that so

As women do in divers countries go
So doth, so is Religion; and this blind-
Ness too much light breeds; but unmoved thou
Of force must one, and forc'd but one allow;
And the right? ask thy father which is she,
Let him ask his; though truth and falsehood be
Near twins yet truth a little elder is;

Be busy to seek her. Believe me this,
He 's not of none, nor worst, that seeks the best.

Such verse is certainly not smooth or melodious. Yet the effect is studied and is not inappropriate to the theme and spirit of the poem. Donne's verse resembles Jonson's much more closely than either Hall's or Marston's. He had certainly classical models in view—Martial and Persius and Horace. But imitation alone will not account for Donne's peculiarities. Of the minor [char] of verse, he is always a little careless; but if there is one thing more distinctive than another of Donne's best work it is the closeness with which the verse echoes the sense and soul of the poem. And so it is in the satires. Their abrupt, harsh verse reflects the spirit in which they are written. Horace, quite as much as Persius, is Donne's teacher in satire; and it is Horace he believes himself to be following in adopting a verse in harmony with the unpoetic temper of his work:

And this unpolish'd rugged verse I chose,
As fittest for discourse and nearest prose.

The urbane spirit of Horace was not caught at once by those who, like Donne and Jonson, believed themselves to be following in his footsteps. The style of Donne's satires has neither the intentional obscurity of Hall's more ambitious imitations of Juvenal, nor the vague bluster of Marston's onslaughts upon vice. If we allow for corruptions of the text, one might say that Donne is never obscure. His wit is a succession of disconcerting surprises; his thought original and often profound; his expression, though condensed and harsh, is always perfectly precise. His out-of-the-way learning, too, which supplies puzzles for modern readers, is used with a pedantic precision, even when fantastically applied, to which his editors have not always done justice.

In substance, Donne's satires are not only wittier than those of his contemporaries, but weightier in their serious criticism of life, and happier in their portrayal of manners and types. In this respect, some of them are an interesting pendant to Jonson's comedies. The first describes a walk through London with a giddy ape of fashion, which is limned with a lightness and vivacity wanting to Jonson's more laboured studies of Fastidous Brisk and his fellows. The second, opening with a skit on the lawyer turned poet, passes into a trenchant onslaught—obscured by some corruptions of the text—upon the greedy and unprincipled exacter of fines from recusant Catholics, and "purchasour" of men's lands:

Shortly (as the sea) he 'll compass all the land;
From Scots to Wight; from Mount to Dover strand.

He is the lineal descendant of Chaucer's Man of Law, to whom all was fee-simple in effect, drawn in more angry colours. The third stands by itself, being a grave and eloquent plea for the serious pursuit of religious truth, as opposed to capricious or indolent acquiescence, on the one hand, and contemptuous indifference on the other. The lines which are quoted above in illustration of Donne's verse, and, indeed, the whole poem, were probably in Dryden's mind when he wrote his first plea for the careful quest of religious truth, and concluded that,

't is the safest way
To learn what unsuspected ancients say.

These three satires are ascribed in a note on one manuscript collection to the year 1593. Whether this be strictly correct or not, they seem to reflect what we may take to have been the mind of Donne during his early years in London, at the inns of court, when he was familiar with the life of the town, but not yet an *habitué* of the court, and in a state of intellectual detachment as regards religion, with a lingering prejudice in favour of the faith of his fathers. The last two satires were written in 1597, or the years immediately following, when Donne was in the service of the lord keeper, and they bear the mark of the budding statesman.

The first is a long and somewhat over-elaborated satire on the fashions and follies of court-life at the end of queen Elizabeth's reign. The picture of the bore was doubtless suggested by Horace's *Ibam forte via sacra,* but, like all Donne's types, is drawn from the life, and with the same amplification of detail and satiric point which are to be found in Pope's renderings from Horace. The last of Donne's genuine satires is a descant on the familiar theme of Spenser's laments, the miseries of suitors. Donne's satires were very popular, and, to judge from the extant copies or fragments of copies as well as from contemporary allusions, appear to have circulated more freely than the songs and elegies, which were doubtless confined so far as possible, like the *Paradoxes* and *BIA[char]ANATO[char],* to the circle of the poet's private friends. A Roman Catholic controversialist, replying to *Pseudo-Martyr,* expresses his regret that Donne has "passed beyond his old occupation of making Satires, wherein he hath some talent and may play the fool without control."

Such a writer, had he known them, could hardly have failed to make polemical use of the more daring and outrageous *Elegies* and those songs which strike a similar note. But, though less widely known, the *Songs and Sonnets* and the *Elegies* contain the most intimate and vivid record of his inner soul in these ardent years, as the religious sonnets and hymns do of his later life. And the influence of these on English poetry was deeper, and, despite the temporary eclipse of metaphysical poetry, more enduring, than that of his pungent satires, or of his witty but often laboured and extravagant eulogies in verse letter and funeral elegy.

Chapter 6

Donne as a Love Poet

TAKEN together, John Donne's *Songs and Sonets,* along with many of the erotic elegies, constitute a varied, even sporadic meditation on the experience and significance of love. Despite the apparent contradictions in the collection—the outbursts of bawdiness, arrogance, and cynicism among the reiterated, if often problematic, assertions of love's transcendence of what is base and banal—these poems finally evoke a unified vision of what Monsignor Martin C. D'Arcy calls "the mind and heart of love."

In fact, it is precisely the candid acknowledgment of the contradictions in human attitudes that enables the complex irony of Donne's witty eloquence to dramatize the approach to that "decisive moment" when a man genuinely recognizes the common human identity of the desired other, and" `love' now takes on its proper meaning". As D'Arcy also says, "It is always, we must remember, a full human person who loves, and in that love there are sure to be many different strands". Love is an arresting exemplar of the paradoxical structure of reality as it is perceived by men and women; and poetry, understood broadly as a creative literary fiction (a "golden world," if you will), is our most compelling means of manifesting that perception for the contemplation of "a full human person." Few poets have achieved more in this line than John Donne.

Amid the current atmosphere of ideological intimidation, which looms like a menacing gray mist, spawned by some academic El Nino, over the once temperate vale of Donne scholarship, these must seem quixotic assertions. This is, after all, the same John Donne who has been accused of apostasy (Carey 15-36), phallocentrism (Mueller 148), servile submissiveness to an absurdly repellent embodiment of patriarchal royal absolutism (Goldberg 111-12), and even bulimia The most ambitious twelve-step programme may seem hardly sufficient to restore to a man of such vicious compulsions his former status as the most persuasive love poet in English literature.

These gloomy assessments of Donne and his work arise, however, from a misconception both of love and of poetry. Both of these vital human activities have been "defined down" in this therapeutic agejudged as something less than the sum of their parts. The vital abundance and mysterious subtlety of love have been subjected to a diminished appraisal in a fashion analogous to the "demystification" of the inventive copia and wit of Donne's poetry. The recovery can be managed only by the constructive work of literary criticism and scholarship—a kind of joint operation seeking to rescue meaning from a wind-swept sea of floating signifiers.

The interpretation of Donne's love poetry offered here depends upon a vision of human love as an experience fraught with tension. D'Arcy refers to "the twofold character of love, in which respect it is compared to the struggle of opposites in nature". At the heart of this "struggle" is the tension between Eros and Agape– in the simplest terms, possessive and and self-sacrificing love, desire and charity. The great value of D'Arcy's work lies in his insistence that simply to favor agape over eros will not sufficeperfect agape is possible only for God whose fund of benevolence is infinite and inexhaustible. A man or a woman cannot give absolutely because we are finite creaturesa measure of self-assertive egotism, of possessive eros, is (literally) essential for us in order to retain an identity to be sacrificed or surrendered.

Herein the paradox of the human situationour most transcendent aspirations are as limitless and insatiable as our most sulphurous desires, while our capacity for each alternative is strictly limited. What is more, our divergent longings often seem not merely simultaneous, but even indistinguishable. The swoon of ecstatic self-immolation is whirled about in the slaver of predatory anticipation. The resolution of this dilemma by means of supernatural grace is matter for another essay. My topic here is just the enigma of earthly, profane love, which embodies so much of what is admirable and delightful, reprehensible and mortifying, in human nature and conduct.

This tension at the centre of human life finds its analogue in the tension that is central to poetry, a tension that attains its exemplary literary form in irony. "Irony" in this context means a poetic figure or a rhetorical device; but it refers as well to a particular vision of reality that is marked by an acute awareness of the fallibility of human knowledge, the uncertainty of human enterprise, the contingency of human existence itself. Such considerations are far more pertinent to this discussion than worries about whether irony is excessively "elitist" (Hutcheon 94) or inappropriate—not to say incorrect—in certain political contexts. The concern here is less with irony as a "political issue" (Hutcheon 2) than with Cleanth Brooks' concept of "irony as a principle of structure." Brooks' 1949 essay describes irony as "a dynamic structure—a pattern of thrust and counterthrust"; and after listing apparently contradictory implications in a poem by Randall Jarrell, Brooks argues that what results is not incoherence, but a complex of ironic tension:

> None of these meanings cancels out the others. All are relevant, and each meaning contributes to the total meaning. Indeed, there is not a facet of significance which does not receive illumination from the figure.

The concept of irony as a structure of semantic tension, however, offers an obvious parallel to Monsignor D'Arcy's conception of love as a tension of eros and agape. Together the two concepts provide a means of interpreting Donne's love poetry as the ironic embodiment of a vision of love as a version of concordia discors. The same violent yoking that Dr. Johnson finds in the metaphysical style Brooks attributes to irony:

> Irony, then, in this further sense, is not only an acknowledgment of the pressures of context. Invulnerability

to irony is the stability of a context in which the internal pressures balance and mutually support each other. The stability is like that of the archthe very forces which are calculated to drag the stones to the ground actually provide the principle of support—a principle in which thrust and counterthrust become the means of stability.

Poetic irony is thus the perfect counterpart to D'Arcy's notion of love as "the struggle of opposites in nature." Where Brooks' formulation perhaps falls short is in neglecting to show how the stability of the poem—of any work of art—is the ultimate ironic turn of the screw. In his closing chapter, D'Arcy observes that love only reaches its culminating resolution—its "stability"—in the eternal perfection of the love of God. Following T. S. Eliot and I. A. Richards, Brooks maintains that sentimentality is avoided by that poetry "which does not leave out what is apparently hostile to its dominant tone, and which, because it is able to fuse the irrelevant and the discordant, has come to terms with itself and is invulnerable to irony" . In the realm in which irony is the only antidote to irony—a world of what is "hostile," "irrelevant," "discordant"—we have no lasting city, and no lasting love. Thus the stability of the love poem forged out of the clash of ironic tensions is the ultimate ironic comment on the realm of human experience that the poem evokes.

Not only Donne's notorious "metaphysical" conceits, but indeed the entire fabric of particular poems corresponds to Brooks' "conceit" of ironya typical Donne love poem is a surprising fusion and distillation of hostility, irrelevance, and discord. A privileged recipient of a manuscript of Donne's elegy "The Bracelet" in the 1590s would have been struck first of all by the poem's topicality. The Acts of the Privy Council contains this item for 20 August 1591:

Robert Henlack has petitioned the Council for redress against certain men who robbed him. He complains that while he was absent in the night a confederacy of certain evil disposed persons broke open his chamber door in the house of Isabel Piggott in Thames Street and took away goods and money to the value of 400 [pounds sterling]. Further, one

Nathaniel Baxter hath since then robbed him of 12 [pounds sterling] more, pretending that by casting a figure he would help him to his goods and money again.

The probable reader of "The Bracelet," a Londoner, perhaps an Inns of Court man like Donne himself, might well recall this incident, or one like it, when he read in Donne's poem of "many angled figures, in the booke / Of some great Conjurer" (lines 34-35); and the memory would be reinforced by the desperate persona's effort to satisfy his mistress by any device short of melting down his "twelve righteous Angels" (line 9) to replace her lost chain:

Or let mee creepe to some dread Conjurer,
Which with phantastique scheames fils full much paper;
Which hath divided heaven in tenements,
And with whores, theeves, and murderers stuft his rents
So full, that though hee passe them all in sinne,
He leaves himself no roome to enter in.

This same reader might also be reminded by "The Bracelet" of Sir Edward Coke's opening statement in the prosecution of the Portuguese Jew, Dr. Roderigo Lopez, for attempting to poison the Queen in 1594. Maintaining that Dr. Lopez was in the pay of Philip II, Coke remarked, "the King of Spain and his priests, despairing of prevailing by valour, turned to cowardly treachery, and what they could not do by cannon, they attempted by crowns" (Harrison 307). Surely this notorious affair would have been brought to mind by Donne's ability to exceed the wit of Coke's cannon / crowns alliteration with a pun on "pistolets":

Or were they Spanish Stamps, still travelling,
That are become as Catholique as their King,
Those unlickt beare-whelps, unfil'd pistolets
That (more than Canon shot) availes or lets.

Allusions such as these, along with the colloquial texture of the language of Donne's strong lines, would anchor the elegy firmly in the world of popular gossip and scandal of the last decade of Elizabeth's reign.

The generic designation elegy, however, which apparently was attached to this poem and more than a dozen others in the early manuscripts, would have signalled to an educated Elizabethan reader that the poet was engaged in the learned humanist activity of imitating the classics as well as remarking the kind of sensational "news" that was the preoccupation of broadside ballads. Any reasonably well-read contemporary of Donne would recognize the reference to the love poetry, especially the elegiacs, of Catullus, Propertius, Tibullus, and Ovid.Beyond the mere use of the term, Donne succeeds in evoking the atmosphere of the Roman elegy more successfully than any other Renaissance poet known to me. Donne is less an imitator of particular phrases, stylistic devices, themes, or episodes of this or that poem by his ancient predecessors than a triumphant rival, who has recreated in toto the Roman genre and transposed it into his own late Elizabethan milieu. "The Bracelet," for example, captures the mingling of passionate desire, bitter cynicism, and wry irony that mark the classical erotic elegy without drawing on any specific classical poem. Indeed, its chief incident, the lover forced to search the town for a lost bracelet given him by his mistress, may parody, as Grierson and Gardner point out, Soliman and Perseda, a "foolishly romantic play" probably by Thomas Kyd (Gardner 112, 116).

What emerges from this congeries—references to the "news" or gossip of the day, a form modelled on classical antiquity, allusions to contemporaneous popular literature—is a love poem in which "Love's not so pure, and abstract, as they use / To say, which have no Mistresse but their Muse" ("Love's Growth" 11-12). The "impurity" derives, in large part, from the improbable melangeit is a lover who speaks the poem, but his love is shaped by the poet's response to a generic clash. The Roman erotic elegy is, as Paul Veyne says, "one of the most sophisticated art forms in the entire history of literature", and in Donne it collides with the crude Petrarchanism of so much of the poetry and drama of the Elizabethan age. This is a lover who, as he addresses the beloved, is acutely aware of the world of business and boredom, of perfidy and peril, of avarice and ambition, of vileness and violence—all that from which love is so often sought as an escape. The scene of

Donne's elegy is thus littered with elements that are "hostile," "discordant," and "irrelevant" to the conventional sense of loveit is irony that brings these antagonistic forces together in a single poetic structure. For despite the disparate elements jostling about among its lines, "The Bracelet" attains not only unity but even dramatic cogency. Whether it amuses or appalls, attracts or repels, the voice of this poem is alive and consistent with human experience, because its exasperated speaker is so credibly torn between two familiar human motivationslust and greed. The first of these impulses is sufficiently strong that we infer that he will, however reluctantly, submit to the demand of his imperious mistress:

But, thou art resolute; Thy will be done;
Yet with such anguish, as her onely sonne
The Mother in the hungry grave doth lay,
Unto the fire these Martyrs I betray.

The harsh flirtation with blasphemy evoked by the echo of the Our Father ("Thy will be done"), by the hyperbolic term "Martyrs," and by the hinted reference to the Blessed Virgin at the burial of Christ undercuts the familiar idealism of the Petrarchan deifying of the beloved by a mockingly excessive solemnity. This lover laments the loss of his money more than a mother the death of her child, more than Mary the death of Jesus; and yet the mistress is divine—her "will" must "be done." The angry tone of this reluctant erotic worshipper reveals that his devotion can hardly be spiritual, especially since he has already observed that his very act of appeasement will serve only to diminish her favor:

But, shall my harmlesse angels perish? Shall
I lose my guard, my ease, my food, my all?
Much hope which they should nourish will be dead.
Much of my able youth, and lustyhead
Will vanish; if thou love let them alone,
For thou will love me lesse when they are gone...

The final irony of course is, that despite his compulsive yet reluctant yielding to a less than ideal mistress, the speaker of the poem still cannot relinquish his attachment to his "angels." The woman disappears from the last twenty-four lines in the persona's obsessive brooding over the "wretched finder" of the bracelet:

But, I forgive; repent thee honest man:
Gold is Restorative, restore it then:
Or if with it thou beest loath to'depart,

Because 'tis cordiall, would twere at thy heart.This feverish, fickle preoccupation with the hypothetical possessor of the bracelet is an ironic mirror image of his odi et amo relationship with his rather dubious mistress.

This is a bitterly cynical vision of love as possessive passionthe parallel between the irresistible desire for the erotic favor of a woman, whose chief attributes seem to be greed and arrogance, and the lover's own grasping avarice is a finely distilled solvent for the amorous idealism prevalent in a literary culture dominated by love-sonnet sequences. The final comic irony arises from the absurdity of the speaker's own situationhe is, after all, no better off than the deluded Petrarchist whom he implicitly scorns. Like the saturnine speaker of "Loves Alchymie," he has seen through the sham of love, knows that women are hardly human much less divine; but for all his blase sophistication he is still as frustrated, every bit as much a slave to passion as Astrophil. Here again, without imitating a particular classical poem, Donne has succeeded in capturing the flavour of the Roman erotic elegy. "I myself," writes Paul Veyne, believe that Propertius, or rather the Ego he brings on stage, does not so much suffer from the pangs of jealousy as regard the chains of passion as something dreadful. Indeed, the ancient Roman considered the effects of passion a form of tragic fate, a form of slavery, a special form of unhappiness.

This reflection gives the alternate titles of Donne's poem that refer to the bracelet as a "chaine" rather more resonancethe persona is surely bound to his mistress by the "lost chain."

Here among the love poems of John Donne we find a very acrid view of love, but we find very little about John Donne himself. In a qualified way I wish to endorse the perception of Judith Scherer Herz that "in his poems... Donne is rarely there, indeed in some poems never there," and I agree that Donne is "the master of complex, unsettling, prickly poems, poems that simply will not resolve," and that we must "not look for consistency beyond the boundaries of any single poem, indeed not even necessarily within those boundaries," and that we may thus recover "the Donne of linguistic surprise, of ventriloquistic virtuosity, of theological and philosophical inconsistency, the Donne who will say anything if the poem seems to need it". Such attributes, however, do not define his character. He is writing poems, and a poet is precisely that man or woman "who will say anything if the poem seems to need it"—"for the Poet, he nothing affirmes, and therefore neuer lyeth" (Sidney 184). As John Shawcross points out, "The false specter of Romantic effusion has blighted poetic criticism for a long time—as if the poet cannot write without parallel experience, as if all that is said is fully and firmly believed as he or she writes". I would go even further than Shawcross in defending the essay by Wimsatt and Beardsley, "The Intentional Fallacy," because it accepts absolutely one of the poet's intentions, the intention to write a poem. This brings us back to the issue of inconsistency between and within poems. The persona of "The Bracelet" is surely inconsistent, a monument of tergiversationhe regards his mistress' will as divine, but her person as less "angelic" than his money; he speculates about someone recovering the gold chain who is now a "wretched finder," now "an honest man," and finally the object of what we may call a heartfelt curse.

The discourse represented by the poem is inconsistent because its speaker is inconsistent. Of course Donne himself was also inconsistent, but then so are you and I, and so are most men and women in every era. In the sixteenth century the leading proponent of Neo-Stoicism, the author of De Constantia (1584), was Justus Lipsius (1547-1606), who wandered restlessly from one European university to another and changed his religion at least four times, earning no little scorn among contemporaneous English writers (Gottlieb). Yet Lipsius was himself at least "indifferent honest." There is, then, inconsistency within and among Donne's poems because they deal with the reality of human existence, which is a tissue of inconsistencies; but the poems as such are not inconsistent. The philosopher, as Sidney reminds us, deals in abstractions only tangentially connected to human life; the historian is in danger of drowning in the chaotic flood of experience"the Historian, wanting the precept, is so tyed, not to what shoulde bee but to what is, to the particular truth of things and not to the general reason of things, that hys example draweth no necessary consequence, and therefore a lesse fruitfull doctrine." It is only "the peerelesse Poet" who "coupleth the generall notion with the particuler example". This "coupling," or layering of inconsistencies into whatever the pattern of the poem requires, is irony —"irony as a principle of structure." It is the fundamental irony of poetry that it produces consistent formal structures out of the turbid swirl of inconsistency that constitutes human experience, that it reveals meaning—the "precept"—in what may seem meaningless.

THE distinction between poetic intention and the personal life of the poet becomes more complex in those works of Donne where we find what seems an indisputable indication of "parallel experience" providing the origin of the incidents or situation of a poem. If the tone is even more elusive than that of "The Bracelet" and falls into Gardner's category of "poems of mutual love", then critical preoccupation with the autobiographical features of the poem becomes almost irresistible. There is no better example than "The Sunne Rising." The persona who brashly proclaims his satisfaction at having thrown away the opportunity for preferment in the royal court for the sake of love bears a suspicious resemblance to the historical John Donne, who, we may surmise, had plenty of time to wile away in bed with his teenage bride, since he had no place in the busy world of education, politics, and trade. The seventh line, "Goe tell Court-huntsmen, that the King will ride," cries out to be associated with the court gossip of the years shortly after Donne's elopement, as retailed by that ubiquitous busybody, John Chamberlain, in a letter to Ralph Winwood:

The Kinge went to Roiston two dayes after Twelfetide, where and thereabout he hath continued ever since, and findes such felicitie in that hunting life, that he hath written to the counsaile, that yt is the onely meanes to maintain his health, (which being the health and welfare of us all) he desires them to undertake the charge and burden of affaires, and foresee that he be not interrupted nor troubled with too much business.

This looks like fairly solid evidence that the poem was written sometime after the accession of James Stuart as James I of England, when his new subjects had become acquainted with his habits; however, there was some notice in England of James' addiction to hunting when he was still just King of Scotland. It was bruited about London at least as early as 1591 that, despite the threat of rebellious Earls to James' safety, he would not "be restrained from the fields or in his pastime, for any respect" (Harrison 13). The detail of a hunting king could have been picked up from political gossip during the last decade of Elizabeth's reign in England as well as during the first decade of James' reign. The poem powerfully evokes certain details of what we know of Donne's life during the latter time, but we cannot be sure when it was written, and, finally, it does not matter. We must also take into account, again, the element of literary imitation. It is a commonplace to notice that the opening lines of "The Sunne Rising" echo even as they transform the corresponding lines of Ovid, Amores I. xiiiIam super oceanum venit a seniore marito flava pruinoso quae vehit axe diem. "Quo properas, Aurora? mane!—sic Memnonis umbris annua sollemni caede parentet avis! [Already the blonde who drives the day in her frosty carriage is coming over the ocean from her aged husband.

What's your hurry, Aurora? Wait! —And so may a bird appease Memnon's shade each year with solemn slaughter! But if Donne is, in part, seeking to outdo the wit of Ovid with his own more extravagant conceits, it also seems that he may be parodying "A Hymn to Aurora" of a more recent Latin poet, Marcantonio Flaminio (1498-1550). The opening of his Hymnus in Aurora offers a picture of the dawn goddess that contrasts sharply with Ovid's:

Ecce ab extremo veniens Eoo

roscidas Aurora refert quadrigas
et sinu lucern roseo nitentem
candida portat.

[Behold Aurora coming from the farthest East brings round again her dewy four-horse team and brightly bears the shining light within her rosy bosom.]

Besides the fact that Flaminio portrays the Dawn's conveyance as "dewy" (roscidas) rather than "frosty" (pruinoso), this is an altogether more engaging portrait of the goddess as the embodiment of refulgence, and it seems to be a direct reply to Ovid. The moral edification of the closing sapphics may have especially caught Donne's attention:

Te sine aeterna iaceant sepulti
nocte mortales, sine te nec ullus
sit colour rebus neque vita doctas
culta per artes.
Tu gravem pigris oculis soporem
excutis—leti sopor est imago—
evocans tectis sua quemque laetum ad
munia mittis.
Exsilit stratis rapidus viator,
ad iugum fortes redeunt iuvenci,
laetus in silvas properat citato
cum grege pastor.
Ast amans carae thalamum puellae
deserit flens et tibi verba dicit
aspera, amplexu tenerae cupito a-
vulsus amicae.
Ipse amet noctis latebras dolosae,
me iuvet semper bona luxnitentem
da mihi lucem, dea magna, longos
cernere in annos!

[Without you mortals would lie buried in eternal night, and without you things would have no colors and life would not be enriched with learned arts. You expel heavy sleep from sluggish eyes—sleep is the image of death—calling from the roof-tops you send each one joyful to his duties.

The swift traveller leaps from the covers, the strong

bullocks return to the yoke, the happy shepherd hastens quickly to the woods with his hurried flock. But weeping the lover forsakes the bed of his darling girl and speaks harsh words to you, torn away from the desired embrace of his yielding mistress. Let him love the lairs of deceitful night, let me always rejoice in the good lightpermit me, great goddess, to receive the shining light through the long years!

The weeping lover who speaks harsh words to Aurora would seem to be Flaminio's version of the irreverent persona of Ovid's Amores. This lover of dark dens and loose women is reproved by contrast to the man who rejoices in the light and hastens eagerly to his duties.

Donne reverts to the tone of the Amores, painting a very different scene from Flaminio's sturdy bullocks, eager traveller, and happy shepherd who go off to work whistling like the seven dwarfs:

Sawcy pedantique wretch, goe chide
Late schoole boyes, and sowre prentices,
Goe tell Court-huntsmen, that the King will ride
Call countrey ants to harvest offices...

"The Sunne Rising" undoubtedly celebrates mutually fulfilling love, but the celebration takes place in a context that recalls the limits even of such a love. Donne would have expected his readers to be aware of other claims on human time and attention amidst this exaltation of erotic bliss and sleeping-in. Perhaps neither the poet nor his audience knew this particular poem by Flaminio, but they surely knew poems or prose exhortations like it. There is obvious humour in Donne's mockery of this kind of earnest solemnity; however, even Ovid must have occasionally had to be somewhere on time. Donne calls attention to the equivocal status of the claims made in the poem by their very extravagance. Ovid is never so brash with Aurora as Donne is with the "Sunne," which he calls "Busie old foole" and "Sawcy pedantique wretch." The very excessiveness of his emulation of Ovid and parody of Flaminio discloses the tension between the notion of love's sufficiency and the civic and economic demands of the world:

If her eyes have not blinded thine,

Looke, and to morrow late, tell mee,
Whether both the'India's of spice and Myne
Be where thou leftst them, or lie here with mee.
Aske for those Kings whom thou saw'st yesterday,
And thou shalt heare, All here in one bed lay.

There are times when we have all believed this, or at least wished to do so; and it is a truth of human experience that love is finally more important than money or power. What makes this poem so much more than a conventional assertion of the transcendent power of human love is the structural ironyits subtle incorporation of the contrasting reality that love—certainly the sort that is enacted in the lovers' four-poster bed—is a fragile enterprise indeed without the economic and social where-with-all to sustain it. Cleanth Brooks did not perhaps sufficiently allow for the way the irony is deepened not only by such intertextual resonance as is afforded by Ovid and Flaminio, but also by our knowledge of the historical situation of John Donnethe irony of his radical defiance of accepted social norms is surely rendered more piquant by the disastrous results of his elopement with Anne More. Donne the man could stay in bed every morning because he had no office.

But Brooks is finally rightthe irony is discernible in the structure of "The Sun Rising" though it were as anonymous as Beowulf. As evidence I offer the last stanza, which highlights the conflicting norms of conventional society precisely by rejecting them so outrageously. Are the lovers lingering in their bed alienated from the "busie" world to which the "unruly Sunne" awakens them? It is no matter because they not only transcend that world; they epitomize it:

She'is all States, and all Princes, I,
Nothing else is.
Princes do but play us; compar'd to this,
All honor's mimique; All wealth alchimie...

The "real world" thus fades before the sublime bliss of the shared bed. The high-spirited absurdity of these assertions seems so self-evident that there hardly seems any point in refuting Jonathan Goldberg's assertion that here "the speaker makes the absolutist declaration toward which the entire poem tends... The absorption of the lovers in each other, their replication of the power of the world, constitutes an appropriation of and reversal of the language of state secrets". Likewise, in a generally sympathetic essay, Camille Wells Slights seems to be straining at a gnat when she defends "The Sunne Rising" from the charge that it "reinscribes the culture's gender hierarchy" by arguing that "as third- and first-person singular pronouns give way to first-person plural, the topic becomes not the lovers but their relationship". Carey gets closer to the mark in noticing the tension in the conceits, but he seems altogether oblivious to the tone"Donne's vaunting language is, like all vaunting language, an expression of insecurity, and this makes the poem more human.

The pretension to kingship that he voices amounts to an acknowledgement of personal insufficiency". The speaker of the poem, however, knows this as well as Professor Careythe "vaunting language" sounds like an effort to deflect by means of laughter an anxious question about, say, where the rent money is coming from this month. The woman whose lover or husband has just proclaimed his universal sovereignty over the empire of the bedroom probably has more concrete worries than being colonized by the hegemony of absolutist patriarchal ideology. At the same time, there would have been some compensation even to genteel poverty in the company of such a roguish wit. Most of us are capable of stale, reassuring compliments like "I think the world of you." Donne works out the details of the cliche and creates a superbly preposterous conceit in which the cosmos becomes thalamocentric:

Thou sunne art halfe as happy'as wee,
In that the world's contracted thus.
Thine age askes ease, and since thy duties bee
To warme the world, that's done in warming us.
Shine here to us, and thou art every where;
This bed thy centre is, these walls, thy spheare.

Ovid chides Aurora for her haste to leave her aged husband:

Tithono vellem de te narrare liceret;

fabula non caelo turpior ulla foret.
ilium dum refugis, longo quia grandior aevo,
surgis ad invisas a sene mane rotas.
(Amores I.xiii.35-38)

If only Tithonus were allowed to tell a tale of you; nothing more scandalous would be told in heaven. While you shrink from him, since he is a long age older, early in the day you leap to the chariot odious to the old man. Donne's sly sympathy for the aging sun is a comically inventive variation on the Ovidian theme, and it hints at the reality of human aging, which undermines the speaker's jaunty erotic optimism. This is a man ruefully amused at the human limitations he so brazenly denies. Donne evidently was able to laugh at himself, a capacity some of his modern critics might well consider emulating. The vision of love in "The Sunne Rising" is decidedly more affirmative than what we find in "The Bracelet." Anthony Low has argued persuasively that the former poem marks an important step in "the reinvention of love" at the threshold of modern times whereby lovers, wedded or otherwise, create their own private world over against the claims of the larger community"Surprisingly, the two lovers in Donne's private room enact one of the central rituals of carnival.

They assume the personae of the dominant authority figures of their diurnal society and mockingly invert the social order" . The reference to carnival catches the tone of "The Sunne Rising" very well, and it distinguishes Donne's more equivocal notion of the private world of love from the exacting idealism and solemnity of Milton's divorce tracts and his intense portrait of marital love in Paradise Lost. Donne's pervasive wit precludes even a shadow of sentimentalityhe retains an inescapable awareness of the proclivity of erotic desire for self-absorption and special pleading. "The Dream" provides a striking example. This poem weaves conceits that challenge the most idealistic Petrarchan manner. The beloved mistress is no mere donna angelicata; in her intuition of the speaker's mind she is more than an angel with implicitly divine knowledge:

As lightning, or a Tapers light,

Thine eyes, and not thy noise wak'd mee;
Yet I thought thee
(For thou lovest truth) an Angell, at first sight,
But when I saw thou sawest my heart,
And knew'st my thoughts, beyond an Angels art,
When thou knew'st what I dreamt, when thou knew'st when
Excesse of joy would wake me, and cam'st then,
I doe confesse, it could not chuse but bee
Prophane, to thinke thee any thing but thee.

This stanza is both rather grandiose in its language and yet at the same times an example of strictly verbal ironyto say that it is "prophane" to think a woman less than herself, when less means angelic, is in fact profane because the assertion implies that a mortal creature is divine. Both the comedy and the complexity increase in the following stanza when the lady's divinity is put in doubt because of her reluctance to "act the rest" of the speaker's "dreame":

Comming and staying show'd thee, thee,
But rising makes me doubt, that now,
Thou art not thou.
That love is weake, where feare's as strong as hee;
'Tis not all spirit, pure and brave,
If mixture it of Feare, Shame, Honour, have;
Perchance as torches which must ready bee,
Men light and put out, so thou deal'st with mee,
Thou cam'st to kindle, goest to come; Then I
Will dreame that hope againe, but else would die.

There is a great deal here of sheer metaphysical mockery of the pretensions of erotic idealismthe slangy puns on "Comming" and "die"; the outrageously phallic torch, lit only to be put by in readiness, that suggests the woman to be tease; and, above all, the pseudo-Scholastic speculation about how a woman is not who she is and love "not all spirit, pure, and brave" except when it is realized in the flesh. It is a seducer's paradox that argues for the identification of purity and spirituality with physical consummation.

Yet there is a gentleness, even a tenderness, in "The Dreame" that elevates it above a mere cynical irony. The difference is apparent in the contrast with the bitterness of another famous poem about a woman coming into a man's bedroom"They fle from me that sometyme did me seke/With naked fote stalking in my chambre" (Wyatt 1-3). Readers who know Donne's history will be drawn to set the scene of the poem in York House, and picture the charming intruder in the persona's chamber as a very young Anne More, both daring and diffident, drawn irresistibly to, and yet somewhat afraid of, the witty, sophisticated courtier with the dubious reputation, rather unaccountably employed by her step-uncle. The poem's delicate blend of wry humour and breathless ardor bespeaks both the love and lust of a man who thought his mistress a goddess, but liked his goddess to be flesh and blood—a carnal substitute, perhaps, for the deity incarnate in the sacrament of the Altar that the actual, historical John Donne must have been relinquishing about the time he met Anne More.

However, before casting the roles for this BBC costume drama, we must remember that erotic dreams would have represented a familiar poetic topic for Donne and his contemporaries. "Dreams are not unusual in the Roman love elegy," Clifford Endres observes as he comments on the strikingly original imitation of the motif by Joannes Secundus (1511-1536), who was in turn imitated by other sixteenth-century poets, both Neo-Latin and vernacular . As in "The Dreame," the speaker of Secundus' Somnium is concerned about the tension between his desires to possess his beloved sexually and the restraints imposed by social and familial disapproval:

Non fora, non portus, non jam populosa theatra,
Templaque sunt nostris conscia blanditiis.
Mater abest, digitis legem quae ponat, et ori,
Et cogat tremulo murmure pauca loqui,
Osculaque aridulis non continuanda labellis
Carpere, quae juret barbara, quisquis amat,
Et celare faces, et amici obtexere nomen,
Multaque quae solers fingere discit Amor. (Elegiae I.x.7-14)

[Now no markets, no warehouses, no packed theaters, no

temples are privy to our pleasures. The mother is away who imposes law on fingers and mouths, and constrains us to speak few words in a low murmur, to reap no lingering kisses on parched lips (which any lover would regard as barbarous) to hide our burning torches, to weave the name of friend, and to feign many things which ingenious Love learns.]

Secundus not only anticipates Donne's torch, he also describes a beloved mistress as a source of light"I hold thee, my Light, my Light, I hold thee" (24"Te teneo, mea Lux, Lux mea, te teneo"). But in fact the two previous elegies (viii and ix) have described Julia's wedding to another man, and her appearance in the speaker's bed turns out to be only a dream:

Julia, te teneosuperi, teneatis Olympum.
Quid loquor? an vere, Julia, te teneo?
Dormione? an vigilo? vera haec? an somnia sunt haec?
Somnia seu, seu sunt vera, fruamur, age!
Somnia si sunt haec, durent haec somnia longum,
Nec vigilem faciat me, precor, ulla dies.

[Julia, I am holding youlet the Gods above hold on to their Olympus. What am I saying? Do I truly, Julia, hold you? Do I sleep? Or do I wake? Is this real or is this a dream? Whether dream or reality let's enjoy it, let's do it! If this is a dream, may it last a long time, and let no daylight, I pray, awaken me.]

Like the lover of Secundus' Somnium, the speaker of "A most rare, and excellent Dreame, learnedly set downe by a woorthy Gentleman," which appeared in The Phoenix Nest in 1593, is consoled only by a dream, and unlike the resourceful persona of the Neo-Latin poem, he cannot even manage to stay asleep. The pace of the poem is leisurelyit runs to 60 stanzas of rime royal and includes a learned disquisition on the origin and nature of dreams worthy of Chaunticleer. After the distraught, unrequited lover finally lapses into sleep out of sheer exhaustion, "Slumber" brings him, "To mitigate the anguish of my thought," the vision of "a Ladie faire " who, at the end of a twelve-stanza blazon, turns out to be "the portraict of the Saint, / Which deepe ingraued in my hart I beare, / The Mistress of my hope, my feare, my plaint". The lady's explanation for her appearance in the gentleman's bedchamber is disarmingly innocent:

With vnperceiued motion drawing ny,
Vnto the bed of my distresse and feare,
She with hir hand doth put the curtaine by,
And sits her downe vpon the one side there:
My wasted spirits quite amazed were,
To see the sudden morning of those eies,
Within the darke thus inexpected rise.
Being abrode (quoth she) I lately hard,
That you were falne into a sudden feuer,
And solitarie in your chamber bard,
From companie you did your selfe disseffeuer,
To charitie it appertaineth euer,
In duties to our neighbors for to sticke,
And visit the afflicted and the sicke.

The first of these two stanzas bears an obvious similarity to the situation at the beginning of Donne's "The Dreame," including again an emphasis upon the woman as bearer of light into the darkness. The lady in The Phoenix Nest, however, is devoid of that equivocal blend of daring and diffidence that characterizes her counterpart in Donne's poem. It takes several stanzas for her to realise that her lover expects her to cure his "feuer" without recourse to her garden herbs or "closet of conserues." When she finally understands what he is asking, they argue for several pages the standard love vs. honour theme, with the lady defending rational self-control against blind passion"The argument is dull, and nothing quicke, / Bicause that I am faire, you should be sicke". The lover's only effective counter-argument is a death-like faint, which leads the lady to relent and recall him to life "with a kisse." Unfortunately his joy is so great that the dream is broken and he awakens to "The vanitie and falsehood of these ioyes".

PERUSING a volume like The Phoenix Nest is a forceful reminder of the power and originality of Donne's love poetry. "The Dreame" treats exactly the same dilemma as "A most rare, and excellent Dreame, learnedly set downe by a woorthy Gentelman"namely, the internal clash in a man between love and lust, between the longing to cherish with honour and to possess with casual pleasure, between the image of a woman as angelic, saintly, or divine and the predatory perception of a woman as a quarry. The poem printed in The Phoenix Nest, in keeping with the length of its title, spends 420 lines rehearsing a series of predictable, though loosely strung-together commonplaces. In just thirty lines Donne's poem evokes a world.

The young woman who slips into her lover's room, listens to his blandishments, with their mixture of wry wit and anxious pleading, and then, suddenly panicked, draws back—she comes vividly to life in the words of Donne's poetic persona. There is no need for her to speak; we should probably imagine her hushing his expostulations with her finger at her lips, fascinated and fearful at the same time. She is so real that she generates a tremendous urge to find her in history, to re-create her biography.

But what, in fact, makes her real is precisely the comparison of the poem in which she takes shape with the dreary litter of Phoenix Nests in their thousands despoiling the literary landscape. It is Donne's capacity to interact creatively with literary tradition that makes his poetry so much more than conventional literature. There is an element of truth in Northrop Frye's assertion that poems are made out of other poems, but all poems are not therefore equal.

But a good poet does not have to react against bad poems. Perhaps the most resonant context for Donne's "The Dreame" comes at the end of the very first canto of The Faerie Queene. Could any reader of poetry in the 1590s pick up Donne's account of a man awaking to find the woman of his dreams there at his bedside and not think of the Redcrosse Knight awaking to a demonic apparition of his beloved? There is a striking inverted parallel insofar as Spenser's hero is beguiled into mistaking an evil spirit—that is, a fallen angel—for the real Una, who allegorically represents the Truth; while Donne's persona at first mistakes the real woman for a mere "Angel." Donne's poem differs most notably from the first two bits of poetic context that we have considered insofar as "The

Dreame" is not just a dream—the lady actually shows up in the bedroom. The difference with the scene created by Spenser is still more significantUna bears a grave symbolic burden as the representation of the transcendental truth and the idea of the true Church. When the Redcrosse Knight finally chases the counterfeit out of his room—much unlike Donne's persona, who urges the lady to stay—it is as if the Truth itself has failed:

Long after lay he musing at her mood,
Much griev'd to thinke that gentle dame so light,
For whose defence he was to shed his blood.
The Faerie Queene.

It is no surprise when, several cantos later, in the company of that very different woman, the false "Fidessa," his iron resolve fails "Poured out in looseness on the grassy grownd, / Both carelesse of his health and of his fame".

"The Dreame" thus flashes a derisive smile at Spenser's aggressively Protestant, rigorously Neo-Platonic idea of Truth. It also gives point to what is clearly the superior reading of line seven"Thou art so truth, that thoughts of thee suffice, / To make dreames truths; and fables histories" . If the lady in Donne's poem who enters the bedroom is contrasted with Spenser's Una, then Gardner's reading "so true" instead of "so truth" must be rejected; and the relevance of Grierson's citation of St. Thomas, which she dismisses, becomes clear (Gardner 209). Donne is proposing that truth is a flesh and blood woman, not a Platonic abstraction.

The being of God, St. Thomas writes, is not only consistent with his understanding, but it even is his act of understanding; and his act of understanding is the measure and cause of every other being, and of every other understanding; and he is himself his own being and understanding. Hence it follows that not only is he truth in himself, but that he is the first and highest truth itself.

In other words, God is truth itself because He is absolutely and completely Himself in a way impossible to any creature. The ironic exception is, of course, the lady who enters the bedroom in "The Dreame"she is "so truth" that she too is divine—but only so long as she stays:

Comming and staying show'd thee, thee,
But rising makes me doubt, that now,
Thou art not thou.

The woman in his bed, in his arms, is truth itselfpalpable, concrete, existential reality. Gardner finds "`so truth' a very forced expression and the repetition of `truth... truth' unpleasing to the ear" , but if the woman in "The Dreame" is set against Una as a differing version of truth, then Donne has provided an Aristotelian/Thomist vision to counter Spenser's Neo-Platonism.

To be sure, "The Dreame," as well as many other poems among The Songs and Sonnets, offers a very irreverent version of Thomism or more generally of Catholic doctrine and practice. It behooves us to recall, again, that in the course of writing these poems Donne was moving away from the faith of his youth. Most especially, he was relinquishing the Real Presence of the Body and Blood of Christ in the Sacrament of the Altar—the ultimate manifestation of God's truth in the Catholic liturgy. If the poet's reckless marriage to Anne More was the decisive event in his spiritual journey, then he can be said to have surrendered the Body of Christ for the body of a woman, the flesh and blood present on the altar for the "divine" presence of the woman in the bed.

"What Donne proposes in his most idealized love lyrics," writes Anthony Low, "is a union between lovers that is essentially communal, sacred, and religious in a certain sense, but neither Christian nor social" . While Spenser tries to reconcile human sexual love with a militantly Protestant, Platonically spiritual version of truth, Donne attempts to forge a dramatic account of the truth of Eros that is ironically modeled on Catholicism at its most incarnational and sacramental. This convergence of conflicting elements—religious and political strife, philosophical and literary competition, the clash of Petrarchan idealism and cynical libertinism—results in the equivocal tension and the pervasive irony that mark the love poetry of John Donne.

An historical individual named John Donne with all his individual quirks and personal experiences; literary conventions derived from ancient elegy, from Medieval Scholasticism, from courtly love lyric, from Renaissance Petrarchanism, and from many other sources; ideas about love of religious, philosophical, and social origin—all these elements converge in the love poetry of John Donne along with many more too numerous to list. What holds them together and forges them into a unity is wit. Baltasar Gracifin calls this agudeza—literally "sharpness" or "keenness"—which finds its literary manifestation in the conceit"What beauty is for the eyes, what harmony is for the ears, the conceit is that for the understanding".

The literary result is ironythe perception of the incongruous and contradictory suspended together in a verbal matrix. Gracifin goes on to define the conceit (concepto) as "an act of the understanding that expresses the correspondence that is found among objects"—found or invented by "the artifice of ingenuity" (242; artificio del ingenio).Literature is thus fundamentally ironic insofar as it acknowledges the incongruousness of human existence. Donne's love poetry is "a well wrought urne" precisely in recognizing its own heroic insufficiency against the temporal and material forces always threatening to overwhelm it. The wit and irony of Donne's poetry are very much akin to what a modern poet, Wallace Stevens, calls "nobility":

It is a violence from within that protects us from a violence from without. It is the imagination pressing back against the pressure of reality. It seems, in the last analysis, to have something to do with our self-preservation; and that, no doubt, is why the expression of it, the sound of its words, helps us to live our lives.

Chapter 7

Donne and His Poetry

John Donne was born in 1572 to a London merchant and his wife. Donne's parents were both Catholic at a time when England was deeply divided over matters of religion; Queen Elizabeth persecuted the Catholics and upheld the Church of England established by her father, Henry VIII. The subsequent ruler, James I, tolerated Catholicism, but advised Donne that he would achieve advancement only in the Church of England. Having renounced his Catholic faith, Donne was ordained in the Church of England in 1615. Donne's father died when he was very young, as did several of his brothers and sisters, and his mother remarried twice during his lifetime. Donne was educated at Hart's Hall, Oxford, and Lincoln's Inn; he became prodigiously learned, speaking several languages and writing poems in both English and Latin.

Donne's adult life was colorful, varied, and often dangerous; he sailed with the royal fleet and served as both a Member of Parliament and a diplomat. In 1601, he secretly married a woman named Ann More, and he was imprisoned by her father, Sir George More; however, after the Court of Audiences upheld his marriage several months later, he was released and sent to live with his wife's cousin in Surrey, his fortunes now in tatters. For the next several years, Donne moved his family throughout England, traveled extensively in France and Italy, and attempted unsuccessfully to gain positions that might improve his financial situation. In 1615, Donne was ordained a priest in the Anglican Church; in 1621, he became the Dean of St. Paul's Cathedral, a post that he retained for the rest of his life. A very successful priest, Donne preached several times before royalty; his sermons were famous for their power and directness. For the last decade of his life, before his death in 1630, Donne concentrated more on writing sermons than on writing poems, and today he is admired for the former as well as the latter. (One of his most famous sermons contains the passage beginning, "No man is an island" and ending, "Therefore ask not for whom the bell tolls; it tolls for thee.") However, it is for his extraordinary poems that Donne is primarily remembered; and it was on the basis of his poems that led to the revival of his reputation at the beginning of the 20th century, following years of obscurity. (The renewed interest in Donne was led by a new generation of writers at the turn of the century, including T.S. Eliot.) Donne was the leading exponent of a style of poetry called "metaphysical poetry," which flourished in the late sixteenth and early seventeenth centuries.

Metaphysical poetry features elaborate conceits and surprising symbols, wrapped up in original, challenging language structures, with learned themes that draw heavily on eccentric chains of reasoning. Donne's verse, like that of George Herbert, Andrew Marvell, and many of their contemporaries, exemplifies these traits. But Donne is also a highly individual poet, and his consistently ingenious treatment of his great theme—the conflict between spiritual piety and physical carnality, as embodied in religion and love—remains unparalleled.

John Donne, whose poetic reputation languished before he was rediscovered in the early part of the twentieth century, is remembered today as the leading exponent of a style of verse known as "metaphysical poetry," which flourished in the late sixteenth and early seventeenth centuries. (Other great metaphysical poets include Andrew Marvell, Robert Herrick, and George Herbert.) Metaphysical poetry typically employs unusual verse forms, complex figures of speech applied to elaborate and surprising metaphorical conceits, and learned themes discussed according to eccentric and unexpected chains of reasoning. Donne's poetry exhibits each of these characteristics. His jarring, unusual meters; his proclivity for abstract puns and double entendres; his often bizarre metaphors (in one poem he compares love to a carnivorous fish; in another he pleads with God to make him pure by raping him); and his process of oblique reasoning are all characteristic traits of the metaphysicals, unified in Donne as in no other poet.

Donne is valuable not simply as a representative writer but also as a highly unique one. He was a man of contradictionsAs a minister in the Anglican Church, Donne possessed a deep spirituality that informed his writing throughout his life; but as a man, Donne possessed a carnal lust for life, sensation, and experience. He is both a great religious poet and a great erotic poet, and perhaps no other writer (with the possible exception of Herbert) strove as hard to unify and express such incongruous, mutually discordant passions. In his best poems, Donne mixes the discourses of the physical and the spiritual; over the course of his career, Donne gave sublime expression to both realms.

His conflicting proclivities often cause Donne to contradict himself. (For example, in one poem he writes, "Death be not proud, though some have called thee / Mighty and dreadful, for thou art not so." Yet in another, he writes, "Death I recant, and say, unsaid by me / Whate'er hath slipped, that might diminish thee.") However, his contradictions are representative of the powerful contrary forces at work in his poetry and in his soul, rather than of sloppy thinking or inconsistency. Donne, who lived a generation after Shakespeare, took advantage of his divided nature to become the greatest metaphysical poet of the seventeenth century; among the poets of inner conflict, he is one of the greatest of all time.

Chapter 8

Complete Text Poems by John Donne

Songs and Sonnets

The Flea

MARK but this flea, and mark in this,
How little that which thou deniest me is;
It suck'd me first, and now sucks thee,
And in this flea our two bloods mingled be.
Thou know'st that this cannot be said
A sin, nor shame, nor loss of maidenhead;
Yet this enjoys before it woo,
And pamper'd swells with one blood made of two;
And this, alas ! is more than we would do.
O stay, three lives in one flea spare,
Where we almost, yea, more than married are.
This flea is you and I, and this
Our marriage bed, and marriage temple is.
Though parents grudge, and you, we're met,
And cloister'd in these living walls of jet.
Though use make you apt to kill me,
Let not to that self-murder added be,
And sacrilege, three sins in killing three.
Cruel and sudden, hast thou since
Purpled thy nail in blood of innocence?
Wherein could this flea guilty be,
Except in that drop which it suck'd from thee?

Yet thou triumph'st, and say'st that thou
Find'st not thyself nor me the weaker now.
'Tis true; then learn how false fears be;
Just so much honour, when thou yield'st to me,
Will waste, as this flea's death took life from thee

The Good-Morrow

I WONDER by my troth, what thou and I
Did, till we loved ? were we not wean'd till then ?
But suck'd on country pleasures, childishly ?
Or snorted we in the Seven Sleepers' den ?
'Twas so; but this, all pleasures fancies be;
If ever any beauty I did see,
Which I desired, and got, 'twas but a dream of thee.
And now good-morrow to our waking souls,
Which watch not one another out of fear;
For love all love of other sights controls,
And makes one little room an everywhere.
Let sea-discoverers to new worlds have gone;
Let maps to other, worlds on worlds have shown;
Let us possess one world; each hath one, and is one.
My face in thine eye, thine in mine appears,
And true plain hearts do in the faces rest;
Where can we find two better hemispheres
Without sharp north, without declining west ?
Whatever dies, was not mix'd equally;
If our two loves be one, or thou and I
Love so alike that none can slacken, none can die.

Song Go and Catch a Falling Star

GO and catch a falling star,
Get with child a mandrake root,
Tell me where all past years are,
Or who cleft the devil's foot,
Teach me to hear mermaids singing,
Or to keep off envy's stinging,
And find
What wind

Serves to advance an honest mind.
If thou be'st born to strange sights,
Things invisible to see,
Ride ten thousand days and nights,
Till age snow white hairs on thee,
Thou, when thou return'st, wilt tell me,
All strange wonders that befell thee,
And swear,
No where
Lives a woman true and fair.
If thou find'st one, let me know,
Such a pilgrimage were sweet;
Yet do not, I would not go,
Though at next door we might meet,
Though she were true, when you met her,
And last, till you write your letter,
Yet she
Will be
False, ere I come, to two, or three.

Woman's Constancy.

NOW thou hast loved me one whole day,
To-morrow when thou leavest, what wilt thou say ?
Wilt thou then antedate some new-made vow ?
Or say that now
We are not just those persons which we were ?
Or that oaths made in reverential fear
Of Love, and his wrath, any may forswear ?
Or, as true deaths true marriages untie,
So lovers' contracts, images of those,
Bind but till sleep, death's image, them unloose ?
Or, your own end to justify,
For having purposed change and falsehood, you
Can have no way but falsehood to be true ?
Vain lunatic, against these 'scapes I could
Dispute, and conquer, if I would;
Which I abstain to do,
For by to-morrow I may think so too.

The Undertaking.

I HAVE done one braver thing
Than all the Worthies did;
And yet a braver thence doth spring,
Which is, to keep that hid.
It were but madness now to impart
The skill of specular stone,
When he, which can have learn'd the art
To cut it, can find none.
So, if I now should utter this,
Others—because no more
Such stuff to work upon, there is—
Would love but as before.
But he who loveliness within
Hath found, all outward loathes,
For he who colour loves, and skin,
Loves but their oldest clothes.
If, as I have, you also do
Virtue in woman see,
And dare love that, and say so too,
And forget the He and She;
And if this love, though placèd so,
From profane men you hide,
Which will no faith on this bestow,
Or, if they do, deride;
Then you have done a braver thing
Than all the Worthies did;
And a braver thence will spring,
Which is, to keep that hid.

The Indifferent.

I CAN love both fair and brown;
Her whom abundance melts, and her whom want betrays;
Her who loves loneness best, and her who masks and plays;
Her whom the country form'd, and whom the town;
Her who believes, and her who tries;
Her who still weeps with spongy eyes,

And her who is dry cork, and never cries.
I can love her, and her, and you, and you;
I can love any, so she be not true.
Will no other vice content you ?
Will it not serve your turn to do as did your mothers ?
Or have you all old vices spent, and now would find out others ?
Or doth a fear that men are true torment you ?
O we are not, be not you so;
Let me—and do you—twenty know;
Rob me, but bind me not, and let me go.
Must I, who came to travel thorough you,
Grow your fix'd subject, because you are true ?
Venus heard me sigh this song;
And by love's sweetest part, variety, she swore,
She heard not this till now; and that it should be so no more.
She went, examined, and return'd ere long,
And said, "Alas ! some two or three
Poor heretics in love there be,
Which think to stablish dangerous constancy.
But I have told them, 'Since you will be true,
You shall be true to them who're false to you.'

Love's Usury

FOR every hour that thou wilt spare me now,
I will allow,
Usurious god of love, twenty to thee,
When with my brown my gray hairs equal be.
Till then, Love, let my body range, and let
Me travel, sojourn, snatch, plot, have, forget,
Resume my last year's relict; think that yet
We'd never met.
Let me think any rival's letter mine,
And at next nine
Keep midnight's promise; mistake by the way
The maid, and tell the lady of that delay;
Only let me love none; no, not the sport

From country grass to confitures of court,
Or city's *quelque-choses*; let not report
My mind transport.
This bargain's good; if when I'm old, I be
Inflamed by thee,
If thine own honour, or my shame and pain,
Thou covet most, at that age thou shalt gain.
Do thy will then; then subject and degree
And fruit of love, Love, I submit to thee.
Spare me till then; I'll bear it, though she be
One that love me.

The Canonization

FOR God's sake hold your tongue, and let me love;
Or chide my palsy, or my gout;
My five gray hairs, or ruin'd fortune flout;
With wealth your state, your mind with arts improve;
Take you a course, get you a place,
Observe his Honour, or his Grace;
Or the king's real, or his stamp'd face
Contemplate; what you will, approve,
So you will let me love.
Alas ! alas ! who's injured by my love?
What merchant's ships have my sighs drown'd?
Who says my tears have overflow'd his ground?
When did my colds a forward spring remove?
When did the heats which my veins fill
Add one more to the plaguy bill?
Soldiers find wars, and lawyers find out still
Litigious men, which quarrels move,
Though she and I do love.
Call's what you will, we are made such by love;
Call her one, me another fly,
We're tapers too, and at our own cost die,
And we in us find th' eagle and the dove.
The phoenix riddle hath more wit
By us; we two being one, are it;
So, to one neutral thing both sexes fit.

We die and rise the same, and prove
Mysterious by this love.
We can die by it, if not live by love,
And if unfit for tomb or hearse
Our legend be, it will be fit for verse;
And if no piece of chronicle we prove,
We'll build in sonnets pretty rooms;
As well a well-wrought urn becomes
The greatest ashes, as half-acre tombs,
And by these hymns, all shall approve
Us canonized for love;
And thus invoke us, "You, whom reverend love
Made one another's hermitage;
You, to whom love was peace, that now is rage;
Who did the whole world's soul contract, and drove
Into the glasses of your eyes;
So made such mirrors, and such spies,
That they did all to you epitomize—
Countries, towns, courts beg from above
A pattern of your love."

The Triple Fool.

I am two fools, I know,
For loving, and for saying so
In whining poetry;
But where's that wise man, that would not be I,
If she would not deny ?
Then as th' earth's inward narrow crooked lanes
Do purge sea water's fretful salt away,
I thought, if I could draw my pains
Through rhyme's vexation, I should them allay.
Grief brought to numbers cannot be so fierce,
For he tames it, that fetters it in verse.
But when I have done so,
Some man, his art and voice to show,
Doth set and sing my pain;
And, by delighting many, frees again
Grief, which verse did restrain.

To love and grief tribute of verse belongs,
But not of such as pleases when 'tis read.
Both are increasèd by such songs,
For both their triumphs so are published,
And I, which was two fools, do so grow three.
Who are a little wise, the best fools be.

Lovers' Infiniteness

IF yet I have not all thy love,
Dear, I shall never have it all;
I cannot breathe one other sigh, to move,
Nor can intreat one other tear to fall;
And all my treasure, which should purchase thee,
Sighs, tears, and oaths, and letters I have spent;
Yet no more can be due to me,
Than at the bargain made was meant.
If then thy gift of love were partial,
That some to me, some should to others fall,
Dear, I shall never have thee all.
Or if then thou gavest me all,
All was but all, which thou hadst then;
But if in thy heart since there be or shall
New love created be by other men,
Which have their stocks entire, and can in tears,
In sighs, in oaths, and letters, outbid me,
This new love may beget new fears,
For this love was not vow'd by thee.
And yet it was, thy gift being general;
The ground, thy heart, is mine; what ever shall
Grow there, dear, I should have it all.
Yet I would not have all yet.
He that hath all can have no more;
And since my love doth every day admit
New growth, thou shouldst have new rewards in store;
Thou canst not every day give me thy heart,
If thou canst give it, then thou never gavest it;
Love's riddles are, that though thy heart depart,
It stays at home, and thou with losing savest it;

But we will have a way more liberal,
Than changing hearts, to join them; so we shall
Be one, and one another's all.

SongSweetest Love, I do not go

SWEETEST love, I do not go,
For weariness of thee,
Nor in hope the world can show
A fitter love for me;
But since that I
At the last must part, 'tis best,
Thus to use myself in jest
By feigned deaths to die.
Yesternight the sun went hence,
And yet is here to-day;
He hath no desire nor sense,
Nor half so short a way;
Then fear not me,
But believe that I shall make
Speedier journeys, since I take
More wings and spurs than he.
O how feeble is man's power,
That if good fortune fall,
Cannot add another hour,
Nor a lost hour recall;
But come bad chance,
And we join to it our strength,
And we teach it art and length,
Itself o'er us to advance.
When thou sigh'st, thou sigh'st not wind,
But sigh'st my soul away;
When thou weep'st, unkindly kind,
My life's blood doth decay.
It cannot be
That thou lovest me as thou say'st,
If in thine my life thou waste,
That art the best of me.
Let not thy divining heart

Forethink me any ill;
Destiny may take thy part,
And may thy fears fulfil.
But think that we
Are but turn'd aside to sleep.
They who one another keep
Alive, ne'er parted be.

The Legacy

WHEN last I died, and, dear, I die
As often as from thee I go,
Though it be but an hour ago
—And lovers' hours be full eternity—
I can remember yet, that I
Something did say, and something did bestow;
Though I be dead, which sent me, I might be
Mine own executor, and legacy.
I heard me say, "Tell her anon,
That myself," that is you, not I,
" Did kill me," and when I felt me die,
I bid me send my heart, when I was gone;
But I alas ! could there find none;
When I had ripp'd, and search'd where hearts should lie,
It kill'd me again, that I who still was true
In life, in my last will should cozen you.
Yet I found something like a heart,
But colours it, and corners had;
It was not good, it was not bad,
It was entire to none, and few had part;
As good as could be made by art
It seem'd, and therefore for our loss be sad.
I meant to send that heart instead of mine,
But O ! no man could hold it, for 'twas thine.

A Fever

O ! DO not die, for I shall hate
All women so, when thou art gone,
That thee I shall not celebrate,

When I remember thou wast one.
But yet thou canst not die, I know;
To leave this world behind, is death;
But when thou from this world wilt go,
The whole world vapours with thy breath.
Or if, when thou, the world's soul, go'st,
It stay, 'tis but thy carcase then;
The fairest woman, but thy ghost,
But corrupt worms, the worthiest men.
O wrangling schools, that search what fire
Shall burn this world, had none the wit
Unto this knowledge to aspire,
That this her feaver might be it?
And yet she cannot waste by this,
Nor long bear this torturing wrong,
For more corruption needful is,
To fuel such a fever long.
These burning fits but meteors be,
Whose matter in thee is soon spent;
Thy beauty, and all parts, which are thee,
Are unchangeable firmament.
Yet 'twas of my mind, seizing thee,
Though it in thee cannot persévér;
For I had rather owner be
Of thee one hour, than all else ever.

Air and Angels

TWICE or thrice had I loved thee,
Before I knew thy face or name;
So in a voice, so in a shapeless flame
Angels affect us oft, and worshipp'd be.
Still when, to where thou wert, I came,
Some lovely glorious nothing did I see.
But since my soul, whose child love is,
Takes limbs of flesh, and else could nothing do,
More subtle than the parent is
Love must not be, but take a body too;
And therefore what thou wert, and who,

I bid Love ask, and now
That it assume thy body, I allow,
And fix itself in thy lip, eye, and brow.
Whilst thus to ballast love I thought,
And so more steadily to have gone,
With wares which would sink admiration,
I saw I had love's pinnace overfraught;
Thy every hair for love to work upon
Is much too much; some fitter must be sought;
For, nor in nothing, nor in things
Extreme, and scattering bright, can love inhere;
Then as an angel face and wings
Of air, not pure as it, yet pure doth wear,
So thy love may be my love's sphere;
Just such disparity
As is 'twixt air's and angels' purity,
'Twixt women's love, and men's, will ever be.

Break of Day

STAY, O sweet, and do not rise;
The light that shines comes from thine eyes;
The day breaks not, it is my heart,
Because that you and I must part.
Stay, or else my joys will die,
And perish in their infancy

Another of The Same, Break of the day

'TIS true, 'tis day; what though it be?
O, wilt thou therefore rise from me?
Why should we rise because 'tis light?
Did we lie down because 'twas night?
Love, which in spite of darkness brought us hither,
Should in despite of light keep us together.
Light hath no tongue, but is all eye;
If it could speak as well as spy,
This were the worst that it could say,
That being well I fain would stay,
And that I loved my heart and honour so

That I would not from him, that had them, go.
Must business thee from hence remove?
O ! that's the worst disease of love,
The poor, the foul, the false, love can
Admit, but not the busied man.
He which hath business, and makes love, doth do
Such wrong, as when a married man doth woo.

The Anniversary

ALL kings, and all their favourites,
All glory of honours, beauties, wits,
The sun it self, which makes time, as they pass,
Is elder by a year now than it was
When thou and I first one another saw.
All other things to their destruction draw,
Only our love hath no decay;
This no to-morrow hath, nor yesterday;
Running it never runs from us away,
But truly keeps his first, last, everlasting day.
Two graves must hide thine and my corse;
If one might, death were no divorce.
Alas ! as well as other princes, we
—Who prince enough in one another be—
Must leave at last in death these eyes and ears,
Oft fed with true oaths, and with sweet salt tears;
But souls where nothing dwells but love
—All other thoughts being inmates—then shall prove
This or a love increasèd there above,
When bodies to their graves, souls from their graves remove.
And then we shall be throughly blest;
But now no more than all the rest.
Here upon earth we're kings, and none but we
Can be such kings, nor of such subjects be.
Who is so safe as we? where none can do
Treason to us, except one of us two.
True and false fears let us refrain,
Let us love nobly, and live, and add again

Years and years unto years, till we attain
To write threescore; this is the second of our reign.

A Valediction of My Name, In the Window

I

MY name engraved herein
Doth contribute my firmness to this glass,
Which ever since that charm hath been
As hard, as that which graved it was;
Thine eye will give it price enough, to mock
The diamonds of either rock.

II

'Tis much that glass should be
As all-confessing, and through-shine as I;
'Tis more that it shows thee to thee,
And clear reflects thee to thine eye.
But all such rules love's magic can undo;
Here you see me, and I am you.

III

As no one point, nor dash,
Which are but accessories to this name,
The showers and tempests can outwash
So shall all times find me the same;
You this entireness better may fulfill,
Who have the pattern with you still.

IV

Or if too hard and deep
This learning be, for a scratch'd name to teach,
It as a given death's head keep,
Lovers' mortality to preach;
Or think this ragged bony name to be
My ruinous anatomy.

V

Then, as all my souls be
Emparadised in you—in whom alone
I understand, and grow, and see—
The rafters of my body, bone,
Being still with you, the muscle, sinew, and vein

Which tile this house, will come again.

VI

Till my return repair
And recompact my scatter'd body so,
As all the virtuous powers which are
Fix'd in the stars are said to flow
Into such characters as gravèd be
When these stars have supremacy.

VII

So since this name was cut,
When love and grief their exaltation had,
No door 'gainst this name's influence shut.
As much more loving, as more sad,
'Twill make thee; and thou shouldst, till I return,
Since I die daily, daily mourn.

VIII

When thy inconsiderate hand
Flings open this casement, with my trembling name,
To look on one, whose wit or land
New battery to thy heart may frame,
Then think this name alive, and that thou thus
In it offend'st my Genius.

IX

And when thy melted maid,
Corrupted by thy lover's gold and page,
His letter at thy pillow hath laid,
Disputed it, and tamed thy rage,
And thou begin'st to thaw towards him, for this,
May my name step in, and hide his.

X

And if this treason go
To an overt act and that thou write again,
In superscribing, this name flow
Into thy fancy from the pane;
So, in forgetting thou remembʼrest right,
And unaware to me shalt write.

XI

But glass and lines must be

No means our firm substantial love to keep;
Near death inflicts this lethargy,
And this I murmur in my sleep;
Inpute this idle talk, to that I go,
For dying men talk often so.

Twickenham Garden

BLASTED with sighs, and surrounded with tears,
Hither I come to seek the spring,
And at mine eyes, and at mine ears,
Receive such balms as else cure every thing.
But O ! self-traitor, I do bring
The spider Love, which transubstantiates all,
And can convert manna to gall;
And that this place may thoroughly be thought
True paradise, I have the serpent brought.
'Twere wholesomer for me that winter did
Benight the glory of this place,
And that a grave frost did forbid
These trees to laugh and mock me to my face;
But that I may not this disgrace
Endure, nor yet leave loving, Love, let me
Some senseless piece of this place be;
Make me a mandrake, so I may grow here,
Or a stone fountain weeping out my year.
Hither with crystal phials, lovers, come,
And take my tears, which are love's wine,
And try your mistress' tears at home,
For all are false, that taste not just like mine.
Alas ! hearts do not in eyes shine,
Nor can you more judge women's thoughts by tears,
Than by her shadow what she wears.
O perverse sex, where none is true but she,
Who's therefore true, because her truth kills me.

Valediction to his Book

I'LL tell thee now (dear love) what thou shalt do
To anger destiny, as she doth us;

How I shall stay, though she eloign me thus,
And how posterity shall know it too;
How thine may out-endure
Sibyl's glory, and obscure
Her who from Pindar could allure,
And her, through whose help Lucan is not lame,
And her, whose book (they say) Homer did find, and name.
Study our manuscripts, those myriads
Of letters, which have past 'twixt thee and me;
Thence write our annals, and in them will be
To all whom love's subliming fire invades,
Rule and example found;
There the faith of any ground
No schismatic will dare to wound,
That sees, how Love this grace to us affords,
To make, to keep, to use, to be these his records.
This book, as long-lived as the elements,
Or as the world's form, this all-gravèd tome
In cypher writ, or new made idiom;
We for Love's clergy only are instruments;
When this book is made thus,
Should again the ravenous
Vandals and Goths invade us,
Learning were safe; in this our universe,
Schools might learn sciences, spheres music, angels verse.
Here Love's divines—since all divinity
Is love or wonder—may find all they seek,
Whether abstract spiritual love they like,
Their souls exhaled with what they do not see;
Or, loth so to amuse
Faith's infirmity, they choose
Something which they may see and use;
For, though mind be the heaven, where love doth sit,
Beauty a convenient type may be to figure it.
Here more than in their books may lawyers find,
Both by what titles mistresses are ours,
And how prerogative these states devours,

Transferr'd from Love himself, to womankind;
Who, though from heart and eyes,
They exact great subsidies,
Forsake him who on them relies;
And for the cause, honour, or conscience give;
Chimeras vain as they or their prerogative.
Here statesmen—or of them, they which can read—
May of their occupation find the grounds;
Love, and their art, alike it deadly wounds,
If to consider what 'tis, one proceed.
In both they do excel
Who the present govern well,
Whose weakness none doth, or dares tell;
In this thy book, such will there something see,
As in the Bible some can find out alchemy.
Thus vent thy thoughts; abroad I'll study thee,
As he removes far off, that great heights takes;
How great love is, presence best trial makes,
But absence tries how long this love will be;
To take a latitude
Sun, or stars, are fitliest view'd
At their brightest, but to conclude
Of longitudes, what other way have we,
But to mark when and where the dark eclipses be?

Community

GOOD we must love, and must hate ill,
For ill is ill, and good good still;
But there are things indifferent,
Which wee may neither hate, nor love,
But one, and then another prove,
As we shall find our fancy bent.
If then at first wise Nature had
Made women either good or bad,
Then some wee might hate, and some choose;
But since she did them so create,
That we may neither love, nor hate,
Only this rests, all all may use.

If they were good it would be seen;
Good is as visible as green,
And to all eyes itself betrays.
If they were bad, they could not last;
Bad doth itself, and others waste;
So they deserve nor blame, nor praise.
But they are ours as fruits are ours;
He that but tastes, he that devours,
And he that leaves all, doth as well;
Changed loves are but changed sorts of meat;
And when he hath the kernel eat,
Who doth not fling away the shell?

Love's Growth

I SCARCE believe my love to be so pure
As I had thought it was,
Because it doth endure
Vicissitude, and season, as the grass;
Methinks I lied all winter, when I swore
My love was infinite, if spring make it more.
But if this medicine, love, which cures all sorrow
With more, not only be no quintessence,
But mix'd of all stuffs, vexing soul, or sense,
And of the sun his active vigour borrow,
Love's not so pure, and abstract as they use
To say, which have no mistress but their Muse;
But as all else, being elemented too,
Love sometimes would contemplate, sometimes do.
And yet no greater, but more eminent,
Love by the spring is grown;
As in the firmament
Stars by the sun are not enlarged, but shown,
Gentle love deeds, as blossoms on a bough,
From love's awakened root do bud out now.
If, as in water stirr'd more circles be
Produced by one, love such additions take,
Those like so many spheres but one heaven make,
For they are all concentric unto thee;

And though each spring do add to love new heat,
As princes do in times of action get
New taxes, and remit them not in peace,
No winter shall abate this spring's increase.

Love's Exchange

LOVE, any devil else but you
Would for a given soul give something too.
At court your fellows every day
Give th' art of rhyming, huntsmanship, or play,
For them which were their own before;
Only I have nothing, which gave more,
But am, alas ! by being lowly, lower.
I ask no dispensation now,
To falsify a tear, or sigh, or vow;
I do not sue from thee to draw
A *non obstante* on nature's law;
These are prerogatives, they inhere
In thee and thine; none should forswear
Except that he Love's minion were.
Give me thy weakness, make me blind,
Both ways, as thou and thine, in eyes and mind;
Love, let me never know that this
Is love, or, that love childish is;
Let me not know that others know
That she knows my paines, lest that so
A tender shame make me mine own new woe.
If thou give nothing, yet thou 'rt just,
Because I would not thy first motions trust;
Small towns which stand stiff, till great shot
Enforce them, by war's law condition not;
Such in Love's warfare is my case;
I may not article for grace,
Having put Love at last to show this face.
This face, by which he could command
And change th' idolatry of any land,
This face, which, wheresoe'er it comes,
Can call vow'd men from cloisters, dead from tombs,

And melt both poles at once, and store
Deserts with cities, and make more
Mines in the earth, than quarries were before.
For this Love is enraged with me,
Yet kills not; if I must example be
To future rebels, if th' unborn
Must learn by my being cut up and torn,
Kill, and dissect me, Love; for this
Torture against thine own end is;
Rack'd carcasses make ill anatomies.

Confined Love

Some man unworthy to be possessor
Of old or new love, himself being false or weak,
Thought his pain and shame would be lesser,
If on womankind he might his anger wreak;
And thence a law did grow,
One might but one man know;
But are other creatures so?
Are sun, moon, or stars by law forbidden
To smile where they list, or lend away their light?
Are birds divorced or are they chidden
If they leave their mate, or lie abroad a night?
Beasts do no jointures lose
Though they new lovers choose;
But we are made worse than those.
Who e'er rigg'd fair ships to lie in harbours,
And not to seek lands, or not to deal with all?
Or built fair houses, set trees, and arbours,
Only to lock up, or else to let them fall?
Good is not good, unless
A thousand it possess,
But doth waste with greediness.

The Dream

DEAR love, for nothing less than thee
Would I have broke this happy dream;
It was a theme

For reason, much too strong for fantasy.
Therefore thou waked'st me wisely; yet
My dream thou brokest not, but continued'st it.
Thou art so true that thoughts of thee suffice
To make dreams truths, and fables histories;
Enter these arms, for since thou thought'st it best,
Not to dream all my dream, let's act the rest.
As lightning, or a taper's light,
Thine eyes, and not thy noise waked me;
Yet I thought thee
—For thou lovest truth—an angel, at first sight;
But when I saw thou saw'st my heart,
And knew'st my thoughts beyond an angel's art,
When thou knew'st what I dreamt, when thou knew'st when
Excess of joy would wake me, and camest then,
I must confess, it could not choose but be
Profane, to think thee any thing but thee.
Coming and staying show'd thee, thee,
But rising makes me doubt, that now
Thou art not thou.
That love is weak where fear's as strong as he;
'Tis not all spirit, pure and brave,
If mixture it of fear, shame, honour have;
Perchance as torches, which must ready be,
Men light and put out, so thou deal'st with me;
Thou camest to kindle, go'st to come; then I
Will dream that hope again, but else would die.

A Valediction of Weeping

LET me pour forth
My tears before thy face, whilst I stay here,
For thy face coins them, and thy stamp they bear,
And by this mintage they are something worth.
For thus they be
Pregnant of thee;
Fruits of much grief they are, emblems of more;
When a tear falls, that thou fall'st which it bore;

So thou and I are nothing then, when on a divers shore.
On a round ball
A workman, that hath copies by, can lay
An Europe, Afric, and an Asia,
And quickly make that, which was nothing, all.
So doth each tear,
Which thee doth wear,
A globe, yea world, by that impression grow,
Till thy tears mix'd with mine do overflow
This world, by waters sent from thee, my heaven dissolvèd so.
O! more than moon,
Draw not up seas to drown me in thy sphere;
Weep me not dead, in thine arms, but forbear
To teach the sea, what it may do too soon;
Let not the wind
Example find
To do me more harm than it purposeth:
Since thou and I sigh one another's breath,
Whoe'er sighs most is cruellest, and hastes the other's death.

Love's Alchemy

Some that have deeper digg'd love's mine than I,
Say, where his centric happiness doth lie.
I have loved, and got, and told,
But should I love, get, tell, till I were old,
I should not find that hidden mystery.
O ! 'tis imposture all;
And as no chemic yet th' elixir got,
But glorifies his pregnant pot,
If by the way to him befall
Some odoriferous thing, or medicinal,
So, lovers dream a rich and long delight,
But get a winter-seeming summer's night.
Our ease, our thrift, our honour, and our day,
Shall we for this vain bubble's shadow pay?
Ends love in this, that my man

Can be as happy as I can, if he can
Endure the short scorn of a bridegroom's play?
That loving wretch that swears,
'Tis not the bodies marry, but the minds,
Which he in her angelic finds,
Would swear as justly, that he hears,
In that day's rude hoarse minstrelsy, the spheres.
Hope not for mind in women; at their best,
Sweetness and wit they are, but mummy, possess'd.

The Curse

WHOEVER guesses, thinks, or dreams, he knows
Who is my mistress, wither by this curse;
Him, only for his purse
May some dull whore to love dispose,
And then yield unto all that are his foes;
May he be scorn'd by one, whom all else scorn,
Forswear to others, what to her he hath sworn,
With fear of missing, shame of getting, torn.
Madness his sorrow, gout his cramps, may he
Make, by but thinking who hath made him such;
And may he feel no touch
Of conscience, but of fame, and be
Anguish'd, not that 'twas sin, but that 'twas she;
Or may he for her virtue reverence
One that hates him only for impotence,
And equal traitors be she and his sense.
May he dream treason, and believe that he
Meant to perform it, and confesses, and die,
And no record tell why;
His sons, which none of his may be,
Inherit nothing but his infamy;
Or may he so long parasites have fed,
That he would fain be theirs whom he hath bred,
And at the last be circumcised for bread.
The venom of all stepdames, gamesters' gall,
What tyrants and their subjects interwish,
What plants, mine, beasts, fowl, fish,

Can contribute, all ill, which all
Prophets or poets spake, and all which shall
Be annex'd in schedules unto this by me,
Fall on that man; For if it be a she
Nature beforehand hath out-cursèd me.

The Message

SEND home my long stray'd eyes to me,
Which, O ! Too long have dwelt on thee;
yet since there they have learn'd such ill,
such forced fashions,
and false passions,
That they be
Made by thee
Fit for no good sight, keep them still.
Send home my harmless heart again,
Which no unworthy thought could stain;
Which if it be taught by thine
To make jestings
Of protestings,
And break both
Word and oath,
Keep it, for then 'tis none of mine.
Yet send me back my heart and eyes,
That I may know, and see thy lies,
And may laugh and joy, when thou
Art in anguish
And dost languish
For some one
That will none,
Or prove as false as thou art now.

A Nocturnal Upon St. Lucy's Day

BEING THE SHORTEST DAY.
'TIS the year's midnight, and it is the day's,
Lucy's, who scarce seven hours herself unmasks;
The sun is spent, and now his flasks
Send forth light squibs, no constant rays;

The world's whole sap is sunk;
The general balm th' hydroptic earth hath drunk,
Whither, as to the bed's-feet, life is shrunk,
Dead and interr'd; yet all these seem to laugh,
Compared with me, who am their epitaph.
Study me then, you who shall lovers be
At the next world, that is, at the next spring;
For I am every dead thing,
In whom Love wrought new alchemy.
For his art did express
A quintessence even from nothingness,
From dull privations, and lean emptiness;
He ruin'd me, and I am re-begot
Of absence, darkness, death—things which are not.
All others, from all things, draw all that's good,
Life, soul, form, spirit, whence they being have;
I, by Love's limbec, am the grave
Of all, that's nothing. Oft a flood
Have we two wept, and so
Drown'd the whole world, us two; oft did we grow,
To be two chaoses, when we did show
Care to aught else; and often absences
Withdrew our souls, and made us carcasses.
But I am by her death—which word wrongs her—
Of the first nothing the elixir grown;
Were I a man, that I were one
I needs must know; I should prefer,
If I were any beast,
Some ends, some means; yea plants, yea stones detest,
And love; all, all some properties invest.
If I an ordinary nothing were,
As shadow, a light, and body must be here.
But I am none; nor will my sun renew.
You lovers, for whose sake the lesser sun
At this time to the Goat is run
To fetch new lust, and give it you,
Enjoy your summer all,
Since she enjoys her long night's festival.

Let me prepare towards her, and let me call
This hour her vigil, and her eve, since this
Both the year's and the day's deep midnight is.

The Prohibition.

TAKE heed of loving me;
At least remember, I forbade it thee;
Not that I shall repair my unthrifty waste
Of breath and blood, upon thy sighs and tears,
By being to thee then what to me thou wast;
But so great joy our life at once outwears.
Then, lest thy love by my death frustrate be,
If thou love me, take heed of loving me.
Take heed of hating me,
Or too much triumph in the victory;
Not that I shall be mine own officer,
And hate with hate again retaliate;
But thou wilt lose the style of conqueror,
If I, thy conquest, perish by thy hate.
Then, lest my being nothing lessen thee,
If thou hate me, take heed of hating me.
Yet love and hate me too;
So these extremes shall ne'er their office do;
Love me, that I may die the gentler way,
Hate me, because thy love's too great for me;
Or let these two, themselves, not me, decay;
So shall I live thy stage, not triumph be.
Lest thou thy love and hate, and me undo,
O let me live, yet love and hate me too.

Witchcraft By a Picture

I FIX mine eye on thine, and there
Pity my picture burning in thine eye;
My picture drown'd in a transparent tear,
When I look lower I espy;
Hadst thou the wicked skill
By pictures made and marr'd, to kill,
How many ways mightst thou perform thy will?

But now I've drunk thy sweet salt tears,
And though thou pour more, I'll depart;
My picture vanished, vanish all fears
That I can be endamaged by that art;
Though thou retain of me
One picture more, yet that will be,
Being in thine own heart, from all malice free.

The Bait

COME live with me, and be my love,
And we will some new pleasures prove
Of golden sands, and crystal brooks,
With silken lines and silver hooks.
There will the river whisp'ring run
Warm'd by thy eyes, more than the sun;
And there th' enamour'd fish will stay,
Begging themselves they may betray.
When thou wilt swim in that live bath,
Each fish, which every channel hath,
Will amorously to thee swim,
Gladder to catch thee, than thou him.
If thou, to be so seen, be'st loth,
By sun or moon, thou dark'nest both,
And if myself have leave to see,
I need not their light, having thee.
Let others freeze with angling reeds,
And cut their legs with shells and weeds,
Or treacherously poor fish beset,
With strangling snare, or windowy net.
Let coarse bold hands from slimy nest
The bedded fish in banks out-wrest;
Or curious traitors, sleeve-silk flies,
Bewitch poor fishes' wand'ring eyes.
For thee, thou need'st no such deceit,
For thou thyself art thine own bait:
That fish, that is not catch'd thereby,
Alas ! Is wiser far than I.

The Apparition

WHEN by thy scorn, O murd'ress, I am dead,
And that thou thinkst thee free
From all solicitation from me,
Then shall my ghost come to thy bed,
And thee, feign'd vestal, in worse arms shall see:
Then thy sick taper will begin to wink,
And he, whose thou art then, being tired before,
Will, if thou stir, or pinch to wake him, think
Thou call'st for more,
And, in false sleep, will from thee shrink:
And then, poor aspen wretch, neglected thou
Bathed in a cold quicksilver sweat wilt lie,
A verier ghost than I.
What I will say, I will not tell thee now,
Lest that preserve thee; and since my love is spent,
I'd rather thou shouldst painfully repent,
Than by my threatenings rest still innocent.

The Broken Heart

He is stark mad, whoever says,
That he hath been in love an hour,
Yet not that love so soon decays,
But that it can ten in less space devour;
Who will believe me, if I swear
That I have had the plague a year?
Who would not laugh at me, if I should say
I saw a flash of powder burn a day?
Ah, what a trifle is a heart,
If once into love's hands it come!
All other griefs allow a part
To other griefs, and ask themselves but some;
They come to us, but us love draws;
He swallows us and never chaws;
By him, as by chain'd shot, whole ranks do die;
He is the tyrant pike, our hearts the fry.
If 'twere not so, what did become

Of my heart when I first saw thee?
I brought a heart into the room,
But from the room I carried none with me.
If it had gone to thee, I know
Mine would have taught thine heart to show
More pity unto me; but Love, alas!
At one first blow did shiver it as glass.
Yet nothing can to nothing fall,
Nor any place be empty quite;
Therefore I think my breast hath all
Those pieces still, though they be not unite;
And now, as broken glasses show
A hundred lesser faces, so
My rags of heart can like, wish, and adore,
But after one such love, can love no more.

A Valediction Forbidding Mourning

AS virtuous men pass mildly away,
And whisper to their souls to go,
Whilst some of their sad friends do say,
"Now his breath goes," and some say, "No."
So let us melt, and make no noise,
No tear-floods, nor sigh-tempests move;
'Twere profanation of our joys
To tell the laity our love.
Moving of th' earth brings harms and fears;
Men reckon what it did, and meant;
But trepidation of the spheres,
Though greater far, is innocent.
Dull sublunary lovers' love
—Whose soul is sense—cannot admit
Of absence, 'cause it doth remove
The thing which elemented it.
But we by a love so much refined,
That ourselves know not what it is,
Inter-assurèd of the mind,
Care less, eyes, lips and hands to miss.
Our two souls therefore, which are one,

Though I must go, endure not yet
A breach, but an expansion,
Like gold to aery thinness beat.
If they be two, they are two so
As stiff twin compasses are two;
Thy soul, the fix'd foot, makes no show
To move, but doth, if th' other do.
And though it in the centre sit,
Yet, when the other far doth roam,
It leans, and hearkens after it,
And grows erect, as that comes home.
Such wilt thou be to me, who must,
Like th' other foot, obliquely run;
Thy firmness makes my circle just,
And makes me end where I begun.

The Ecstacy

WHERE, like a pillow on a bed,
A pregnant bank swell'd up, to rest
The violet's reclining head,
Sat we two, one another's best.
Our hands were firmly cemented
By a fast balm, which thence did spring;
Our eye-beams twisted, and did thread
Our eyes upon one double string.
So to engraft our hands, as yet
Was all the means to make us one;
And pictures in our eyes to get
Was all our propagation.
As, 'twixt two equal armies, Fate
Suspends uncertain victory,
Our souls—which to advance their state,
Were gone out—hung 'twixt her and me.
And whilst our souls negotiate there,
We like sepulchral statues lay;
All day, the same our postures were,
And we said nothing, all the day.
If any, so by love refined,

That he soul's language understood,
And by good love were grown all mind,
Within convenient distance stood,
He—though he knew not which soul spake,
Because both meant, both spake the same—
Might thence a new concoction take,
And part far purer than he came.
This ecstasy doth unperplex
(We said) and tell us what we love;
We see by this, it was not sex;
We see, we saw not, what did move:
But as all several souls contain
Mixture of things they know not what,
Love these mix'd souls doth mix again,
And makes both one, each this, and that.
A single violet transplant,
The strength, the colour, and the size—
All which before was poor and scant—
Redoubles still, and multiplies.
When love with one another so
Interanimates two souls,
That abler soul, which thence doth flow,
Defects of loneliness controls.
We then, who are this new soul, know,
Of what we are composed, and made,
For th' atomies of which we grow
Are souls, whom no change can invade.
But, O alas! so long, so far,
Our bodies why do we forbear?
They are ours, though not we; we are
Th' intelligences, they the spheres.
We owe them thanks, because they thus
Did us, to us, at first convey,
Yielded their senses' force to us,
Nor are dross to us, but allay.
On man heaven's influence works not so,
But that it first imprints the air;
For soul into the soul may flow,

Though it to body first repair.
As our blood labours to beget
Spirits, as like souls as it can;
Because such fingers need to knit
That subtle knot, which makes us man;
So must pure lovers' souls descend
To affections, and to faculties,
Which sense may reach and apprehend,
Else a great prince in prison lies.
To our bodies turn we then, that so
Weak men on love reveal'd may look;
Love's mysteries in souls do grow,
But yet the body is his book.
And if some lover, such as we,
Have heard this dialogue of one,
Let him still mark us, he shall see
Small change when we're to bodies gone.

Love's Deity

I LONG to talk with some old lover's ghost,
Who died before the god of love was born.
I cannot think that he, who then loved most,
Sunk so low as to love one which did scorn.
But since this god produced a destiny,
And that vice-nature, custom, lets it be,
I must love her that loves not me.
Sure, they which made him god, meant not so much,
Nor he in his young godhead practised it.
But when an even flame two hearts did touch,
His office was indulgently to fit
Actives to passives. Correspondency
Only his subject was; it cannot be
Love, till I love her, who loves me.
But every modern god will now extend
His vast prerogative as far as Jove.
To rage, to lust, to write to, to commend,
All is the purlieu of the god of love.
O! Were we waken'd by this tyranny

To ungod this child again; it could not be
I should love her, who loves not me.
Rebel and atheist too, why murmur I,
As though I felt the worst that love could do?
Love might make me leave loving, or might try
A deeper plague, to make her love me too;
Which, since she loves before, I'm loth to see.
Falsehood is worse than hate; and that must be,
If she whom I love, should love me.

Love's Diet

TO what a cumbersome unwieldiness
And burdenous corpulence my love had grown,
But that I did, to make it less,
And keep it in proportion,
Give it a diet, made it feed upon
That which love worst endures, discretion
Above one sigh a day I allow'd him not,
Of which my fortune, and my faults had part;
And if sometimes by stealth he got
A she sigh from my mistress' heart,
And thought to feast upon that, I let him see
'Twas neither very sound, nor meant to me.
If he wrung from me a tear, I brined it so
With scorn and shame, that him it nourish'd not;
If he suck'd hers, I let him know
'Twas not a tear which he had got;
His drink was counterfeit, as was his meat;
For eyes, which roll towards all, weep not, but sweat.
Whatever he would dictate I writ that,
But burnt her letters when she writ to me;
And if that favour made him fat,
I said, "If any title be
Convey'd by this, ah ! What doth it avail,
To be the fortieth name in an entail?"
Thus I reclaim'd my buzzard love, to fly
At what, and when, and how, and where I choose.
Now negligent of sports I lie,

And now, as other falconers use,
I spring a mistress, swear, write, sigh, and weep;
And the game kill'd, or lost, go talk or sleep.

The Will

BEFORE I sigh my last gasp, let me breathe,
Great Love, some legacies; I here bequeath
Mine eyes to Argus, if mine eyes can see;
If they be blind, then, Love, I give them thee;
My tongue to Fame; to ambassadors mine ears;
To women, or the sea, my tears;
Thou, Love, hast taught me heretofore
By making me serve her who had twenty more,
That I should give to none, but such as had too much before.
My constancy I to the planets give;
My truth to them who at the court do live;
My ingenuity and openness,
To Jesuits; to buffoons my pensiveness;
My silence to any, who abroad hath been;
My money to a Capuchin:
Thou, Love, taught'st me, by appointing me
To love there, where no love received can be,
Only to give to such as have an incapacity.
My faith I give to Roman Catholics;
All my good works unto the Schismatics
Of Amsterdam; my best civility
And courtship to an University;
My modesty I give to soldiers bare;
My patience let gamesters share:
Thou, Love, taught'st me, by making me
Love her that holds my love disparity,
Only to give to those that count my gifts indignity.
I give my reputation to those
Which were my friends; mine industry to foes;
To schoolmen I bequeath my doubtfulness;
My sickness to physicians, or excess;
To nature all that I in rhyme have writ;

And to my company my wit:
Thou, Love, by making me adore
Her, who begot this love in me before,
Taught'st me to make, as though I gave, when I do but restore.
To him for whom the passing-bell next tolls,
I give my physic books; my written rolls
Of moral counsels I to Bedlam give;
My brazen medals unto them which live
In want of bread; to them which pass among
All foreigners, mine English tongue:
Though, Love, by making me love one
Who thinks her friendship a fit portion
For younger lovers, dost my gifts thus disproportion.
Therefore I'll give no more, but I'll undo
The world by dying, because love dies too.
Then all your beauties will be no more worth
Than gold in mines, where none doth draw it forth;
And all your graces no more use shall have,
Than a sun-dial in a grave:
Thou, Love, taught'st me by making me
Love her who doth neglect both me and thee,
To invent, and practise this one way, to annihilate all three.

The Funeral

WHOEVER comes to shroud me, do not harm,
Nor question much,
That subtle wreath of hair, which crowns my arm;
The mystery, the sign, you must not touch;
For 'tis my outward soul,
Viceroy to that, which then to heaven being gone,
Will leave this to control
And keep these limbs, her provinces, from dissolution.
For if the sinewy thread my brain lets fall
Through every part
Can tie those parts, and make me one of all,
Those hairs which upward grew, and strength and art
Have from a better brain,

Can better do 't; except she meant that I
By this should know my pain,
As prisoners then are manacled, when they're condemn'd to die.
Whate'er she meant by it, bury it with me,
For since I am
Love's martyr, it might breed idolatry,
If into other hands these relics came.
As 'twas humility
To afford to it all that a soul can do,
So 'tis some bravery,
That since you would have none of me, I bury some of you.

The Blossom

LITTLE think'st thou, poor flower,
Whom I've watch'd six or seven days,
And seen thy birth, and seen what every hour
Gave to thy growth, thee to this height to raise,
And now dost laugh and triumph on this bough,
Little think'st thou,
That it will freeze anon, and that I shall
To-morrow find thee fallen, or not at all.
Little think'st thou, poor heart,
That labourest yet to nestle thee,
And think'st by hovering here to get a part
In a forbidden or forbidding tree,
And hopest her stiffness by long siege to bow,
Little think'st thou
That thou to-morrow, ere the sun doth wake,
Must with the sun and me a journey take.
But thou, which lovest to be
Subtle to plague thyself, wilt say,
Alas ! if you must go, what's that to me?
Here lies my business, and here I will stay
You go to friends, whose love and means present
Various content
To your eyes, ears, and taste, and every part;

If then your body go, what need your heart?
Well then, stay here; but know,
When thou hast stay'd and done thy most,
A naked thinking heart, that makes no show,
Is to a woman but a kind of ghost.
How shall she know my heart; or having none,
Know thee for one?
Practice may make her know some other part;
But take my word; she doth not know a heart.
Meet me in London, then,
Twenty days hence, and thou shalt see
Me fresher and more fat, by being with men,
Than if I had stay'd still with her and thee.
For God's sake, if you can, be you so too;
I will give you
There to another friend, whom we shall find
As glad to have my body as my mind.

The Primrose, Being At Montgomery Castle

UPON THE HILL, ON WHICH IT IS SITUATE.
UPON this Primrose hill,
Where, if heaven would distil
A shower of rain, each several drop might go
To his own primrose, and grow manna so;
And where their form, and their infinity
Make a terrestrial galaxy,
As the small stars do in the sky;
I walk to find a true love; and I see
That 'tis not a mere woman, that is she,
But must or more or less than woman be.
Yet know I not, which flower
I wish; a six, or four;
For should my true-love less than woman be,
She were scarce anything; and then, should she
Be more than woman, she would get above
All thought of sex, and think to move
My heart to study her, and not to love.
Both these were monsters; since there must reside

Falsehood in woman, I could more abide,
She were by art, than nature falsified.
Live, primrose, then, and thrive
With thy true number five;
And, woman, whom this flower doth represent,
With this mysterious number be content;
Ten is the farthest number; if half ten
Belongs to each woman, then
Each woman may take half us men;
Or—if this will not serve their turn—since all
Numbers are odd, or even, and they fall
First into five, women may take us all.

The Relic

WHEN my grave is broke up again
Some second guest to entertain,
—For graves have learn'd that woman-head,
To be to more than one a bed—
And he that digs it, spies
A bracelet of bright hair about the bone,
Will he not let us alone,
And think that there a loving couple lies,
Who thought that this device might be some way
To make their souls at the last busy day
Meet at this grave, and make a little stay?
If this fall in a time, or land,
Where mass-devotion doth command,
Then he that digs us up will bring
Us to the bishop or the king,
To make us relics; then
Thou shalt be a Mary Magdalen, and I
A something else thereby;
All women shall adore us, and some men.
And, since at such time miracles are sought,
I would have that age by this paper taught
What miracles we harmless lovers wrought.
First we loved well and faithfully,
Yet knew not what we loved, nor why;

Difference of sex we never knew,
No more than guardian angels do;
Coming and going we
Perchance might kiss, but not between those meals;
Our hands ne'er touch'd the seals,
Which nature, injured by late law, sets free.
These miracles we did; but now alas !
All measure, and all language, I should pass,
Should I tell what a miracle she was.

The Dissolution

SHE's dead; and all which die
To their first elements resolve;
And we were mutual elements to us,
And made of one another.
My body then doth hers involve,
And those things whereof I consist hereby
In me abundant grow, and burdenous,
And nourish not, but smother.
My fire of passion, sighs of air,
Water of tears, and earthly sad despair,
Which my materials be,
But near worn out by love's security,
She, to my loss, doth by her death repair.
And I might live long wretched so,
But that my fire doth with my fuel grow.
Now, as those active kings
Whose foreign conquest treasure brings,
Receive more, and spend more, and soonest break,
This —which I am amazed that I can speak—
This death, hath with my store
My use increased.
And so my soul, more earnestly released,
Will outstrip hers; as bullets flown before
A latter bullet may o'ertake, the powder being more.

The Damp

WHEN I am dead, and doctors know not why,

And my friends' curiosity
Will have me cut up to survey each part,
When they shall find your picture in my heart,
You think a sudden damp of love
Will thorough all their senses move,
And work on them as me, and so prefer
Your murder to the name of massacre,
Poor victories; but if you dare be brave,
And pleasure in your conquest have,
First kill th' enormous giant, your Disdain;
And let th' enchantress Honour, next be slain;
And like a Goth and Vandal rise,
Deface records and histories
Of your own arts and triumphs over men,
And without such advantage kill me then,
For I could muster up, as well as you,
My giants, and my witches too,
Which are vast Constancy and Secretness;
But these I neither look for nor profess;
Kill me as woman, let me die
As a mere man; do you but try
Your passive valour, and you shall find then,
Naked you have odds enough of any man.

A Jet Ring Sen

THOU art not so black as my heart,
Nor half so brittle as her heart, thou art;
What would'st thou say? shall both
our properties by thee be spoke,
—Nothing more endless, nothing sooner broke?
Marriage rings are not of this stuff;
Oh, why should ought less precious, or less tough
Figure our loves? except in thy name thou
have bid it say,
"—I'm cheap, and nought but fashion; fling me away."
Yet stay with me since thou art come,
Circle this finger's top, which didst her thumb;
Be justly proud, and gladly safe, that thou dost

dwell with me;
She that, O! broke her faith, would soon break thee.

Negative Love

I NEVER stoop'd so low, as they
Which on an eye, cheek, lip, can prey;
Seldom to them which soar no higher
Than virtue, or the mind to admire.
For sense and understanding may
Know what gives fuel to their fire;
My love, though silly, is more brave;
For may I miss, whene'er I crave,
If I know yet what I would have.
If that be simply perfectest,
Which can by no way be express'd
But negatives, my love is so.
To all, which all love, I say no.
If any who deciphers best,
What we know not—ourselves—can know,
Let him teach me that nothing. This
As yet my ease and comfort is,
Though I speed not, I cannot miss.

The Expiration

SO, so, break off this last lamenting kiss,
Which sucks two souls, and vapours both away;
Turn, thou ghost, that way, and let me turn this,
And let ourselves benight our happiest day.
We ask none leave to love; nor will we owe
Any so cheap a death as saying, "Go."
Go; and if that word have not quite killed thee,
Ease me with death, by bidding me go too.
Or, if it have, let my word work on me,
And a just office on a murderer do.
Except it be too late, to kill me so,
Being double dead, going, and bidding, "Go."

The Computation

FOR my first twenty years, since yesterday,

I scarce believed thou couldst be gone away;
For forty more I fed on favours past,
And forty on hopes that thou wouldst they might last;
Tears drown'd one hundred, and sighs blew out two;
A thousand, I did neither think nor do,
Or not divide, all being one thought of you;
Or in a thousand more, forgot that too.
Yet call not this long life; but think that I
Am, by being dead, immortal; can ghosts die?

The Paradox

NO lover saith, I love, nor any other
Can judge a perfect lover;
He thinks that else none can or will agree,
That any loves but he;
I cannot say I loved, for who can say
He was kill'd yesterday.
Love with excess of heat, more young than old,
Death kills with too much cold;
We die but once, and who loved last did die,
He that saith, twice, doth lie;
For though he seem to move, and stir a while,
It doth the sense beguile.
Such life is like the light which bideth yet
When the life's light is set,
Or like the heat which fire in solid matter
Leaves behind, two hours after.
Once I loved and died; and am now become
Mine epitaph and tomb;
Here dead men speak their last, and so do I;
Love-slain, lo! here I die.

SongSoul's Joy, Now I am Gone

SOUL'S joy, now I am gone,
And you alone,
—Which cannot be,
Since I must leave myself with thee,
And carry thee with me—

Yet when unto our eyes
Absence denies
Each other's sight,
And makes to us a constant night,
When others change to light;
O give no way to grief,
But let belief
Of mutual love
This wonder to the vulgar prove,
Our bodies, not we move.
Let not thy wit beweep
Words but sense deep;
For when we miss
By distance our hope's joining bliss,
Even then our souls shall kiss;
Fools have no means to meet,
But by their feet;
Why should our clay
Over our spirits so much sway,
To tie us to that way?
O give no way to grief, &c.

Farewell To Love

WHILST yet to prove
I thought there was some deity in love,
So did I reverence, and gave
Worship; as atheists at their dying hour
Call, what they cannot name, an unknown power,
As ignorantly did I crave.
Thus when
Things not yet known are coveted by men,
Our desires give them fashion, and so
As they wax lesser, fall, as they size, grow.
But, from late fair,
His highness sitting in a golden chair,
Is not less cared for after three days
By children, than the thing which lovers so
Blindly admire, and with such worship woo;

Being had, enjoying it decays;
And thence,
What before pleased them all, takes but one sense,
And that so lamely, as it leaves behind
A kind of sorrowing dulness to the mind.
Ah cannot we,
As well as cocks and lions, jocund be
After such pleasures, unless wise
Nature decreed—since each such act, they say,
Diminisheth the length of life a day—
This; as she would man should despise
The sport,
Because that other curse of being short,
And only for a minute made to be
Eager, desires to raise posterity.
Since so, my mind
Shall not desire what no man else can find;
I'll no more dote and run
To pursue things which had endamaged me;
And when I come where moving beauties be,
As men do when the summer's sun
Grows great,
Though I admire their greatness, shun their heat.
Each place can afford shadows; if all fail,
Tis but applying worm-seed to the tail.

A Lecture Upon The Shadow

STAND still, and I will read to thee
A lecture, Love, in Love's philosophy.
These three hours that we have spent,
Walking here, two shadows went
Along with us, which we ourselves produced.
But, now the sun is just above our head,
We do those shadows tread,
And to brave clearness all things are reduced.
So whilst our infant loves did grow,
Disguises did, and shadows, flow
From us and our cares; but now 'tis not so.

That love hath not attain'd the highest degree,
Which is still diligent lest others see.
Except our loves at this noon stay,
We shall new shadows make the other way.
As the first were made to blind
Others, these which come behind
Will work upon ourselves, and blind our eyes.
If our loves faint, and westerwardly decline,
To me thou, falsely, thine
And I to thee mine actions shall disguise.
The morning shadows wear away,
But these grow longer all the day;
But O ! love's day is short, if love decay.
Love is a growing, or full constant light,
And his short minute, after noon, is night.

A Dialogue Between Sir Henry Wotton And

MR. DONNE.

W

IF her disdain least change in you can move,
You do not love,
For when that hope gives fuel to the fire,
You sell desire.
Love is not love, but given free;
And so is mine; so should yours be.

D

Her heart, that weeps to hear of others' moan,
To mine is stone.
Her eyes, that weep a stranger's eyes to see,
Joy to wound me.
Yet I so well affect each part,
As—caused by them—I love my smart.

W

Say her disdainings justly must be graced
With name of chaste;
And that she frowns lest longing should exceed,
And raging breed;
So her disdains can ne'er offend,
Unless self-love take private end.

D

'Tis love breeds love in me, and cold disdain
Kills that again,
As water causeth fire to fret and fume,
Till all consume.
Who can of love more rich gift make,
That to Love's self for love's own sake?
I'll never dig in quarry of an heart
To have no part,
Nor roast in fiery eyes, which always are
Canicular.
Who this way would a lover prove,
May show his patience, not his love.
A frown may be sometimes for physic good,
But not for food;
And for that raging humour there is sure
A gentler cure.
Why bar you love of private end,
Which never should to public tend?

Self-Love.

HE that cannot choose but love,
And strives against it still,
Never shall my fancy move,
For he loves against his will;
Nor he which is all his own,
And cannot pleasure choose;
When I am caught he can be gone,
And when he list refuse;
Nor he that loves none but fair,
For such by all are sought;
Nor he that can for foul ones care,
For his judgement then is nought;
Nor he that hath wit, for he
Will make me his jest or slave;
Nor a fool when others —
He can neither —
Nor he that still his mistress prays,

For she is thrall'd therefore;
Nor he that pays, not, for he says
Within, she's worth no more.
Is there then no kind of men
Whom I may freely prove?
I will vent that humour then
In mine own self-love.

The Token.

SEND me some tokens, that my hope may live
Or that my easeless thoughts may sleep and rest;
Send me some honey, to make sweet my hive,
That in my passions I may hope the best.
I beg nor ribbon wrought with thine own hands,
To knit our loves in the fantastic strain
Of new-touch'd youth; nor ring to show the stands
Of our affection, that, as that's round and plain,
So should our loves meet in simplicity;
No, nor the corals, which thy wrist enfold,
Laced up together in congruity,
To show our thoughts should rest in the same hold;
No, nor thy picture, though most gracious,
And most desired, 'cause 'tis like the best
Nor witty lines, which are most copious,
Within the writings which thou hast address'd.
Send me nor this nor that, to increase my score,
But swear thou think'st I love thee, and no more.

Epithalamion or Marriage Song

AN EPITHALAMION, OR MARRIAGE SONG
ON THE LADY ELIZABETH AND COUNT
PALATINE BEING MARRIED ON ST.VALENTINE'S
DAY.

I

HAIL Bishop Valentine, whose day this is;
All the air is thy diocese,
And all the chirping choristers
And other birds are thy parishioners;

Thou marriest every year
The lyric lark, and the grave whispering dove,
The sparrow that neglects his life for love,
The household bird with the red stomacher;
Thou makest the blackbird speed as soon,
As doth the goldfinch, or the halcyon;
The husband cock looks out, and straight is sped,
And meets his wife, which brings her feather-bed.
This day more cheerfully than ever shine;
This day, which might enflame thyself, old Valentine.

II

Till now, thou warmd'st with multiplying loves
Two larks, two sparrows, or two doves;
All that is nothing unto this;
For thou this day couplest two phoenixes;
Thou makst a taper see
What the sun never saw, and what the ark
—Which was of fouls and beasts the cage and park—
Did not contain, one bed contains, through thee;
Two phoenixes, whose joined breasts
Are unto one another mutual nests,
Where motion kindles such fires as shall give
Young phoenixes, and yet the old shall live;
Whose love and courage never shall decline,
But make the whole year through, thy day, O Valentine.

III

Up then, fair phoenix bride, frustrate the sun;
Thyself from thine affection
Takest warmth enough, and from thine eye
All lesser birds will take their jollity.
Up, up, fair bride, and call
Thy stars from out their several boxes, take
Thy rubies, pearls, and diamonds forth, and make
Thyself a constellation of them all;
And by their blazing signify
That a great princess falls, but doth not die.
Be thou a new star, that to us portends
Ends of much wonder; and be thou those ends.

Since thou dost this day in new glory shine,
May all men date records from this day, Valentine.

IV

Come forth, come forth, and as one glorious flame
Meeting another grows the same,
So meet thy Frederick, and so
To an inseparable union go,
Since separation
Falls not on such things as are infinite,
Nor things, which are but one, can disunite.
You're twice inseparable, great, and one;
Go then to where the bishop stays,
To make you one, his way, which divers ways
Must be effected; and when all is past,
And that you're one, by hearts and hands made fast,
You two have one way left, yourselves to entwine,
Besides this bishop's knot, of Bishop Valentine.

V

But O, what ails the sun, that here he stays,
Longer to-day than other days?
Stays he new light from these to get?
And finding here such star, is loth to set?
And why do you two walk,
So slowly paced in this procession?
Is all your care but to be look'd upon,
And be to others spectacle, and talk?
The feast with gluttonous delays
Is eaten, and too long their meat they praise;
The masquers come late, and I think, will stay,
Like fairies, till the cock crow them away.
Alas! did not antiquity assign
A night as well as day, to thee, old Valentine?

VI

They did, and night is come; and yet we see
Formalities retarding thee.
What mean these ladies, which—as though
They were to take a clock in pieces—go
So nicely about the bride?

A bride, before a "Good-night" could be said,
Should vanish from her clothes into her bed,
As souls from bodies steal, and are not spied.
But now she's laid; what though she be?
Yet there are more delays, for where is he?
He comes and passeth through sphere after sphere;
First her sheets, then her arms, then anywhere.
Let not this day, then, but this night be thine;
Thy day was but the eve to this, O Valentine.

VII

Here lies a she sun, and a he moon there;
She gives the best light to his sphere;
Or each is both, and all, and so
They unto one another nothing owe;
And yet they do, but are
So just and rich in that coin which they pay,
That neither would, nor needs forbear, nor stay;
Neither desires to be spared nor to spare.
They quickly pay their debt, and then
Take no acquittances, but pay again;
They pay, they give, they lend, and so let fall
No such occasion to be liberal.
More truth, more courage in these two do shine,
Than all thy turtles have and sparrows, Valentine.

VIII

And by this act these two phoenixes
Nature again restorèd is;
For since these two are two no more,
There's but one phoenix still, as was before.
Rest now at last, and we—
As satyrs watch the sun's uprise—will stay
Waiting when your eyes opened let out day,
Only desired because your face we see.
Others near you shall whispering speak,
And wagers lay, at which side day will break,
And win by observing, then, whose hand it is
That opens first a curtain, hers or his:
This will be tried to-morrow after nine,
Till which hour, we thy day enlarge, O Valentine.

Epithalamion Made at Lincoln's Inn.

HAIL sun-beams in the east are spread;
Leave, leave, fair bride, your solitary bed;
No more shall you return to it alone;
It nurseth sadness, and your body's print,
Like to a grave, the yielding down doth dint;
You, and your other you, meet there anon.
Put forth, put forth, that warm balm-breathing thigh,
Which when next time you in these sheets will smother,
There it must meet another,
Which never was, but must be, oft, more nigh.
Come glad from thence, go gladder than you came;
To-day put on perfection, and a woman's name.
Daughters of London, you which be
Our golden mines, and furnish'd treasury;
You which are angels, yet still bring with you
Thousands of angels on your marriage days;
Help with your presence, and devise to praise
These rites, which also unto you grow due;
Conceitedly dress her, and be assign'd,
By you fit place for every flower and jewel;
Make her for love fit fuel,
As gay as Flora and as rich as Ind;
So may she, fair and rich in nothing lame,
To-day put on perfection, and a woman's name.
And you frolic patricians,
Sons of those senators, wealth's deep oceans;
Ye painted courtiers, barrels of other's wits;
Ye countrymen, who but your beasts love none;
Ye of those fellowships, whereof he's one,
Of study and play made strange hermaphrodites,
Here shine; this bridegroom to the temple bring.
Lo, in yon path which store of strew'd flowers graceth,
The sobre virgin paceth;
Except my sight fail, 'tis no other thing.
Weep not, nor blush, here is no grief nor shame,
To-day put on perfection, and a woman's name.
Thy two-leaved gates, fair temple, unfold,

And these two in thy sacred bosom hold,
Till mystically join'd but one they be;
Then may thy lean and hunger-starvèd womb
Long time expect their bodies, and their tomb,
Long after their own parents fatten thee.
All elder claims, and all cold barrenness,
All yielding to new loves, be far for ever,
Which might these two dissever;
Always, all th'other may each one possess;
For the best bride, best worthy of praise and fame,
To-day puts on perfection, and a woman's name.
Winter days bring much delight,
Not for themselves, but for they soon bring night;
Other sweets wait thee than these diverse meats,
Other disports than dancing jollities,
Other love-tricks than glancing with the eyes,
But that the sun still in our half sphere sweats;
He flies in winter, but he now stands still.
Yet shadows turn; noon point he hath attain'd;
His steeds will be restrain'd,
But gallop lively down the western hill.
Thou shalt, when he hath run the heaven's half frame,
To-night put on perfection, and a woman's name.
The amorous evening star is rose,
Why then should not our amorous star Inclose
Herself in her wish'd bed?Release your strings,
Musicians; and dancers take some truce
With these your pleasing labours, for great use
As much weariness as perfection brings.
You, and not only you, but all toil'd beasts
Rest duly; at night all their toils are dispensed;
But in their beds commenced
Are other labours, and more dainty feasts.
She goes a maid, who, lest she turn the same,
To-night puts on perfection, and a woman's name.
Thy virgin's girdle now untie,
And in thy nuptial bed, love's altar, lie
A pleasing sacrifice; now dispossess

Thee of these chains and robes, which were put on
To adorn the day, not thee; for thou, alone,
Like virtue and truth, art best in nakedness.
This bed is only to virginity
A grave, but to a better state, a cradle.
Till now thou wast but able
To be, what now thou art; then, that by thee
No more be said, " I may be," but, " I am,"
To-night put on perfection, and a woman's name.
Even like a faithful man content,
That this life for a better should be spent,
So she a mother's rich stile doth prefer,
And at the bridegroom's wish'd approach doth lie,
Like an appointed lamb, when tenderly
The priest comes on his knees to embowel her.
Now sleep or watch with more joy; and, O light
Of heaven, to-morrow rise thou hot, and early;
This sun will love so dearly
Her rest, that long, long we shall want her sight.
Wonders are wrought, for she, which had no maim,
To-night puts on perfection, and a woman's name.

Eclogue

I6I3, DECEMBER 26.
ALLOPHANESFINDINGIDIOSINTHECOUNTRYIN CHRISTMAS TIME,REPREHENDSHISABSENCE FROM COURT, AT THE MARRIAGE OF THE EARL OFSOMERSET;IDIOSGIVES AN ACCOUNT OF HISPURPOSETHEREIN,ANDOF HISACTIONS THERE.
ALLOPHANES.
UNSEASONABLE man, statue of ice,
What could to countries solitude entice
Thee, in this year's cold and decrepit time?
Nature's instinct draws to the warmer clime
Even smaller birds, who by that courage dare
In numerous fleets sail through their sea, the air.
What delicacy can in fields appear,

Whilst Flora herself doth a frieze jerkin wear?
Whilst winds do all the trees and hedges strip
Of leaves, to furnish rods enough to whip
Thy madness from thee, and all springs by frost
Have taken cold, and their sweet murmurs lost?
If thou thy faults or fortunes wouldst lament
With just solemnity, do it in Lent.
At court the spring already advanced is,
The sun stays longer up; and yet not his
The glory is; far other, other fires.
First, zeal to prince and state, then love's desires
Burn in one breast, and like heaven's two great lights,
The first doth govern days, the other, nights.
And then that early light which did appear
Before the sun and moon created were,
The princes favour is diffused o'er all,
From which all fortunes, names, and natures fall.
Then from those wombs of stars, the bride's bright eyes,
At every glance, a constellation flies,
And sows the court with stars, and doth prevent
In light and power, the all-eyed firmament.
First her eyes kindle other ladies' eyes,
Then from their beams their jewels' lustres rise,
And from their jewels torches do take fire,
And all is warmth, and light, and good desire.
Most other courts, alas!are like to hell,
Where in dark places, fire without light doth dwell;
Or but like stoves; for lust and envy get
Continual, but artificial heat.
Here zeal and love grown one all clouds digest,
And make our court an everlasting east.
And canst thou be from thence?
IDIOS.No, I am there;
As heaven—to men disposed—is everywhere,
So are those courts, whose princes animate
Not only all their house but all their state.
Let no man think, because he's full, he hath all.
Kings—as their pattern, God—are liberal

Not only in fullness, but capacity,
Enlarging narrow men to feel and see,
And comprehend the blessings they bestow.
So, reclused hermits oftentimes do know
More of heaven's glory than a worldling can.
As man is of the world, the heart of man
Is an epitome of God's great book
Of creatures, and man need no farther look;
So is the country of courts, where sweet peace doth,
As their one common soul, give life to both;
And am I then from court?
ALLOPHANES.
Dreamer, thou art:
Think'st thou, fantastic, that thou hast a part
In the Indian fleet, because thou hast
A little spice or amber in thy taste?
Because thou art not frozen, art thou warm?
Seest thou all good, because thou seest no harm?
The earth doth in her inner bowels hold
Stuff well-disposed, and which would fain be gold;
But never shall, except it chance to lie
So upward, that heaven gild it with his eye.
As, for divine things, faith comes from above,
So, for best civil use, all tinctures move
From higher powers; from God religion springs,
Wisdom and honour from the use of kings:
Then unbeguile thyself, and know with me,
That angels, though on earth employ'd they be,
Are still in heaven, so is he still at home
That doth abroad to honest actions come.
Chide thyself then, O fool, which yesterday
Mightst have read more than all thy books bewray;
Hast thou a history, which doth present
A court, where all affections do assent
Unto the king's, and that that king's are just;
And where it is no levity to trust;
Where there is no ambition, but to obey;
Where men need whisper nothing, and yet may;

Where the king's favours are so placed, that all
Find that the king therein is liberal
To them, in him, because his favours bend
To virtue, to the which they all pretend?
Thou hast no such; yet here was this, and more.
An earnest lover, wise then, and before,
Our little Cupid hath sued livery,
And is no more in his minority;
He is admitted now into that breast
Where the king's counsels and his secrets rest.
What hast thou lost, O ignorant man?
IDIOS.
I knew
All this, and only therefore I withdrew.
To know and feel all this, and not to have
Words to express it, makes a man a grave
Of his own thoughts; I would not therefore stay
At a great feast, having no grace to say.
And yet I 'scaped not here; for being come
Full of the common joy, I utter'd some.
Read then this nuptial song, which was not made
Either the court or men's hearts to invade;
But since I am dead and buried, I could frame
No epitaph, which might advance my fame
So much as this poor song, which testifies
I did unto that day some sacrifice.

I

THE TIME OF THE MARRIAGE.
Thou art reprieved, old year, thou shalt not die;
Though thou upon thy death-bed lie,
And should'st within five days expire,
Yet thou art rescued by a mightier fire,
Than thy old soul, the sun,
When he doth in his largest circle run.
The passage of the west or east would thaw,
And open wide their easy liquid jaw
To all our ships, could a Promethean art
Either unto the northern pole impart

The fire of these inflaming eyes, or of this loving heart.

II

EQUALITY OF PERSONS.

But undiscerning Muse, which heart, which eyes,
In this new couple, dost thou prize,
When his eye as inflaming is
As hers, and her heart loves as well as his?
Be tried by beauty, and then
The bridegroom is a maid, and not a man;
If by that manly courage they be tried,
Which scorns unjust opinion; then the bride
Becomes a man.Should chance or envy's art
Divide these two, whom nature scarce did part,
Since both have the inflaming eye, and both the loving heart?

III

RAISING OF THE BRIDEGROOM.

Though it be some divorce to think of you
Single, so much one are you two,
Let me here contemplate thee,
First, cheerful bridegroom, and first let me see,
How thou prevent'st the sun,
And his red foaming horses dost outrun;
How, having laid down in thy Sovereign's breast
All businesses, from thence to reinvest
Them when these triumphs cease, thou forward art
To show to her, who doth the like impart,
The fire of thy inflaming eyes, and of thy loving heart.

IV

RAISING OF THE BRIDE.

But now to thee, fair bride, it is some wrong,
To think thou wert in bed so long.
Since soon thou liest down first, 'tis fit
Thou in first rising shouldst allow for it.
Powder thy radiant hair,
Which if without such ashes thou wouldst wear,
Thou which, to all which come to look upon,

Wert meant for Phoebus, wouldst be Phaëton.
For our ease, give thine eyes th' unusual part
Of joy, a tear; so quench'd, thou mayst impart,
To us that come, thy inflaming eyes; to him, thy loving heart.

V

HER APPARELLING.
Thus thou descend'st to our infirmity,
Who can the sun in water see.
So dost thou, when in silk and gold
Thou cloud'st thyself; since we which do behold
Are dust and worms, 'tis just,
Our objects be the fruits of worms and dust.
Let every jewel be a glorious star,
Yet stars are not so pure as their spheres are;
And though thou stoop, to appear to us, in part,
Still in that picture thou entirely art,
Which thy inflaming eyes have made within his loving heart.

VI

GOING TO THE CHAPEL.
Now from your easts you issue forth, and we,
As men, which through a cypress see
The rising sun, do think it two;
So, as you go to church, do think of you;
But that veil being gone,
By the church rites you are from thenceforth one.
The church triumphant made this match before,
And now the militant doth strive no more.
Then, reverend priest, who God's Recorder art,
Do, from his dictates, to these two impart
All blessings which are seen, or thought, by angel's eye or heart.

VII

THE BENEDICTION.
Blest pair of swans, O may you interbring
Daily new joys, and never sing;
Live, till all grounds of wishes fail,

Till honour, yea, till wisdom grow so stale,
That new great heights to try,
I must serve your ambition, to die;
Raise heirs, and may here, to the world's end, live
Heirs from this king, to take thanks, you, to give.
Nature and grace do all, and nothing art;
May never age or error overthwart
With any west these radiant eyes, with any north
this heart.

VIII

FEASTS AND REVELS.
But you are over-blest.Plenty this day
Injures;it causeth time to stay;
The tables groan, as though this feast
Would, as the flood, destroy all fowl and beast.
And were the doctrine new
That the earth moved, this day would make it true;
For every part to dance and revel goes,
They tread the air, and fall not where they rose.
Though six hours since the sun to bed did part,
The masks and banquets willnot yet impart
A sunset to these weary eyes, a centre to this heart.

IX

THE BRIDE'S GOING TO BED.
What mean'st thou, bride, this company to keep?
To sit up, till thou fain wouldst sleep?
Thou mayst not, when thou'rt laid, do so;
Thyself must to him a new banquet grow;
And you must entertain
And do all this day's dances o'er again.
Know that if sun and moon together do
Rise in one point, they do not set so too.
Therefore thou mayst, fair bride, to bed depart;
Thou art not gone, being gone; where'er thou art,
Thou leavest in him thy watchful eyes, in him thy
loving heart.

X

THE BRIDEGROOM'S COMING.

As he that sees a star fall, runs apace,
And finds a jelly in the place,
So doth the bridegroom haste as much,
Being told this star is fallen, and finds her such.
And as friends may look strange,
By a new fashion, or apparel's change,
Their souls, though long acquainted they had been,
These clothes, their bodies, never yet had seen.
Therefore at first she modestly might start,
But must forthwith surrender every part,
As freely as each to each before gave either eye or heart.

XI

THE GOOD-NIGHT.
Now, as in Tullia's tomb, one lamp burnt clear,
Unchanged for fifteen hundred year,
May these love-lamps we here enshrine,
In warmth, light, lasting, equal the divine.
Fire ever doth aspire,
And makes all like itself, turns all to fire,
But ends in ashes; which these cannot do,
For none of these is fuel, but fire too.
This is joy's bonfire, then, where love's strong arts
Make of so noble individual parts
One fire of four inflaming eyes, and of two loving hearts.
IDIOS.As I have brought this song, that I may do
A perfect sacrifice, I'll burn it too.
ALLOPHANES.No, sir.This paper I have justly got,
For, in burnt incense, the perfume is not
His only that presents it, but of all;
Whatever celebrates this festival
Is common, since the joy thereof is so.
Nor may yourself be priest; but let me go
Back to the court, and I will lay it upon
Such altars, as prize your devotion.

Elegies

Elegy I

JEALOUSY

FOND woman, which wouldst have thy husband die,
And yet complain'st of his great jealousy;
If, swollen with poison, he lay in his last bed,
His body with a sere bark covered,
Drawing his breath as thick and short as can
The nimblest crocheting musician,
Ready with loathsome vomiting to spew
His soul out of one hell into a new,
Made deaf with his poor kindred's howling cries,
Begging with few feign'd tears great legacies,—
Thou wouldst not weep, but jolly, and frolic be,
As a slave, which to-morrow should be free.
Yet weep'st thou, when thou seest him hungerly
Swallow his own death, heart's-bane jealousy?
O give him many thanks, he's courteous,
That in suspecting kindly warneth us.
We must not, as we used, flout openly,
In scoffing riddles, his deformity;
Nor at his board together being sat,
With words, nor touch, scarce looks, adulterate.
Nor when he, swollen and pamper'd with great fare,
Sits down and snorts, caged in his basket chair,
Must we usurp his own bed any more,
Nor kiss and play in his house, as before.
Now I see many dangers; for it is
His realm, his castle, and his diocese.
But if—as envious men, which would revile
Their prince, or coin his gold, themselves exile
Into another country, and do it there—
We play in another house, what should we fear?
There we will scorn his household policies,
His silly plots, and pensionary spies,
As the inhabitants of Thames' right side
Do London's mayor, or Germans the Pope's pride.

Elegy II.

THE ANAGRAM.

MARRY, and love thy Flavia, for she
Hath all things, whereby others beauteous be;

For, though her eyes be small, her mouth is great;
Though they be ivory, yet her teeth be jet;
Though they be dim, yet she is light enough;
And though her harsh hair fall, her skin is tough;
What though her cheeks be yellow, her hair's red,
Give her thine, and she hath a maidenhead.
These things are beauty's elements; where these
Meet in one, that one must, as perfect, please.
If red and white, and each good quality
Be in thy wench, ne'er ask where it doth lie.
In buying things perfumed, we ask, if there
Be musk and amber in it, but not where.
Though all her parts be not in th' usual place,
She hath yet an anagram of a good face.
If we might put the letters but one way,
In that lean dearth of words, what could we say?
When by the gamut some musicians make
A perfect song, others will undertake,
By the same gamut changed, to equal it.
Things simply good can never be unfit;
She's fair as any, if all be like her;
And if none be, then she is singular.
All love is wonder; if we justly do
Account her wonderful, why not lovely too?
Love built on beauty, soon as beauty, dies;
Choose this face, changed by no deformities.
Women are all like angels; the fair be
Like those which fell to worse; but such as she,
Like to good angels, nothing can impair:
'Tis less grief to be foul, than to have been fair.
For one night's revels, silk and gold we choose,
But, in long journeys, cloth and leather use.
Beauty is barren oft; best husbands say,
There is best land, where there is foulest way.
Oh, what a sovereign plaster will she be,
If thy past sins have taught thee jealousy!
Here needs no spies, nor eunuchs; her commit
Safe to thy foes, yea, to a marmoset.

When Belgia's cities the round country drowns,
That dirty foulness guards and arms the towns,
So doth her face guard her; and so, for thee,
Which forced by business, absent oft must be,
She, whose face, like clouds, turns the day to night;
Who, mightier than the sea, makes Moors seem white;
Who, though seven years she in the stews had laid,
A nunnery durst receive, and think a maid;
And though in childbed's labour she did lie,
Midwives would swear 'twere but a tympany;
Whom, if she accuse herself, I credit less
Than witches, which impossibles confess;
One like none, and liked of none, fittest were;
For things in fashion every man will wear.

Elegy III

CHANGE.
ALTHOUGH thy hand and faith, and good works too,
Have sealed thy love which nothing should undo,
Yea, though thou fall back, that apostasy
Confirm thy love, yet much, much I fear thee.
Women are like the arts, forced unto none,
Open to all searchers, unprized, if unknown.
If I have caught a bird, and let him fly,
Another fowler using these means, as I,
May catch the same bird; and, as these things be,
Women are made for men, not him nor me.
Foxes, and goats—all beasts—change when they please.
Shall women, more hot, wily, wild than these,
Be bound to one man, and did nature then
Idly make them apter to endure than men?
They're our clogs, not their own; if a man be
Chain'd to a galley, yet the galley's free.
Who hath a plough-land, casts all his seed corn there,
And yet allows his ground more corn should bear;
Though Danuby into the sea must flow,
The sea receives the Rhine, Volga, and Po.
By nature, which gave it, this liberty

Thou lovest, but O! canst thou love it and me?
Likeness glues love; and if that thou so do,
To make us like and love, must I change too?
More than thy hate, I hate it; rather let me
Allow her change, then change as oft as she,
And so not teach, but force my opinion,
To love not any one, nor every one.
To live in one land is captivity,
To run all countries a wild roguery.
Waters stink soon, if in one place they bide,
And in the vast sea are more putrified;
But when they kiss one bank, and leaving this
Never look back, but the next bank do kiss,
Then are they purest; change is the nursery
Of music, joy, life and eternity.

Elegy IV

THE PERFUME.

ONCE, and but once, found in thy company,
All thy supposed escapes are laid on me;
And as a thief at bar is question'd there
By all the men that have been robb'd that year,
So am I—by this traiterous means surprized—
By thy hydroptic father catechized.
Though he had wont to search with glazèd eyes,
As though he came to kill a cockatrice;
Though he hath oft sworn that he would remove
Thy beauty's beauty, and food of our love,
Hope of his goods, if I with thee were seen,
Yet close and secret, as our souls, we've been.
Though thy immortal mother, which doth lie
Still buried in her bed, yet will not die,
Takes this advantage to sleep out daylight,
And watch thy entries and returns all night;
And, when she takes thy hand, and would seem kind,
Doth search what rings and armlets she can find;
And kissing notes the colour of thy face;
And fearing lest thou'rt swollen, doth thee embrace;

To try if thou long, doth name strange meats;
And notes thy paleness, blushing, sighs, and sweats;
And politicly will to thee confess
The sins of her own youth's rank lustiness;
Yet love these sorceries did remove, and move
Thee to gull thine own mother for my love.
Thy little brethren, which like fairy sprites
Oft skipp'd into our chamber, those sweet nights,
And kiss'd, and ingled on thy father's knee,
Were bribed next day to tell what they did see;
The grim-eight-foot-high-iron-bound serving-man,
That oft names God in oaths, and only then,
He that, to bar the first gate, doth as wide
As the great Rhodian Colossus stride
—Which, if in hell no other pains there were,
Makes me fear hell, because he must be there—
Though by thy father he were hired to this,
Could never witness any touch or kiss.
But O! too common ill, I brought with me
That, which betray'd me to mine enemy,
A loud perfume, which at my entrance cried
Even at thy father's nose; so were we spied.
When, like a tyrant King, that in his bed
Smelt gunpowder, the pale wretch shivered,
Had it been some bad smell, he would have thought
That his own feet, or breath, that smell had wrought;
But as we in our isle imprisoned,
Where cattle only and diverse dogs are bred,
The precious unicorns strange monsters call,
So thought he good strange, that had none at all.
I taught my silks their whistling to forbear;
Even my oppress'd shoes dumb and speechless were;
Only thou bitter sweet, whom I had laid
Next me, me traiterously hast betray'd,
And unsuspected hast invisibly
At once fled unto him, and stay'd with me.
Base excrement of earth, which dost confound
Sense from distinguishing the sick from sound!

By thee the silly amorous sucks his death
By drawing in a leprous harlot's breath;
By thee the greatest stain to man's estate
Falls on us, to be call'd effeminate;
Though you be much loved in the prince's hall,
There things that seem exceed substantial;
Gods, when ye fumed on altars, were pleased well,
Because you were burnt, not that they liked your smell;
You're loathsome all, being taken simply alone;
Shall we love ill things join'd, and hate each one?
If you were good, your good doth soon decay;
And you are rare; that takes the good away:
All my perfumes I give most willingly
To embalm thy father's corpse; what? will he die?

Elegy V

HIS PICTURE.
HERE take my picture; though I bid farewell,
Thine, in my heart, where my soul dwells, shall dwell.
'Tis like me now, but I dead, 'twill be more,
When we are shadows both, than 'twas before.
When weatherbeaten I come back; my hand
Perhaps with rude oars torn, or sun-beams tann'd,
My face and breast of haircloth, and my head
With care's harsh sudden hoariness o'erspread,
My body a sack of bones, broken within,
And powder's blue stains scatter'd on my skin;
If rival fools tax thee to have loved a man,
So foul and coarse, as, O! I may seem then,
This shall say what I was; and thou shalt say,
" Do his hurts reach me? doth my worth decay?
Or do they reach his judging mind, that he
Should now love less, what he did love to see?
That which in him was fair and delicate,
Was but the milk, which in love's childish state
Did nurse it; who now is grown strong enough
To feed on that, which to weak tastes seems tough."

Elegy VI

O, LET me not serve so, as those men serve,
Whom honour's smokes at once fatten and starve,
Poorly enrich'd with great men's words or looks;
Nor so write my name in thy loving books
As those idolatrous flatterers, which still
Their princes' style with many realms fulfil,
Whence they no tribute have, and where no sway.
Such services I offer as shall pay
Themselves; I hate dead names. O, then let me
Favourite in ordinary, or no favourite be.
When my soul was in her own body sheathed,
Nor yet by oaths betroth'd, nor kisses breathed
Into my purgatory, faithless thee,
Thy heart seemed wax, and steel thy constancy.
So, careless flowers strew'd on the water's face
The curled whirlpools suck, smack, and embrace,
Yet drown them; so the taper's beamy eye
Amorously twinkling beckons the giddy fly,
Yet burns his wings; and such the devil is,
Scarce visiting them who are entirely his.
When I behold a stream, which from the spring
Doth with doubtful melodious murmuring,
Or in a speechless slumber, calmly ride
Her wedded channel's bosom, and there chide,
And bend her brows, and swell, if any bough
Do but stoop down to kiss her upmost brow;
Yet, if her often gnawing kisses win
The traitorous banks to gape, and let her in,
She rusheth violently, and doth divorce
Her from her native and her long-kept course,
And roars, and braves it, and in gallant scorn,
In flattering eddies promising return,
She flouts her channel, which thenceforth is dry;
Then say I; "That is she, and this am I."
Yet let not thy deep bitterness beget
Careless despair in me, for that will whet

My mind to scorn; and O, love dull'd with pain
Was ne'er so wise, nor well arm'd, as disdain.
Then with new eyes I shall survey thee, and spy
Death in thy cheeks, and darkness in thine eye,
Though hope bred faith and love; thus taught, I shall,
As nations do from Rome, from thy love fall;
My hate shall outgrow thine, and utterly
I will renounce thy dalliance; and when I
Am the recusant, in that resolute state
What hurts it me to be excommunicate?

Elegy VII

NATURE'S lay idiot, I taught thee to love,
And in that sophistry, O! thou dost prove
Too subtle; fool, thou didst not understand
The mystic language of the eye nor hand;
Nor couldst thou judge the difference of the air
Of sighs, and say, "This lies, this sounds despair";
Nor by th' eye's water cast a malady
Desperately hot, or changing feverously.
I had not taught thee then the alphabet
Of flowers, how they, devisefully being set
And bound up, might with speechless secrecy
Deliver errands mutely, and mutually.
Remember since all thy words used to be
To every suitor, "Ay, if my friends agree;"
Since household charms, thy husband's name to teach,
Were all the love-tricks that thy wit could reach;
And since an hour's discourse could scarce have made
One answer in thee, and that ill array'd
In broken proverbs, and torn sentences.
Thou art not by so many duties his—
That from th' world's common having sever'd thee,
Inlaid thee, neither to be seen, nor see—
As mine; who have with amorous delicacies
Refined thee into a blissful paradise.
Thy graces and good works my creatures be;
I planted knowledge and life's tree in thee;

Which O! shall strangers taste? Must I, alas!
Frame and enamel plate, and drink in glass?
Chafe wax for other's seals? break a colt's force,
And leave him then, being made a ready horse?

Elegy VIII

THE COMPARISON.

AS the sweet sweat of roses in a still,
As that which from chafed musk cat's pores doth trill,
As the almighty balm of th' early east,
Such are the sweat drops of my mistress' breast;
And on her neck her skin such lustre sets,
They seem no sweat drops, but pearl carcanets.
Rank sweaty froth thy mistress' brow defiles,
Like spermatic issue of ripe menstruous boils,
Or like the scum, which, by need's lawless law
Enforced, Sanserra's starvèd men did draw
From parboil'd shoes and boots, and all the rest
Which were with any sovereign fatness blest;
And like vile lying stones in saffron'd tin,
Or warts, or wheals, it hangs upon her skin.
Round as the world's her head, on every side,
Like to the fatal ball which fell on Ide;
Or that whereof God had such jealousy,
As for the ravishing thereof we die.
Thy head is like a rough-hewn statue of jet,
Where marks for eyes, nose, mouth, are yet scarce set;
Like the first chaos, or flat seeming face
Of Cynthia, when th' earth's shadows her embrace.
Like Proserpine's white beauty-keeping chest,
Or Jove's best fortune's urn, is her fair breast.
Thine's like worm-eaten trunks, clothed in seal's skin,
Or grave, that's dust without, and stink within.
And like that slender stalk, at whose end stands
The woodbine quivering, are her arms and hands.
Like rough-bark'd elm-boughs, or the russet skin
Of men late scourged for madness, or for sin,
Like sun-parch'd quarters on the city gate,

Such is thy tann'd skin's lamentable state;
And like a bunch of ragged carrots stand
The short swollen fingers of thy gouty hand.
Then like the chemic's masculine equal fire,
Which in the limbec's warm womb doth inspire
Into th' earth's worthless dirt a soul of gold,
Such cherishing heat her best loved part doth hold.
Thine's like the dread mouth of a fired gun,
Or like hot liquid metals newly run
Into clay moulds, or like to that Ætna,
Where round about the grass is burnt away.
Are not your kisses then as filthy, and more,
As a worm sucking an envenom'd sore?
Doth not thy fearful hand in feeling quake,
As one which gathering flowers still fears a snake?
Is not your last act harsh and violent,
As when a plough a stony ground doth rent?
So kiss good turtles, so devoutly nice
Are priests in handling reverent sacrifice,
And such in searching wounds the surgeon is,
As we, when we embrace, or touch, or kiss.
Leave her, and I will leave comparing thus,
She and comparisons are odious.

Elegy IX

THE AUTUMNAL.
NO spring, nor summer beauty hath such grace
As I have seen in one autumnal face;
Young beauties force our love, and that's a rape;
This doth but counsel, yet you cannot scape.
If 'twere a shame to love, here 'twere no shame;
Affections here take reverence's name.
Were her first years the Golden Age? that's true,
But now they're gold oft tried, and ever new.
That was her torrid and inflaming time;
This is her tolerable tropic clime.
Fair eyes; who asks more heat than comes from hence,
He in a fever wishes pestilence.

Call not these wrinkles, graves; if graves they were,
They were Love's graves, for else he is nowhere.
Yet lies not Love dead here, but here doth sit,
Vow'd to this trench, like an anachorite,
And here, till hers, which must be his death, come,
He doth not dig a grave, but build a tomb.
Here dwells he; though he sojourn everywhere,
In progress, yet his standing house is here;
Here, where still evening is, not noon, nor night;
Where no voluptuousness, yet all delight.
In all her words, unto all hearers fit,
You may at revels, you at council, sit.
This is love's timber; youth his underwood;
There he, as wine in June, enrages blood;
Which then comes seasonablest, when our taste
And appetite to other things is past.
Xerxes' strange Lydian love, the platane tree,
Was loved for age, none being so large as she;
Or else because, being young, nature did bless
Her youth with age's glory, barrenness.
If we love things long sought, age is a thing
Which we are fifty years in compassing;
If transitory things, which soon decay,
Age must be loveliest at the latest day.
But name not winter faces, whose skin's slack,
Lank as an unthrift's purse, but a soul's sack;
Whose eyes seek light within, for all here's shade;
Whose mouths are holes, rather worn out, than made;
Whose every tooth to a several place is gone,
To vex their souls at resurrection;
Name not these living death-heads unto me,
For these, not ancient, but antique be.
I hate extremes; yet I had rather stay
With tombs than cradles, to wear out a day.
Since such love's motion natural is, may still
My love descend, and journey down the hill,
Not panting after growing beauties; so
I shall ebb out with them who homeward go.

Elegy X

THE DREAM.

IMAGE of her whom I love, more than she,
Whose fair impression in my faithful heart
Makes me her medal, and makes her love me,
As kings do coins, to which their stamps impart
The value; go, and take my heart from hence,
Which now is grown too great and good for me.
Honours oppress weak spirits, and our sense
Strong objects dull; the more, the less we see.
When you are gone, and reason gone with you,
Then fantasy is queen and soul, and all;
She can present joys meaner than you do,
Convenient, and more proportional.
So, if I dream I have you, I have you,
For all our joys are but fantastical;
And so I 'scape the pain, for pain is true;
And sleep, which locks up sense, doth lock out all.
After a such fruition I shall wake,
And, but the waking, nothing shall repent;
And shall to love more thankful sonnets make,
Than if more honour, tears, and pains were spent.
But, dearest heart and dearer image, stay;
Alas! true joys at best are dream enough;
Though you stay here, you pass too fast away,
For even at first life's taper is a snuff.
Fill'd with her love, may I be rather grown
Mad with much heart, than idiot with none.

Elegy XI

THE BRACELET.

UPON THE LOSS OF HIS MISTRESS' CHAIN, FOR WHICH HE MADE SATISFACTION.

NOT that in colour it was like thy hair,
For armlets of that thou mayst let me wear;
Nor that thy hand it oft embraced and kiss'd,
For so it had that good, which oft I miss'd;
Nor for that silly old morality,

That, as these links were knit, our love should be,
Mourn I that I thy sevenfold chain have lost;
Nor for the luck sake; but the bitter cost.
O, shall twelve righteous angels, which as yet
No leaven of vile solder did admit;
Nor yet by any way have stray'd or gone
From the first state of their creation;
Angels, which heaven commanded to provide
All things to me, and be my faithful guide;
To gain new friends, to appease great enemies;
To comfort my soul, when I lie or rise;
Shall these twelve innocents, by thy severe
Sentence, dread judge, my sin's great burden bear?
Shall they be damn'd, and in the furnace thrown,
And punish'd for offenses not their own?
They save not me, they do not ease my pains,
When in that hell they're burnt and tied in chains.
Were they but crowns of France, I carèd not,
For most of these their country's natural rot,
I think, possesseth; they come here to us
So pale, so lame, so lean, so ruinous.
And howsoe'er French kings most Christian be,
Their crowns are circumcised most Jewishly.
Or were they Spanish stamps, still travelling,
That are become as Catholic as their king;
These unlick'd bear-whelps, unfiled pistolets,
That—more than cannon shot—avails or lets;
Which, negligently left unrounded, look
Like many-angled figures in the book
Of some great conjurer that would enforce
Nature, so these do justice, from her course;
Which, as the soul quickens head, feet and heart,
As streams, like veins, run through th' earth's every part,
Visit all countries, and have slily made
Gorgeous France, ruin'd, ragged and decay'd,
Scotland, which knew no state, proud in one day,
And mangled seventeen-headed Belgia.
Or were it such gold as that wherewithal

Almighty chemics, from each mineral
Having by subtle fire a soul out-pull'd,
Are dirtily and desperately gull'd;
I would not spit to quench the fire they're in,
For they are guilty of much heinous sin.
But shall my harmless angels perish? Shall
I lose my guard, my ease, my food, my all?
Much hope which they would nourish will be dead.
Much of my able youth, and lustihead
Will vanish; if thou love, let them alone,
For thou wilt love me less when they are gone;
And be content that some loud squeaking crier,
Well-pleas'd with one lean threadbare groat, for hire,
May like a devil roar through every street,
And gall the finder's conscience, if he meet.
Or let me creep to some dread conjurer,
That with fantastic schemes fills full much paper;
Which hath divided heaven in tenements,
And with whores, thieves, and murderers stuff'd his rents
So full, that though he pass them all in sin,
He leaves himself no room to enter in.
But if, when all his art and time is spent,
He say 'twill ne'er be found; yet be content;
Receive from him that doom ungrudgingly,
Because he is the mouth of destiny.
Thou say'st, alas! the gold doth still remain,
Though it be changed, and put into a chain.
So in the first fallen angels resteth still
Wisdom and knowledge, but 'tis turn'd to ill;
As these should do good works, and should provide
Necessities; but now must nurse thy pride.
And they are still bad angels; mine are none;
For form gives being, and their form is gone.
Pity these angels yet; their dignities
Pass Virtues, Powers, and Principalities.
But thou art resolute; thy will be done;
Yet with such anguish, as her only son
The mother in the hungry grave doth lay,

Unto the fire these martyrs I betray.
Good souls—for you give life to everything—
Good angels—for good messages you bring—
Destined you might have been to such an one,
As would have loved and worshipp'd you alone;
One that would suffer hunger, nakedness,
Yea death, ere he would make your number less;
But, I am guilty of your sad decay;
May your few fellows longer with me stay.
But O! thou wretched finder whom I hate
So, that I almost pity thy estate,
Gold being the heaviest metal amongst all,
May my most heavy curse upon thee fall.
Here fetter'd, manacled, and hang'd in chains,
First mayst thou be; then chain'd to hellish pains;
Or be with foreign gold bribed to betray
Thy country, and fail both of it and thy pay.
May the next thing thou stoop'st to reach, contain
Poison, whose nimble fume rot thy moist brain;
Or libels, or some interdicted thing,
Which negligently kept thy ruin bring.
Lust-bred diseases rot thee; and dwell with thee
Itching desire, and no ability.
May all the evils that gold ever wrought;
All mischief that all devils ever thought;
Want after plenty, poor and gouty age,
The plagues of travellers, love, marriage
Afflict thee, and at thy life's last moment,
May thy swollen sins themselves to thee present.
But, I forgive; repent thee, honest man!
Gold is restorative; restore it then:
But if from it thou be'st loth to depart,
Because 'tis cordial, would 'twere at thy heart.

Elegy XII

COME Fates; I fear you not! All whom I owe
Are paid, but you; then 'rest me ere I go.

But Chance from you all sovereignty hath got;
Love woundeth none but those whom Death dares not;
True if you were, and just in equity,
I should have vanquish'd her, as you did me;
Else lovers should not brave Death's pains, and live;
But 'tis a rule, " Death comes not to relieve."
Or, pale and wan Death's terrors, are they laid
So deep in lovers, they make Death afraid?
Or—the least comfort—have I company?
O'ercame she Fates, Love, Death, as well as me?
Yes, Fates do silk unto her distaff pay,
For ransom, which tax they on us do lay.
Love gives her youth—which is the reason why
Youths, for her sake, some wither and some die.
Poor Death can nothing give; yet, for her sake,
Still in her turn, he doth a lover take.
And if Death should prove false, she fears him not;
Our Muses, to redeem her, she hath got.
That fatal night we last kiss'd, I thus pray'd,
—Or rather, thus despair'd, I should have said—
Kisses, and yet despair! The forbid tree
Did promise (and deceive) no more than she.
Like lambs, that see their teats, and must eat hay,
A food, whose taste hath made me pine away.
Dives, when thou saw'st bliss, and craved'st to touch
A drop of water, thy great pains were such.
Here grief wants a fresh wit, for mine being spent,
And my sighs weary, groans are all my rent.
Unable longer to endure the pain,
They break like thunder, and do bring down rain.
Thus till dry tear solder my eye, I weep;
And then, I dream, how you securely sleep,
And in your dreams do laugh at me. I hate,
And pray Love all may; he pities my state,
But says, I therein no revenge shall find;
The sun would shine, though all the world were blind.
Yet, to try my hate, Love show'd me your tear;

And I had died, had not your smile been there.
Your frown undoes me; your smile is my wealth;
And as you please to look, I have my health.
Methought, Love pitying me, when he saw this,
Gave me your hands, the backs and palms to kiss.
That cured me not, but to bear pain gave strength;
And what is lost in force, is took in length.
I call'd on Love again, who fear'd you so,
That his compassion still proved greater woe;
For, then I dream'd I was in bed with you,
But durst not feel, for fear it should not be true.
This merits not your anger, had it been;
The queen of chastity was naked seen;
And in bed not to feel, the pain I took,
Was more than for Actæon not to look;
And that breast which lay ope, I did not know,
But for the clearness, from a lump of snow;
Nor that sweet teat which on the top it bore
From the rose-bud which for my sake you wore.
These griefs to issue forth, by verse I prove;
Or turn their course by travel and new love.
All would not do; the best at last I tried;
Unable longer to hold out, I died.
And then I found I lost life, death by flying;
Who hundreds live, are but so long in dying.
Charon did let me pass; I'll him requite.
To mark the groves or shades wrongs my delight;
I'll speak but of those ghosts I found alone,
Those thousand ghosts, whereof myself made one,
All images of thee; I asked them why?
The judge told me, all they for thee did die,
And therefore had for their Elysian bliss,
In one another their own loves to kiss.
O here I miss'd not blissh, but being dead;
For lo! I dreamt, I dreamt, and waking said,
" Heaven, if who are in thee there must dwell,
How is't I now was there, and now I fell?"

Elegy XIII

HIS PARTING FROM HER.

SINCE she must go, and I must mourn, come night,
Environ me with darkness, whilst I write;
Shadow that hell unto me, which alone
I am to suffer when my love is gone.
Alas! the darkest magic cannot do it,
Thou and great hell, to boot, are shadows to it.
Should Cynthia quit thee, Venus, and each star,
It would not form one thought dark as mine are.
I could lend them obscureness now, and say
Out of my self, there should be no more day.
Such is already my self-want of sight,
Did not the fire within me force a light.
O Love, that fire and darkness should be mix'd,
Or to thy triumphs such strange torments fix'd!
Is it because thou thyself art blind, that we,
Thy martyrs, must no more each other see?
Or takest thou pride to break us on the wheel,
And view old Chaos in the pains we feel?
Or have we left undone some mutual rite,
That thus with parting thou seek'st us to spite?
No, no. The fault is mine, impute it to me,
Or rather to conspiring destiny,
Which, since I loved in jest before, decreed
That I should suffer, when I loved indeed;
And therefore, sooner now than I can say,
I saw the golden fruit, 'tis rapt away;
Or as I'd watch'd one drop in the vast stream,
And I left wealthy only in a dream.
Yet, Love, thou'rt blinder than myself in this,
To vex my dove-like friend for my amiss;
And where one sad truth may expiate
Thy wrath, to make her fortune run my fate.
So blinded justice doth, when favourites fall,
Strike them, their house, their friends, their favourites all.
Was't not enough that thou didst dart thy fires

Into our bloods, inflaming our desires,
And madest us sigh, and blow, and pant, and burn,
And then thyself into our flames didst turn?
Was't not enough that thou didst hazard us
To paths in love so dark and dangerous,
And those so ambush'd round with household spies,
And over all thy husband's towering eyes,
Inflamed with th' ugly sweat of jealousy;
Yet went we not still on in constancy?
Have we for this kept guards, like spy on spy?
Had correspondence whilst the foe stood by?
Stolen, more to sweeten them, our many blisses
Of meetings, conference, embracements, kisses?
Shadow'd with negligence our best respects?
Varied our language through all dialects
Of becks, winks, looks, and often under boards
Spoke dialogues with our feet far from our words?
Have we proved all the secrets of our art,
Yea, thy pale inwards, and thy panting heart?
And, after all this passed purgatory,
Must sad divorce make us the vulgar story?
First let our eyes be riveted quite through
Our turning brain, and both our lips grow to;
Let our arms clasp like ivy, and our fear
Freeze us together, that we may stick here,
Till Fortune, that would ruin us with the deed,
Strain his eyes open, and yet make them bleed.
For Love it cannot be, whom hitherto
I have accused, should such a mischief do.
O Fortune, thou'rt not worth my least exclaim,
And plague enough thou hast in thy own name.
Do thy great worst; my friend and I have charms,
Though not against thy strokes, against thy harms.
Rend us in sunder; thou canst not divide
Our bodies so, but that our souls are tied,
And we can love by letters still and gifts,
And thoughts and dreams; love never wanteth shifts.
I will not look upon the quickening sun,

But straight her beauty to my sense shall run;
The air shall note her soft, the fire, most pure;
Waters suggest her clear, and the earth sure.
Time shall not lose our passages; the spring,
How fresh our love was in the beginning;
The summer, how it ripen'd in the year;
And autumn, what our golden harvests were;
The winter I'll not think on to spite thee,
But count it a lost season; so shall she.
And dearest friend, since we must part, drown night
With hope of day—burdens well borne are light—;
The cold and darkness longer hang somewhere,
Yet Phoebus equally lights all the sphere;
And what we cannot in like portion pay
The world enjoys in mass, and so we may.
Be then ever yourself, and let no woe
Win on your health, your youth, your beauty; so
Declare yourself base Fortune's enemy,
No less be your contempt than her inconstancy;
That I may grow enamour'd on your mind,
When mine own thoughts I here neglected find.
And this to the comfort of my dear I vow,
My deeds shall still be what my deeds are now;
The poles shall move to teach me ere I start;
And when I change my love, I'll change my heart.
Nay, if I wax but cold in my desire,
Think, heaven hath motion lost, and the world, fire.
Much more I could, but many words have made
That oft suspected which men most persuade.
Take therefore all in this; I love so true,
As I will never look for less in you.

Elegy XIV

JULIA.

HARK, news, O envy; thou shalt hear descried
My Julia; who as yet was ne'er envied.
To vomit gall in slander, swell her veins
With calumny, that hell itself disdains,

Is her continual practice; does her best,
To tear opinion e'en out of the breast
Of dearest friends, and—which is worse than vile—
Sticks jealousy in wedlock; her own child
Scapes not the showers of envy.To repeat
The monstrous fashions how, were alive to eat
Deare reputation; would to God she were
But half so loth to act vice, as to hear
My mild reproof.Lived Mantuan now again
That female Mastix to limn with his pen,
This she Chimera that hath eyes of fire,
Burning with anger—anger feeds desire—
Tongued like the night crow, whose ill boding cries
Give out for nothing but new injuries;
Her breath like to the juice in Tænarus,
That blasts the springs, though ne'er so prosperous;
Her hands, I know not how, used more to spill
The food of others than herself to fill;
But O! her mind, that Orcus, which includes
Legions of mischiefs, countless multitudes
Of formless curses, projects unmade up,
Abuses yet unfashion'd, thoughts corrupt,
Misshapen cavils, palpable untroths,
Inevitable errors, self-accusing loaths.
These, like those atoms swarming in the sun,
Throng in her bosom for creation.
I blush to give her halfe her due; yet say,
No poison's half so bad as Julia.

Elegy XV

A TALE OF A CITIZEN AND HIS WIFE.
I SING no harm, good sooth, to any wight,
To lord or fool, cuckold, beggar, or knight,
To peace-teaching lawyer, proctor, or brave
Reformed or reducèd captain, knave,
Officer, juggler, or justice of peace,
Juror or judge; I touch no fat sow's grease;
I am no libeller, nor will be any,

But—like a true man—say there are too many.
I fear not *ore tenus;* for my tale
Nor count nor counsellor will look red or pale.
A citizen and his wife the other day
Both riding on one horse, upon the way
I overtook; the wench a pretty peat,
And—by her eye—well fitting for the feat.
I saw the lecherous citizen turn back
His head, and on his wife's lip steal a smack;
Whence apprehending that the man was kind,
Riding before to kiss his wife behind,
To get acquaintance with him I began
To sort discourse fit for so fine a man;
I ask'd the number of the plaguing bill;
Ask'd if the custom farmers held out still;
Of the Virginian plot, and whether Ward
The traffic of the island seas had marr'd;
Whether the Britain Burse did fill apace,
And likely were to give th' Exchange disgrace.
Of new-built Aldgate, and the Moor-field crosses,
Of store of bankrupts, and poor merchants' losses
I urgèd him to speak; but he—as mute
As an old courtier worn to his last suit—
Replies with only yeas and nays; at last
—To fit his element—my theme I cast
On tradesmen's gains; that set his tongue a-going.
" Alas! good sir," quoth he, " There is no doing
In court or city now"; she smiled, and I,
And, in my conscience, both gave him the lie
In one met thought; but he went on apace,
And at the present time with such a face
He rail'd, as fray'd me; for he gave no praise
To any but my Lord of Essex' days;
Call'd that the age of action—" True! " quoth I—
" There's now as great an itch of bravery,
And heat of taking up, but cold lay down,
For, put to push of pay, away they run;
Our only city trades of hope now are

Bawd, tavern-keepers, whores, and scriveners.
The much of privileged kinsmen and store
Of fresh protections make the rest all poor.
In the first state of their creation
Though many stoutly stand, yet proves not one
A righteous pay-master." Thus ran he on
In a continued rage; so void of reason
Seem'd his harsh talk, I sweat for fear of treason.
And—troth—how could I less? when in the prayer
For the protection of the wise Lord Mayor,
And his wise brethren's worships, when one prayeth,
He swore that none could say amen with faith.
To get off him from what I glow'd to hear,
In happy time an angel did appear,
The bright sign of a loved and well-tried inn,
Where many citizens with their wives had been
Well used and often; here I pray'd him stay,
To take some due refreshment by the way.
Look, how he look'd that hid the gold, his hope,
And at return found nothing but a rope,
So he at me; refused and made away,
Though willing she pleaded a weary stay.
I found my miss, struck hands, and pray'd him tell—
To hold acquaintance still—where he did dwell.
He barely named the street, promised the wine,
But his kind wife gave me the very sign.

Elegy XVI

THE EXPOSTULATION.
TO make the doubt clear, that no woman's true,
Was it my fate to prove it strong in you?
Thought I, but one had breathèd purest air;
And must she needs be false, because she's fair?
Is it your beauty's mark, or of your youth,
Or your perfection, not to study truth?
Or think you heaven is deaf, or hath no eyes?
Or those it hath smile at your perjuries?
Are vows so cheap with women, or the matter

Whereof they're made, that they are writ in water,
And blown away with wind? Or doth their breath
Both hot and cold, at once make life and death?
Who could have thought so many accents sweet
Form'd into words, so may sighs should meet
As from our hearts, so many oaths, and tears
Sprinkled among, all sweeten'd by our fears,
And the divine impression of stolen kisses,
That seal'd the rest, should now prove empty blisses?
Did you draw bonds to forfeit? sign to break?
Or must we read you quite from what you speak,
And find the truth out the wrong way? or must
He first desire you false, would wish you just?
O! I profane! though most of women be
This kind of beast, my thoughts shall except thee,
My dearest love; though froward jealousy
With circumstance might urge thy inconstancy,
Sooner I'll think the sun will cease to cheer
The teeming earth, and that forget to bear;
Sooner that rivers will run back, or Thames
With ribs of ice in June will bind his streams;
Or nature, by whose strength the world endures,
Would change her course, before you alter yours.
But O! that treacherous breast, to whom weak you
Did drift our counsels, and we both may rue,
Having his falsehood found too late; 'twas he
That made me cast you guilty, and you me;
Whilst he, black wretch, betray'd each simple word
We spake, unto the cunning of a third.
Cursed may he be, that so our love hath slain,
And wander on the earth, wretched as Cain,
Wretched as he, and not deserve least pity.
In plaguing him, let misery be witty;
Let all eyes shun him, and he shun each eye,
Till he be noisome as his infamy;
May he without remorse deny God thrice,
And not be trusted more on his soul's price;
And, after all self-torment, when he dies,

May wolves tear out his heart, vultures his eyes,
Swine eat his bowels, and his falser tongue
That utter'd all, be to some raven flung;
And let his carrion corse be a longer feast
To the king's dogs, than any other beast.
Now have I cursed, let us our love revive;
In me the flame was never more alive.
I could begin again to court and praise,
And in that pleasure lengthen the short days
Of my life's lease; like painters that do take
Delight, not in made work, but whiles they make.
I could renew those times, when first I saw
Love in your eyes, that gave my tongue the law
To like what you liked; and at masks and plays
Commend the self-same actors, the same ways;
Ask how you did, and often with intent
Of being officious, be impertinent;
All which were such soft pastimes, as in these
Love was as subtly catch'd as a disease.
But being got, it is a treasure sweet,
Which to defend is harder than to get;
And ought not be profaned, on either part,
For though 'tis got by chance, 'tis kept by art.

Elegy XVII

ELEGY ON HIS MISTRESS.
By our first strange and fatal interview,
By all desires which thereof did ensue,
By our long starving hopes, by that remorse
Which my words masculine persuasive force
Begot in thee, and by the memory
Of hurts, which spies and rivals threaten'd me,
I calmly beg. But by thy father's wrath,
By all pains, which want and divorcement hath,
I conjure thee, and all the oaths which I
And thou have sworn to seal joint constancy,
Here I unswear, and overswear them thus;
Thou shalt not love by ways so dangerous.

Temper, O fair love, love's impetuous rage;
Be my true mistress still, not my feign'd page.
I'll go, and, by thy kind leave, leave behind
Thee, only worthy to nurse in my mind
Thirst to come back; O! if thou die before,
My soul from other lands to thee shall soar.
Thy else almighty beauty cannot move
Rage from the seas, nor thy love teach them love,
Nor tame wild Boreas' harshness; thou hast read
How roughly he in pieces shivered
Fair Orithea, whom he swore he loved.
Fall ill or good, 'tis madness to have proved
Dangers unurged; feed on this flattery,
That absent lovers one in th' other be.
Dissemble nothing, not a boy, nor change
Thy body's habit, nor mind; be not strange
To thyself only. All will spy in thy face
A blushing womanly discovering grace.
Richly clothed apes are call'd apes, and as soon
Eclipsed as bright, we call the moon the moon.
Men of France, changeable chameleons,
Spitals of diseases, shops of fashions,
Love's fuellers, and the rightest company
Of players, which upon the world's stage be,
Will quickly know thee, and no less, alas!
Th' indifferent Italian, as we pass
His warm land, well content to think thee page,
Will hunt thee with such lust, and hideous rage,
As Lot's fair guests were vex'd. But none of these
Nor spongy hydroptic Dutch shall thee displease,
If thou stay here. O stay here, for for thee
England is only a worthy gallery,
To walk in expectation, till from thence
Our greatest king call thee to his presence.
When I am gone, dream me some happiness;
Nor let thy looks our long-hid love confess;
Nor praise, nor dispraise me, nor bless nor curse
Openly love's force, nor in bed fright thy nurse

With midnight's startings, crying out, O! O!
Nurse, O! my love is slain; I saw him go
O'er the white Alps alone; I saw him, I,
Assail'd, fight, taken, stabb'd, bleed, fall, and die.
Augur me better chance, except dread Jove
Think it enough for me to have had thy love.

Elegy XVIII

THE heavens rejoice in motion; why should I
Abjure my so much loved variety,
And not with many youth and love divide?
Pleasure is none, if not diversified.
The sun that, sitting in the chair of light,
Sheds flame into what else so ever doth seem bright,
Is not contented at one sign to inn,
But ends his year, and with a new begin.
All things do willingly in change delight,
The fruitful mother of our appetite;
Rivers the clearer and more pleasing are,
Where their fair-spreading streams run wide and clear;
And a dead lake, that no strange bark doth greet,
Corrupts itself, and what doth live in it.
Let no man tell me such a one is fair,
And worthy all alone my love to share.
Nature in her hath done the liberal part
Of a kind mistress, and employed her art,
To make her loveable, and I aver
Him not humane, that would turn back from her.
I love her well, and would, if need were, die,
To do her service. But follows it that I
Must serve her only, when I may have choice?
The law is hard, and shall not have my voice.
The last I saw in all extremes is fair,
And holds me in the sunbeams of her hair;
Her nymph-like features such agreements have,
That I could venture with her to the grave.
Another's brown; I like her not the worse;
Her tongue is soft and takes me with discourse.

Others, for that they well descended were,
Do in my love obtain as large a share;
And though they be not fair, 'tis much with me
To win their love only for their degree.
And though I fail of my required ends,
The attempt is glorious and itself commends.
How happy were our sires in ancient time,
Who held plurality of loves no crime.
With them it was accounted charity
To stir up race of all indifferently;
Kindred were not exempted from the bands,
Which with the Persian still in usage stands.
Women were then no sooner ask'd than won,
And what they did was honest and well done.
But since this little Honour hath been used,
Our weak credulity hath been abused;
The golden laws of nature are repeal'd,
Which our first fathers in such reverence held;
Our liberty reversed and charters gone;
And we made servants to Opinion;
A monster in no certain shape attired,
And whose original is much desired,
Formless at first, but growing on its fashions,
And doth prescribe manners and laws to nations.
Here love received immedicable harms,
And was despoiled of his daring arms;
A greater want than is his daring eyes,
He lost those awful wings with which he flies,
His sinewy bow and those immortal darts,
With which he is wont to bruise resisting hearts.
Only some few, strong in themselves and free,
Retain the seeds of ancient liberty,
Following that part of love although depress'd,
Yet make a throne for him within their breast,
In spite of modern censures him avowing
Their sovereign, all service him allowing.
Amongst which troop although I am the least,
Yet equal in perfection with the best,

I glory in subjection of his hand,
Nor ever did decline his least command;
For in whatever form the message came
My heart did open and receive the same,
But time will in his course a point descry
When I this lovèd service must deny;
For our allegiance temporary is;
With firmer age returns our liberties.
What time in years and judgment we reposed,
Shall not so easily be to change disposed,
Nor to the art of several eyes obeying,
But beauty with true worth securely weighing;
Which being found assembled in some one
We'll leave her ever, and love her alone.

Elegy XIX

WHOEVER loves, if he do not propose
The right true end of love, he's one that goes
To sea for nothing but to make him sick.
Love is a bear-whelp bornif we o'er-lick
Our love, and force it new strange shapes to take,
We err, and of a lump a monster make.
Were not a calf a monster, that were grown
Faced like a man, though better than his own?
Perfection is in unity; prefer
One woman first, and then one thing in her.
I, when I value gold, may think upon
The ductileness, the application,
The wholesomeness, the ingenuity,
From rust, from soil, from fire ever free;
But if I love it, 'tis because 'tis made
By our new nature, use, the soul of trade.
All this in women we might think upon,
—If women had them—and yet love but one.
Can men more injure women than to say
They love them for that, by which they're not they?
Makes virtue woman? must I cool my blood
Till I both be, and find one wise and good?

May barren angels love so. But if we
Make love to woman, virtue is not she,
As beauty is not, nor wealth. He that strays thus
From her to hers is more adulterous
Than if he took her maid. Search every sphere
And firmament, our Cupid is not there.
He's an infernal God, and underground
With Pluto dwells, where gold and fire abound.
Men to such gods their sacrificing coals
Did not on altars lay, but pits and holes.
Although we see celestial bodies move
Above the earth, the earth we till and love.
So we her airs contemplate, words and heart,
And virtues, but we love the centric part.
Nor is the soul more worthy, or more fit
For love, than this, as infinite as it.
But in attaining this desired place
How much they err, that set out at the face?
The hair a forest is of ambushes,
Of springes, snares, fetters, and manacles;
The brow becalms us when 'tis smooth and plain,
And when 'tis wrinkled, shipwrecks us again;
Smooth, 'tis a paradise, where we would have
Immortal stay, but wrinkled 'tis a grave.
The nose, like to the first meridian, runs
Not 'twixt an east and west, but 'twixt two suns;
It leaves a cheek, a rosy hemisphere,
On either side, and then directs us where
Upon the islands fortunate we fall,
Not faint Canaries, but ambrosial,
Her swelling lips, to which when we are come,
We anchor there, and think ourselves at home,
For they seem all; there Sirens' songs and there
Wise Delphic oracles do fill the ear.
There, in a creek where chosen pearls do swell,
The remora, her cleaving tongue, doth dwell.
These and the glorious promontory, her chin,

O'erpast, and the straight Hellespont between
The Sestos and Abydos of her breasts,
Not of two lovers, but two loves, the nests,
Succeeds a boundless sea, but yet thine eye
Some island moles may scattered there descry;
And sailing towards her India, in that way
Shall at her fair Atlantic navel stay.
Though there the current be the pilot made,
Yet, ere thou be where thou shouldst be embay'd,
Thou shalt upon another forest set,
Where many shipwreck, and no further get.
When thou art there, consider what this chase
Misspent by thy beginning at the face.
Rather set out below; practise thy art;
Some symmetry the foot hath with that part
Which thou dost seek, and is thy map for that,
Lovely enough to stop, but not stay at.
Least subject to disguise and change it is;
Men say the devil never can change his;
It is the emblem that hath figured
Firmness; 'tis the first part that comes to bed.
Civility we see refined; the kiss,
Which at the face began, transplanted is,
Since to the hand, since to the imperial knee,
Now at the papal foot delights to be.
If kings think that the nearer way, and do
Rise from the foot, lovers may do so too;
For, as free spheres move faster far than can
Birds, whom the air resists, so may that man
Which goes this empty and ethereal way,
Than if at beauty's elements he stay.
Rich Nature in women wisely made
Two purses, and their mouths aversely laid.
They then which to the lower tribute owe,
That way which that exchequer looks must go;
He which doth not, his error is as great,
As who by clyster gives the stomach meat.

Elegy XX

TO HIS MISTRESS GOING TO BED.

COME, madam, come, all rest my powers defy;
Until I labour, I in labour lie.
The foe ofttimes, having the foe in sight,
Is tired with standing, though he never fight.
Off with that girdle, like heaven's zone glittering,
But a far fairer world encompassing.
Unpin that spangled breast-plate, which you wear,
That th' eyes of busy fools may be stopp'd there.
Unlace yourself, for that harmonious chime
Tells me from you that now it is bed-time.
Off with that happy busk, which I envy,
That still can be, and still can stand so nigh.
Your gown going off such beauteous state reveals,
As when from flowery meads th' hill's shadow steals.
Off with your wiry coronet, and show
The hairy diadems which on you do grow.
Off with your hose and shoes; then softly tread
In this love's hallow'd temple, this soft bed.
In such white robes heaven's angels used to be
Revealed to men; thou, angel, bring'st with thee
A heaven-like Mahomet's paradise; and though
Ill spirits walk in white, we easily know
By this these angels from an evil sprite;
Those set our hairs, but these our flesh upright.
Licence my roving hands, and let them go
Before, behind, between, above, below.
O, my America, my Newfoundland,
My kingdom, safest when with one man mann'd,
My mine of precious stones, my empery;
How am I blest in thus discovering thee!
To enter in these bonds, is to be free;
Then, where my hand is set, my soul shall be.
Full nakedness! All joys are due to thee;
As souls unbodied, bodies unclothed must be
To taste whole joys. Gems which you women use

Are like Atlanta's ball cast in men's views;
That, when a fool's eye lighteth on a gem,
His earthly soul might court that, not them.
Like pictures, or like books' gay coverings made
For laymen, are all women thus array'd.
Themselves are only mystic books, which we
—Whom their imputed grace will dignify—
Must see reveal'd. Then, since that I may know,
As liberally as to thy midwife show
Thyself; cast all, yea, this white linen hence;
There is no penance due to innocence:
To teach thee, I am naked first; why then,
What needst thou have more covering than a man?

Holy Sonnets

Holy Sonnets I

THOU hast made me, and shall Thy work decay ?
Repair me now, for now mine end doth haste;
I run to death, and Death meets me as fast,
And all my pleasures are like yesterday.
I dare not move my dim eyes any way;
Despair behind, and Death before doth cast
Such terror, and my feeble flesh doth waste
By sin in it, which it towards hell doth weigh.
Only Thou art above, and when towards Thee
By Thy leave I can look, I rise again;
But our old subtle foe so tempteth me,
That not one hour myself I can sustain.
Thy grace may wing me to prevent his art
And thou like adamant draw mine iron heart.

Holy Sonnets II

AS due by many titles I resign
Myself to thee, O God. First I was made
By Thee; and for Thee, and when I was decay'd
Thy blood bought that, the which before was Thine.
I am Thy son, made with Thyself to shine,
Thy servant, whose pains Thou hast still repaid,

Thy sheep, Thine image, and—till I betray'd
Myself—a temple of Thy Spirit divine.
Why doth the devil then usurp on me ?
Why doth he steal, nay ravish, that's Thy right ?
Except Thou rise and for Thine own work fight,
O ! I shall soon despair, when I shall see
That Thou lovest mankind well, yet wilt not choose me,
And Satan hates me, yet is loth to lose me.

Holy Sonnets III

O ! might those sighs and tears return again
Into my breast and eyes, which I have spent,
That I might in this holy discontent
Mourn with some fruit, as I have mourn'd in vain.
In mine idolatry what showers of rain
Mine eyes did waste ? what griefs my heart did rent ?
That sufferance was my sin, I now repent;
'Cause I did suffer, I must suffer pain.
Th' hydroptic drunkard, and night-scouting thief,
The itchy lecher, and self-tickling proud
Have the remembrance of past joys, for relief
Of coming ills. To poor me is allow'd
No ease; for long, yet vehement grief hath been
Th' effect and cause, the punishment and sin.

Holy Sonnets IV

O, my black soul, now thou art summoned
By sickness, Death's herald and champion;
Thou'rt like a pilgrim, which abroad hath done
Treason, and durst not turn to whence he's fled;
Or like a thief, which till death's doom be read,
Wisheth himself deliver'd from prison,
But damn'd and haled to execution,
Wisheth that still he might be imprisoned.
Yet grace, if thou repent, thou canst not lack;
But who shall give thee that grace to begin ?
O, make thyself with holy mourning black,
And red with blushing, as thou art with sin;

Or wash thee in Christ's blood, which hath this might,
That being red, it dyes red souls to white.

Holy Sonnets V

I am a little world made cunningly
Of elements, and an angelic sprite;
But black sin hath betray'd to endless night
My world's both parts, and, O, both parts must die.
You which beyond that heaven which was most high
Have found new spheres, and of new land can write,
Pour new seas in mine eyes, that so I might
Drown my world with my weeping earnestly,
Or wash it if it must be drown'd no more.
But O, it must be burnt; alas ! the fire
Of lust and envy burnt it heretofore,
And made it fouler; let their flames retire,
And burn me, O Lord, with a fiery zeal
Of Thee and Thy house, which doth in eating heal.

Holy Sonnets VI

This is my play's last scene; here heavens appoint
My pilgrimage's last mile; and my race
Idly, yet quickly run, hath this last pace;
My span's last inch, my minute's latest point;
And gluttonous Death will instantly unjoint
My body and soul, and I shall sleep a space;
But my ever-waking part shall see that face,
Whose fear already shakes my every joint.
Then, as my soul to heaven her first seat takes flight,
And earth-born body in the earth shall dwell,
So fall my sins, that all may have their right,
To where they're bred and would press me to hell.
Impute me righteous, thus purged of evil,
For thus I leave the world, the flesh, the devil.

Holy Sonnets VII

At the round earth's imagined corners blow
Your trumpets, angels, and arise, arise

From death, you numberless infinities
Of souls, and to your scattered bodies go;
All whom the flood did, and fire shall o'erthrow,
All whom war, dea[r]th, age, agues, tyrannies,
Despair, law, chance hath slain, and you, whose eyes
Shall behold God, and never taste death's woe.
But let them sleep, Lord, and me mourn a space;
For, if above all these my sins abound,
'Tis late to ask abundance of Thy grace,
When we are there. Here on this lowly ground,
Teach me how to repent, for that's as good
As if Thou hadst seal'd my pardon with Thy blood.

Holy Sonnets VIII

If faithful souls be alike glorified
As angels, then my father's soul doth see,
And adds this even to full felicity,
That valiantly I hell's wide mouth o'erstride.
But if our minds to these souls be descried
By circumstances, and by signs that be
Apparent in us not immediately,
How shall my mind's white truth by them be tried ?
They see idolatrous lovers weep and mourn,
And stile blasphemous conjurers to call
On Jesu's name, and pharisaical
Dissemblers feign devotion. Then turn,
O pensive soul, to God, for He knows best
Thy grief, for He put it into my breast.

Holy Sonnets IX

If poisonous minerals, and if that tree,
Whose fruit threw death on (else immortal) us,
If lecherous goats, if serpents envious
Cannot be damn'd, alas ! why should I be ?
Why should intent or reason, born in me,
Make sins, else equal, in me more heinous ?
And, mercy being easy, and glorious
To God, in His stern wrath why threatens He ?

But who am I, that dare dispute with Thee ?
O God, O ! of Thine only worthy blood,
And my tears, make a heavenly Lethean flood,
And drown in it my sin's black memory.
That Thou remember them, some claim as debt;
I think it mercy if Thou wilt forget.

Holy Sonnets X

Death, be not proud, though some have called thee
Mighty and dreadful, for thou art not so;
For those, whom thou think'st thou dost overthrow,
Die not, poor Death, nor yet canst thou kill me.
From rest and sleep, which but thy picture[s] be,
Much pleasure, then from thee much more must flow,
And soonest our best men with thee do go,
Rest of their bones, and soul's delivery.
Thou'rt slave to Fate, chance, kings, and desperate men,
And dost with poison, war, and sickness dwell,
And poppy, or charms can make us sleep as well,
And better than thy stroke; why swell'st thou then ?
One short sleep past, we wake eternally,
And Death shall be no more; Death, thou shalt die.

Holy Sonnets XI

Spit in my face, you Jews, and pierce my side,
Buffet, and scoff, scourge, and crucify me,
For I have sinn'd, and sinne', and only He,
Who could do no iniquity, hath died.
But by my death can not be satisfied
My sins, which pass the Jews' impiety.
They kill'd once an inglorious man, but I
Crucify him daily, being now glorified.
O let me then His strange love still admire;
Kings pardon, but He bore our punishment;
And Jacob came clothed in vile harsh attire,
But to supplant, and with gainful intent;
God clothed Himself in vile man's flesh, that so
He might be weak enough to suffer woe.

Holy Sonnets XII

Why are we by all creatures waited on ?
Why do the prodigal elements supply
Life and food to me, being more pure than I,
Simpler and further from corruption ?
Why brook'st thou, ignorant horse, subjection ?
Why dost thou, bull and boar, so sillily
Dissemble weakness, and by one man's stroke die,
Whose whole kind you might swallow and feed upon ?
Weaker I am, woe's me, and worse than you;
You have not sinn'd, nor need be timorous.
But wonder at a greater, for to us
Created nature doth these things subdue;
But their Creator, whom sin, nor nature tied,
For us, His creatures, and His foes, hath died.

Holy Sonnets XIII

What if this present were the world's last night ?
Mark in my heart, O soul, where thou dost dwell,
The picture of Christ crucified, and tell
Whether His countenance can thee affright.
Tears in His eyes quench the amazing light;
Blood fills his frowns, which from His pierced head fell;
And can that tongue adjudge thee unto hell,
Which pray'd forgiveness for His foes' fierce spite ?
No, no; but as in my idolatry
I said to all my profane mistresses,
Beauty of pity, foulness only is
A sign of rigour; so I say to thee,
To wicked spirits are horrid shapes assign'd;
This beauteous form assures a piteous mind.

Holy Sonnets XIV

Batter my heart, three-person'd God; for you
As yet but knock; breathe, shine, and seek to mend;
That I may rise, and stand, o'erthrow me, and bend
Your force, to break, blow, burn, and make me new.

I, like an usurp'd town, to another due,
Labour to admit you, but O, to no end.
Reason, your viceroy in me, me should defend,
But is captived, and proves weak or untrue.
Yet dearly I love you, and would be loved fain,
But am betroth'd unto your enemy;
Divorce me, untie, or break that knot again,
Take me to you, imprison me, for I,
Except you enthrall me, never shall be free,
Nor ever chaste, except you ravish me.

Holy Sonnets XV

Wilt thou love God as he thee ? then digest,
My soul, this wholesome meditation,
How God the Spirit, by angels waited on
In heaven, doth make His temple in thy breast.
The Father having begot a Son most blest,
And still begetting—for he ne'er begun—
Hath deign'd to choose thee by adoption,
Co-heir to His glory, and Sabbath' endless rest.
And as a robb'd man, which by search doth find
His stolen stuff sold, must lose or buy it again,
The Sun of glory came down, and was slain,
Us whom He had made, and Satan stole, to unbind.
'Twas much, that man was made like God before,
But, that God should be made like man, much more.

Holy Sonnets XVI

Father, part of His double interest
Unto Thy kingdom Thy Son gives to me;
His jointure in the knotty Trinity
He keeps, and gives to me his death's conquest.
This Lamb, whose death with life the world hath blest,
Was from the world's beginning slain, and He
Hath made two wills, which with the legacy
Of His and Thy kingdom do thy sons invest.
Yet such are these laws, that men argue yet
Whether a man those statutes can fulfil.

None doth; but thy all-healing grace and Spirit
Revive again what law and letter kill.
Thy law's abridgement, and Thy last command
Is all but love; O let this last Will stand !

Holy Sonnets XVII

Since she whom I loved hath paid her last debt
To Nature, and to hers, and my good is dead,
And her soul early into heaven ravishèd,
Wholly on heavenly things my mind is set.
Here the admiring her my mind did whet
To seek thee, God; so streams do show the head;
But though I have found thee, and thou my thirst hast fed,
A holy thirsty dropsy melts me yet.
But why should I beg more love, whenas thou
Dost woo my soul, for hers offering all thine:
And dost not only fear lest I allow
My love to saints and angels, things divine,
But in thy tender jealousy dost doubt
Lest the world, flesh, yea, devil put thee out.

Holy Sonnets XVIII

Show me, dear Christ, thy spouse so bright and clear.
What! is it she which on the other shore
Goes richly painted? or which, robbed and tore,
Laments and mourns in Germany and here?
Sleeps she a thousand, then peeps up one year?
Is she self-truth, and errs? now new, now outwore?
Doth she, and did she, and shall she evermore
On one, on seven, or on no hill appear?
Dwells she with us, or like adventuring knights
First travel we to seek, and then make love?
Betray, kind husband, thy spouse to our sights,
And let mine amorous soul court thy mild dove,
Who is most true and pleasing to thee then
When she is embraced and open to most men.

Holy Sonnet XIX

Oh, to vex me, contraries meet in one:
Inconstancy unnaturally hath begot
A constant habit; that when I would not
I change in vows, and in devotion.
As humorous is my contrition
As my profane love, and as soon forgot:
As riddlingly distempered, cold and hot,
As praying, as mute; as infinite, as none.
I durst not view heaven yesterday; and today
In prayers and flattering speeches I court God:
Tomorrow I quake with true fear of his rod.
So my devout fits come and go away
Like a fantastic ague; save that here
Those are my best days, when I shake with feare.

The Cross

SINCE Christ embraced the cross itself, dare I
His image, th' image of His cross, deny ?
Would I have profit by the sacrifice,
And dare the chosen altar to despise ?
It bore all other sins, but is it fit
That it should bear the sin of scorning it ?
Who from the picture would avert his eye,
How would he fly his pains, who there did die ?
From me no pulpit, nor misgrounded law,
Nor scandal taken, shall this cross withdraw,
It shall not, for it cannot; for the loss
Of this cross were to me another cross.
Better were worse, for no affliction,
No cross is so extreme, as to have none.
Who can blot out the cross, with th' instrument
Of God dew'd on me in the Sacrament ?
Who can deny me power, and liberty
To stretch mine arms, and mine own cross to be ?
Swim, and at every stroke thou art thy cross;
The mast and yard make one, where seas do toss;

Look down, thou spiest out crosses in small things;
Look up, thou seest birds raised on crossed wings;
All the globe's frame, and spheres, is nothing else
But the meridians crossing parallels.
Material crosses then, good physic be,
But yet spiritual have chief dignity.
These for extracted chemic medicine serve,
And cure much better, and as well preserve.
Then are you your own physic, or need none,
When still'd or purged by tribulation;
For when that cross ungrudged unto you sticks,
Then are you to yourself a crucifix.
As perchance carvers do not faces make,
But that away, which hid them there, do take;
Let crosses, so, take what hid Christ in thee,
And be His image, or not His, but He.
But, as oft alchemists do coiners prove,
So may a self-despising get self-love;
And then, as worst surfeits of best meats be,
So is pride, issued from humility,
For 'tis no child, but monster; therefore cross
Your joy in crosses, else, 'tis double loss.
And cross thy senses, else both they and thou
Must perish soon, and to destruction bow.
For if the eye seek good objects, and will take
No cross from bad, we cannot 'scape a snake.
So with harsh, hard, sour, stinking; cross the rest;
Make them indifferent; call, nothing best.
But most the eye needs crossing, that can roam,
And move; to th' others th' objects must come home.
And cross thy heart; for that in man alone
Pants downwards, and hath palpitation.
Cross those dejections, when it downward tends,
And when it to forbidden heights pretends.
And as the brain through bony walls doth vent
By sutures, which a cross's form present,
So when thy brain works, ere thou utter it,
Cross and correct concupiscence of wit.

Be covetous of crosses; let none fall;
Cross no man else, but cross thyself in all.
Then doth the cross of Christ work faithfully
Within our hearts, when we love harmlessly
That cross's pictures much, and with more care
That cross's children, which our crosses are.

Resurrection, Imperfect

SLEEP, sleep, old sun, thou canst not have repass'd,
As yet, the wound thou took'st on Friday last;
Sleep then, and rest; the world may bear thy stay;
A better sun rose before thee to-day;
Who—not content to enlighten all that dwell
On the earth's face, as thou—enlighten'd hell,
And made the dark fires languish in that vale,
As at thy presence here our fires grow pale;
Whose body, having walk'd on earth, and now
Hasting to heaven, would—that He might allow
Himself unto all stations, and fill all—
For these three days become a mineral.
He was all gold when He lay down, but rose
All tincture, and doth not alone dispose
Leaden and iron wills to good, but is
Of power to make e'en sinful flesh like his.
Had one of those, whose credulous piety
Thought that a soul one might discern and see
Go from a body, at this sepulchre been,
And, issuing from the sheet, this body seen,
He would have justly thought this body a soul,
If not of any man, yet of the whole.

The Annunciation and Passion

TAMELY, frail body, abstain to-day; to-day
My soul eats twice, Christ hither and away.
She sees Him man, so like God made in this,
That of them both a circle emblem is,
Whose first and last concur; this doubtful day
Of feast or fast, Christ came, and went away;

She sees Him nothing, twice at once, who's all;
She sees a cedar plant itself, and fall;
Her Maker put to making, and the head
Of life at once not yet alive, yet dead;
She sees at once the Virgin Mother stay
Reclused at home, public at Golgotha;
Sad and rejoiced she's seen at once, and seen
At almost fifty, and at scarce fifteen;
At once a son is promised her, and gone;
Gabriell gives Christ to her, He her to John;
Not fully a mother, she's in orbity;
At once receiver and the legacy.
All this, and all between, this day hath shown,
Th' abridgement of Christ's story, which makes one—
As in plain maps, the furthest west is east—
Of th' angels *Ave*, and *Consummatum est*.
How well the Church, God's Court of Faculties,
Deals, in sometimes, and seldom joining these.
As by the self-fix'd Pole we never do
Direct our course, but the next star thereto,
Which shows where th'other is, and which we say
—Because it strays not far—doth never stray,
So God by His Church, nearest to him, we know,
And stand firm, if we by her motion go.
His Spirit, as His fiery pillar, doth
Lead, and His Church, as cloud; to one end both.
This Church by letting those days join, hath shown
Death and conception in mankind is one;
Or 'twas in Him the same humility,
That He would be a man, and leave to be;
Or as creation He hath made, as God,
With the last judgment but one period,
His imitating spouse would join in one
Manhood's extremes; He shall come, He is gone;
Or as though one blood drop, which thence did fall,
Accepted, would have served, He yet shed all,
So though the least of His pains, deeds, or words,
Would busy a life, she all this day affords.

This treasure then, in gross, my soul, uplay,
And in my life retail it every day.

Good-friday, 1613, Riding Westward

LET man's soul be a sphere, and then, in this,
Th' intelligence that moves, devotion is;
And as the other spheres, by being grown
Subject to foreign motion, lose their own,
And being by others hurried every day,
Scarce in a year their natural form obey;
Pleasure or business, so, our souls admit
For their first mover, and are whirl'd by it.
Hence is't, that I am carried towards the west,
This day, when my soul's form bends to the East.
There I should see a Sun by rising set,
And by that setting endless day beget.
But that Christ on His cross did rise and fall,
Sin had eternally benighted all.
Yet dare I almost be glad, I do not see
That spectacle of too much weight for me.
Who sees Gods face, that is self-life, must die;
What a death were it then to see God die ?
It made His own lieutenant, Nature, shrink,
It made His footstool crack, and the sun wink.
Could I behold those hands, which span the poles
And tune all spheres at once, pierced with those holes ?
Could I behold that endless height, which is
Zenith to us and our antipodes,
Humbled below us ? or that blood, which is
The seat of all our soul's, if not of His,
Made dirt of dust, or that flesh which was worn
By God for His apparel, ragg'd and torn ?
If on these things I durst not look, durst I
On His distressed Mother cast mine eye,
Who was God's partner here, and furnish'd thus
Half of that sacrifice which ransom'd us ?
Though these things as I ride be from mine eye,
They're present yet unto my memory,

For that looks towards them; and Thou look'st towards me,
O Saviour, as Thou hang'st upon the tree.
I turn my back to thee but to receive
Corrections till Thy mercies bid Thee leave.
O think me worth Thine anger, punish me,
Burn off my rust, and my deformity;
Restore Thine image, so much, by Thy grace,
That Thou mayst know me, and I'll turn my face.

A Litany

I

THE FATHER.
FATHER of Heaven, and Him, by whom
It, and us for it, and all else for us,
Thou madest, and govern'st ever, come
And re-create me, now grown ruinous:
My heart is by dejection, clay,
And by self-murder, red.
From this red earth, O Father, purge away
All vicious tinctures, that new-fashioned
I may rise up from death, before I'm dead.

II

THE SON.
O Son of God, who, seeing two things,
Sin and Death, crept in, which were never made,
By bearing one, tried'st with what stings
The other could Thine heritage invade;
O be Thou nail'd unto my heart,
And crucified again;
Part not from it, though it from Thee would part,
But let it be by applying so Thy pain,
Drown'd in Thy blood, and in Thy passion slain.

III

THE HOLY GHOST.
O Holy Ghost, whose temple I
Am, but of mud walls, and condensèd dust,
And being sacrilegiously

Half wasted with youth's fires of pride and lust,
Must with new storms be weather-beat,
Double in my heart Thy flame,
Which let devout sad tears intend, and let—
Though this glass lanthorn, flesh, do suffer maim—
Fire, sacrifice, priest, altar be the same.

IV

THE TRINITY.
O blessed glorious Trinity,
Bones to philosophy, but milk to faith,
Which, as wise serpents, diversely
Most slipperiness, yet most entanglings hath,
As you distinguish'd, undistinct,
By power, love, knowledge be,
Give me a such self different instinct,
Of these let all me elemented be,
Of power, to love, to know you unnumbered three.

V

THE VIRGIN MARY.
For that fair blessed mother-maid,
Whose flesh redeem'd us, that she-cherubin,
Which unlock'd paradise, and made
One claim for innocence, and disseizèd sin,
Whose womb was a strange heaven, for there
God clothed Himself, and grew,
Our zealous thanks we pour.As her deeds were
Our helps, so are her prayers; nor can she sue
In vain, who hath such titles unto you.

VI

THE ANGELS.
And since this life our nonage is,
And we in wardship to Thine angels be,
Native in heaven's fair palaces
Where we shall be but denizen'd by Thee;
As th' earth conceiving by the sun,
Yields fair diversity,
Yet never knows what course that light doth run;
So let me study that mine actions be

Worthy their sight, though blind in how they see.

VII

THE PATRIARCHS.

And let Thy patriarchs' desire,
—Those great grandfathers of Thy Church, which saw
More in the cloud than we in fire,
Whom nature clear'd more, than us grace and law,
And now in heaven still pray, that we
May use our new helps right—
Be satisfied, and fructify in me;
Let not my mind be blinder by more light,
Nor faith by reason added lose her sight.

VIII

THE PROPHETS.

Thy eagle-sighted prophets too,
—Which were Thy Church's organs, and did sound
That harmony which made of two
One law, and did unite, but not confound;
Those heavenly poets which did see
Thy will, and it express
In rhythmic feet—in common pray for me,
That I by them excuse not my excess
In seeking secrets, or poeticness.

IX

THE APOSTLES.

And thy illustrious zodiac
Of twelve apostles, which engirt this All,
—From whom whosoever do not take
Their light, to dark deep pits throw down and fall;—
As through their prayers Thou'st let me know
That their books are divine,
May they pray still, and be heard, that I go
Th' old broad way in applying; O decline
Me, when my comment would make Thy word mine.

X

THE MARTYRS.

And since Thou so desirously
Didst long to die, that long before Thou couldst,

And long since Thou no more couldst die,
Thou in thy scatter'd mystic body wouldst
In Abel die, and ever since
In Thine; let their blood come
To beg for us a discreet patience
Of death, or of worse life; for O, to some
Not to be martyrs, is a martyrdom.

XI

THE CONFESSORS.
Therefore with Thee triumpheth there
A virgin squadron of white confessors,
Whose bloods betroth'd not married were,
Tender'd, not taken by those ravishers.
They know, and pray that we may know,
In every Christian
Hourly tempestuous persecutions grow;
Temptations martyr us alive; a man
Is to himself a Diocletian.

XII

THE VIRGINS.
The cold white snowy nunnery,
Which, as Thy Mother, their high abbess, sent
Their bodies back again to Thee,
As Thou hadst lent them, clean and innocent;
Though they have not obtain'd of Thee,
That or Thy Church or I
Should keep, as they, our first integrity,
Divorce Thou sin in us, or bid it die,
And call chaste widowhead virginity.

XIII

THE DOCTORS.
The sacred academy above
Of Doctors, whose pains have unclasp'd, and taught
Both books of life to us—for love
To know Thy scriptures tells us, we are wrote
In Thy other book—pray for us there,
That what they have misdone
Or missaid, we to that may not adhere.

Their zeal may be our sin.Lord, let us run
Mean ways, and call them stars, but not the sun.

XIV

And whilst this universal quire,
That Church in triumph, this in warfare here,
Warm'd with one all-partaking fire
Of love, that none be lost, which cost Thee dear,
Prays ceaselessly, and Thou hearken too
—Since to be gracious
Our task is treble, to pray, bear, and do—
Hear this prayer, Lord; O Lord, deliver us
From trusting in those prayers, though pour'd out
thus.

XV

From being anxious, or secure,
Dead clods of sadness, or light squibs of mirth,
From thinking that great courts immure
All, or no happiness, or that this earth
Is only for our prison framed,
Or that Thou'rt covetous
To them whom Thou lovest, or that they are maim'd
From reaching this world's sweet who seek Thee thus,
With all their might, good Lord, deliver us.

XVI

From needing danger, to be good,
From owing Thee yesterday's tears to-day,
From trusting so much to Thy blood
That in that hope we wound our soul away,
From bribing Thee with alms, to excuse
Some sin more burdenous,
From light affecting, in religion, news,
From thinking us all soul, neglecting thus
Our mutual duties, Lord, deliver us.

XVII

From tempting Satan to tempt us,
By our connivance, or slack company,
From measuring ill by vicious
Neglecting to choke sin's spawn, vanity,

From indiscreet humility,
Which might be scandalous
And cast reproach on Christianity,
From being spies, or to spies pervious,
From thirst or scorn of fame, deliver us.

XVIII

Deliver us through Thy descent
Into the Virgin, whose womb was a place
Of middle kind; and Thou being sent
To ungracious us, stay'dst at her full of grace;
And through Thy poor birth, where first Thou
Glorified'st poverty;
And yet soon after riches didst allow,
By accepting kings' gifts in th' Epiphany;
Deliver us, and make us to both ways free.

XIX

And through that bitter agony,
Which is still th' agony of pious wits,
Disputing what distorted Thee,
And interrupted evenness with fits;
And through Thy free confession,
Though thereby they were then
Made blind, so that Thou mightst from them have gone;
Good Lord, deliver us, and teach us when
We may not, and we may, blind unjust men.

XX

Through Thy submitting all, to blows
Thy face, Thy robes to spoil, Thy fame to scorn,
All ways, which rage, or justice knows,
And by which Thou couldst show that Thou wast born;
And through Thy gallant humbleness
Which Thou in death didst show,
Dying before Thy soul they could express;
Deliver us from death, by dying so
To this world, ere this world do bid us go.

XXI

When senses, which Thy soldiers are,
We arm against Thee, and they fight for sin;

When want, sent but to tame, doth war,
And work despair a breach to enter in;
When plenty, God's image, and seal,
Makes us idolatrous,
And love it, not him, whom it should reveal;
When we are moved to seem religious
Only to vent wit; Lord, deliver us.

XXII

In churches, when th' infirmity
Of him which speaks, diminishes the word;
When magistrates do misapply
To us, as we judge, lay or ghostly sword;
When plague, which is Thine angel, reigns,
Or wars, Thy champions, sway;
When heresy, Thy second deluge, gains;
In th' hour of death, th' eve of last Judgment day;
Deliver us from the sinister way.

XXIII

Hear us, O hear us, Lord; to Thee
A sinner is more music, when he prays,
Than spheres' or angels' praises be,
In panegyric alleluias;
Hear us, for till Thou hear us, Lord,
We know not what to say;
Thine ear to our sighs, tears, thoughts, gives voice and word;
O Thou, who Satan heard'st in Job's sick day,
Hear Thyself now, for Thou in us dost pray.

XXIV

That we may change to evenness
This intermitting aguish piety;
That snatching cramps of wickedness
And apoplexies of fast sin may die;
That music of Thy promises,
Not threats in thunder may
Awaken us to our just offices;
What in Thy book Thou dost, or creatures say,
That we may hear, Lord, hear us when we pray.

XXV

That our ears' sickness we may cure,
And rectify those labyrinths aright,
That we by heark'ning not procure
Our praise, nor others' dispraise so invite;
That we get not a slipp'riness
And senselessly decline,
From hearing bold wits jest at kings' excess,
To admit the like of majesty divine;
That we may lock our ears, Lord, open Thine.

XXVI

That living law, the magistrate,
Which to give us, and make us physic, doth
Our vices often aggravate;
That preachers taxing sin, before her growth;
That Satan, and envenom'd men—
Which will, if we starve, dine—
When they do most accuse us, may see then
Us to amendment hear them, Thee decline;
That we may open our ears, Lord, lock Thine.

XXVII

That learning, Thine ambassador,
From Thine allegiance we never tempt;
That beauty, paradise's flower
For physic made, from poison be exempt;
That wit—born apt high good to do—
By dwelling lazily
On nature's nothing be not nothing too;
That our affections kill us not, nor die;
Hear us, weak echoes, O, Thou Ear and Eye.

XXVIII

Son of God, hear us, and since Thou
By taking our blood, owest it us again,
Gain to Thyself, or us allow;
And let not both us and Thyself be slain;
O Lamb of God, which took'st our sin,
Which could not stick to Thee,
O let it not return to us again;

But patient and physician being free,
As sin is nothing, let it nowhere be.

Hymn to God, My God, in My Sickness

SINCE I am coming to that Holy room,
Where, with Thy choir of saints for evermore,
I shall be made Thy music; as I come
I tune the instrument here at the door,
And what I must do then, think here before;
Whilst my physicians by their love are grown
Cosmographers, and I their map, who lie
Flat on this bed, that by them may be shown
That this is my south-west discovery,
Per fretum febris, by these straits to die;
I joy, that in these straits I see my west;
For, though those currents yield return to none,
What shall my west hurt me ? As west and east
In all flat maps—and I am one—are one,
So death doth touch the resurrection.
Is the Pacific sea my home ? Or are
The eastern riches ? Is Jerusalem ?
Anyan, and Magellan, and Gibraltar ?
All straits, and none but straits, are ways to them
Whether where Japhet dwelt, or Cham, or Shem.
We think that Paradise and Calvary,
Christ's cross and Adam's tree, stood in one place;
Look, Lord, and find both Adams met in me;
As the first Adam's sweat surrounds my face,
May the last Adam's blood my soul embrace.
So, in His purple wrapp'd, receive me, Lord;
By these His thorns, give me His other crown;
And as to others' souls I preach'd Thy word,
Be this my text, my sermon to mine own,
"Therefore that He may raise, the Lord throws down."

A Hymn to God the Father

I

WILT Thou forgive that sin where I begun,

Which was my sin, though it were done before?
Wilt Thou forgive that sin, through which I run,
And do run still, though still I do deplore?
When Thou hast done, Thou hast not done,
For I have more.

II

Wilt Thou forgive that sin which I have won
Others to sin, and made my sin their door?
Wilt Thou forgive that sin which I did shun
A year or two, but wallowed in a score?
When Thou hast done, Thou hast not done,
For I have more.

III

I have a sin of fear, that when I have spun
My last thread, I shall perish on the shore;
But swear by Thyself, that at my death Thy Son
Shall shine as he shines now, and heretofore;
And having done that, Thou hast done;
I fear no more.

A Hymn to Christ, at the Author's Last Going Into Germany

IN what torn ship so ever I embark,
That ship shall be my emblem of Thy ark;
What sea soever swallow me, that flood
Shall be to me an emblem of Thy blood;
Though Thou with clouds of anger do disguise
Thy face, yet through that mask I know those eyes,
Which, though they turn away sometimes,
They never will despise.
I sacrifice this island unto Thee,
And all whom I love there, and who loved me;
When I have put our seas 'twixt them and me,
Put thou Thy seas betwixt my sins and Thee.
As the tree's sap doth seek the root below
In winter, in my winter now I go,
Where none but Thee, the eternal root
Of true love, I may know.

Nor Thou nor Thy religion dost control
The amorousness of an harmonious soul;
But Thou wouldst have that love Thyself; as Thou
Art jealous, Lord, so I am jealous now;
Thou lovest not, till from loving more Thou free
My soul; Who ever gives, takes liberty;
Oh, if Thou carest not whom I love,
Alas ! Thou lovest not me.
Seal then this bill of my divorce to all,
On whom those fainter beams of love did fall;
Marry those loves, which in youth scatter'd be
On fame, wit, hopes—false mistresses—to Thee.
Churches are best for prayer, that have least light;
To see God only, I go out of sight;
And to escape stormy days, I choose
An everlasting night.

Chapter 9

Summary and Analysis

The Broken Heart

Summary

The speaker declares that any man who claims he has been in love for an hour is insane; not because love "decays" in so short a time, but because, in an hour, love can "devour" ten men—in other words, not because love itself is destroyed in an hour, but because it will destroy the lover in much less time than that. To explain himself, the speaker uses an analogyHe says that anyone who heard him claim to have had the plague for an entire year would disbelieve him because the plague would have killed him in much less time than that. He also says that anyone who heard him claim to have seen a flask of gunpowder burn for an entire day would laugh at him because the flask would have exploded immediately. Like the plague and the powder-flask, love works violently and swiftly.

"What a trifle is a heart," the speaker says, "If once into Love's hands it come!" Unlike love, other feelings and "other griefs" do not demand the entire heart, only a part of it. Other griefs "come to us" but Love draws us to it, swallowing us whole. Masses of people are felled by Love as ranks of soldiers are felled by chain-shot. Love is like a ravenous pike, and our hearts are like the small fish it feasts on.

Addressing his beloved, the speaker asks her a questionIf what he says about love is false, then what happened to his heart the first time he saw her? He says that he entered the room with a heart, and left the room without one. If his heart had been captured whole by his beloved, he says, it would have taught her to treat him more kindly; instead, the impact of love shattered his heart "as glass."

Still, he says, a thing cannot be so utterly destroyed that it becomes *nothing*; the pieces of his shattered heart are still in his breast. In the same way that a broken mirror reflects "a hundred lesser faces," the speaker says that his "rags of heart" can "like, wish, and adore"; but after experiencing the shock of "one such love," they can never love again.

The four regular stanzas of "The Broken Heart" utilize Donne's characteristically angular iambic meters; each stanza is eight lines long, with lines one, two, three, five, and six in iambic tetrameter, and lines four, seven, and eight in iambic pentameter. (The line-stress pattern, therefore, is 44454455 in each stanza.) Each stanza follows a rhyme scheme of ABABCCDD.

Analysis

"The Broken Heart" is an excellent example of Donne's style in his metaphysical mode, transforming a relatively simple idea (that love destroys the hearts that feel it) into an oblique, elaborate meditation full of startling images (the burning powder-flask, love as a carnivorous fish) and implications. Structurally, the poem looks at its theme from a different angle in each of its stanzas. The first stanza is metaphorical and explanatory, establishing the basic idea of the poem by showing that to be in love for an entire hour would be like having the plague for a year or seeing a flask of gunpowder burn for an entire day; love is instant, like the explosion of the flask. The second stanza personifies love as a kind of monster that destroys human beings, trifling with hearts, swallowing men whole (he "never chaws"), killing whole ranks, and devouring men as a pike devours smaller fish ("He is the tyrant pike, our hearts the fry").

In the third stanza, the speaker departs from the general and enters the specific, addressing his beloved and recalling the moment when love destroyed *his* heart, enabling him to understand that which he now writes in his poem; the instant he saw his beloved, love shattered his heart like glass. The final stanza offers a kind of moral for the poem, opening in a homiletic tone ("nothing can to nothing fall, / Nor any place be empty quite") and detailing what happens to a heart after it has been shattered by the force of love. The heart remains, the speaker claims, in the breast, like shards of a broken mirror, able to reflect lesser emotions, such as hope and affection, but never again to love.

Throughout, "The Broken Heart" typifies the quality of Donne's metaphysical poems. It is often difficult to understand the speaker's language or to see quite where he is coming from (the opening of the poem is particularly difficult), but once the basic idea is grasped, most of the conceptual elements of the poem fall easily into place. It is remarkable for its unusual conception of love—not many poets would compare love to death by a violent disease—and for the surprising angles from which the speaker approaches that conception.

"The Canonization"

Summary

The speaker asks his addressee to be quiet, and let him love. If the addressee cannot hold his tongue, the speaker tells him to criticize him for other shortcomings (other than his tendency to love)his palsy, his gout, his "five grey hairs," or his ruined fortune. He admonishes the addressee to look to his own mind and his own wealth and to think of his position and copy the other nobles ("Observe his Honour, or his Grace, / Or the King's real, or his stamped face / Contemplate.") The speaker does not care what the addressee says or does, as long as he lets him love.

The speaker asks rhetorically, "Who's injured by my love?" He says that his sighs have not drowned ships, his tears have not flooded land, his colds have not chilled spring, and the heat of his veins has not added to the list of those killed by the plague. Soldiers still find wars and lawyers still find litigious men, regardless of the emotions of the speaker and his lover.

The speaker tells his addressee to "Call us what you will," for it is love that makes them so. He says that the addressee can "Call her one, me another fly," and that they are also like candles ("tapers"), which burn by feeding upon their own selves ("and at our own cost die"). In each other, the lovers find the eagle and the dove, and together ("we two being one") they illuminate the riddle of the phoenix, for they "die and rise the same," just as the phoenix does—though unlike the phoenix, it is love that slays and resurrects them.

He says that they can die by love if they are not able to live by it, and if their legend is not fit "for tombs and hearse," it will be fit for poetry, and "We'll build in sonnets pretty rooms." A well-wrought urn does as much justice to a dead man's ashes as does a gigantic tomb; and by the same token, the poems about the speaker and his lover will cause them to be "canonized," admitted to the sainthood of love. All those who hear their story will invoke the lovers, saying that countries, towns, and courts "beg from above / A pattern of your love!"

The five stanzas of "The Canonization" are metered in iambic lines ranging from trimeter to pentameter; in each of the nine-line stanzas, the first, third, fourth, and seventh lines are in pentameter, the second, fifth, sixth, and eighth in tetrameter, and the ninth in trimeter. (The stress pattern in each stanza is 545544543.) The rhyme scheme in each stanza is ABBACCCDD.

Analysis

This complicated poem, spoken ostensibly to someone who disapproves of the speaker's love affair, is written in the voice of a world-wise, sardonic courtier who is nevertheless utterly caught up in his love. The poem simultaneously parodies old notions of love and coins elaborate new ones, eventually concluding that even if the love affair is impossible in the real world, it can become legendary through poetry, and the speaker and his lover will be like saints to later generations of lovers. (Hence the title"The Canonization" refers to the process by which people are inducted into the canon of saints).

In the first stanza, the speaker obliquely details his relationship to the world of politics, wealth, and nobility; by assuming that these are the concerns of his addressee, he indicates his own background amid such concerns, and he also indicates the extent to which he has moved beyond that background. He hopes that the listener will leave him alone and pursue a career in the court, toadying to aristocrats, preoccupied with favor (the King's real face) and money (the King's stamped face, as on a coin). In the second stanza, he parodies contemporary Petrarchan notions of love and continues to mock his addressee, making the point that his sighs have not drowned ships and his tears have not caused floods. (Petrarchan love-poems were full of claims like "My tears are rain, and my sighs storms.") He also mocks the operations of the everyday world, saying that his love will not keep soldiers from fighting wars or lawyers from finding court cases—as though war and legal wrangling were the sole concerns of world outside the confines of his love affair.

In the third stanza, the speaker begins spinning off metaphors that will help explain the intensity and uniqueness of his love. First, he says that he and his lover are like moths drawn to a candle ("her one, me another fly"), then that they are like the candle itself. They embody the elements of the eagle (strong and masculine) and the dove (peaceful and feminine) bound up in the image of the phoenix, dying and rising by love. In the fourth stanza, the speaker explores the possibility of canonization in verse, and in the final stanza, he explores his and his lover's roles as the saints of love, to whom generations of future lovers will appeal for help. Throughout, the tone of the poem is balanced between a kind of arch, sophisticated sensibility ("half-acre tombs") and passionate amorous abandon ("We die and rise the same, and prove / Mysterious by this love").

"The Canonization" is one of Donne's most famous and most written-about poems. Its criticism at the hands of Cleanth Brooks and others has made it a central topic in the argument between formalist critics and historicist critics; the former argue that the poem is what it seems to be, an anti-political love poem, while the latter argue, based on events in Donne's life at the time of the poem's composition, that it is actually a kind of coded, ironic rumination on the "ruined fortune" and dashed political hopes of the first stanza. The choice of which argument to follow is largely a matter of personal temperament. But unless one seeks a purely biographical understanding of Donne, it is probably best to understand the poem as the sort of droll, passionate speech-act it is, a highly sophisticated defence of love against the corrupting values of politics and privilege.

The Flea

Summary

The speaker tells his beloved to look at the flea before them and to note "how little" is that thing that she denies him. For the flea, he says, has sucked first his blood, then her blood, so that now, inside the flea, they are mingled; and that mingling cannot be called "sin, or shame, or loss of maidenhead." The flea has joined them together in a way that, "alas, is more than we would do."

As his beloved moves to kill the flea, the speaker stays her hand, asking her to spare the three lives in the fleahis life, her life, and the flea's own life. In the flea, he says, where their blood is mingled, they are almost married—no, more than married—and the flea is their marriage bed and marriage temple mixed into one. Though their parents grudge their romance and though she will not make love to him, they are nevertheless united and cloistered in the living walls of the flea. She is apt to kill him, he says, but he asks that she not kill herself by killing the flea that contains her blood; he says that to kill the flea would be sacrilege, "three sins in killing three."

"Cruel and sudden," the speaker calls his lover, who has now killed the flea, "purpling" her fingernail with the "blood of innocence." The speaker asks his lover what the flea's sin was, other than having sucked from each of them a drop of blood. He says that his lover replies that neither of them is less noble for having killed the flea. It is true, he says, and it is this very fact that proves that her fears are falseIf she were to sleep with him ("yield to me"), she would lose no more honour than she lost when she killed the flea.

This poem alternates metrically between lines in iambic tetrameter and lines in iambic pentameter, a 4-5 stress pattern ending with two pentameter lines at the end of each stanza. Thus, the stress pattern in each of the nine-line stanzas is 454545455. The rhyme scheme in each stanza is similarly regular, in couplets, with the final line rhyming with the final coupletAABBCCDDD.

Analysis

This funny little poem again exhibits Donne's metaphysical love-poem mode, his aptitude for turning even the least likely images into elaborate symbols of love and romance. This poem uses the image of a flea that has just bitten the speaker and his beloved to sketch an amusing conflict over whether the two will engage in premarital sex. The speaker wants to, the beloved does not, and so the speaker, highly clever but grasping at straws, uses the flea, in whose body his blood mingles with his beloved's, to show how innocuous such mingling can be—he reasons that if mingling in the flea is so innocuous, sexual mingling would be equally innocuous, for they are really the same thing. By the second stanza, the speaker is trying to save the flea's life, holding it up as "our marriage bed and marriage temple."

But when the beloved kills the flea despite the speaker's protestations (and probably as a deliberate move to squash his argument, as well), he turns his argument on its head and claims that despite the high-minded and sacred ideals he has just been invoking, killing the flea did not really impugn his beloved's honour—and despite the high-minded and sacred ideals she has invoked in refusing to sleep with him, doing so would not impugn her honour either. This poem is the cleverest of a long line of sixteenth-century love poems using the flea as an erotic image, a genre derived from an older poem of Ovid. Donne's poise of hinting at the erotic without ever explicitly referring to sex, while at the same time leaving no doubt as to exactly what he means, is as much a source of the poem's humour as the silly image of the flea is; the idea that being bitten by a flea would represent "sin, or shame, or loss of maidenhead" gets the point across with a neat conciseness and clarity that Donne's later religious lyrics never attained.

The Sun Rising

Summary

Lying in bed with his lover, the speaker chides the rising sun, calling it a "busy old fool," and asking why it must bother them through windows and curtains. Love is not subject to season or to time, he says, and he admonishes the sun—the "Saucy pedantic wretch"—to go and bother late schoolboys and sour apprentices, to tell the court-huntsmen that the King will ride, and to call the country ants to their harvesting. Why should the sun think that his beams are strong? The speaker says that he could eclipse them simply by closing his eyes, except that he does not want to lose sight of his beloved for even an instant. He asks the sun—if the sun's eyes have not been blinded by his lover's eyes—to tell him by late tomorrow whether the treasures of India are in the same place they occupied yesterday or if they are now in bed with the speaker. He says that if the sun asks about the kings he shined on yesterday, he will learn that they all lie in bed with the speaker.

The speaker explains this claim by saying that his beloved is like every country in the world, and he is like every king; nothing else is real. Princes simply play at having countries; compared to what he has, all honour is mimicry and all wealth is alchemy. The sun, the speaker says, is half as happy as he and his lover are, for the fact that the world is contracted into their bed makes the sun's job much easier—in its old age, it desires ease, and now all it has to do is shine on their bed and it shines on the whole world. "This bed thy centre is," the speaker tells the sun, "these walls, thy sphere."

The three regular stanzas of "The Sun Rising" are each ten lines long and follow a line-stress pattern of 4255445555—lines one, five, and six are metered in iambic tetrameter, line two is in dimeter, and lines three, four, and seven through ten are in pentameter. The rhyme scheme in each stanza is ABBACDCDEE.

Analysis

One of Donne's most charming and successful metaphysical love poems, "The Sun Rising" is built around a few hyperbolic assertions—first, that the sun is conscious and has the watchful personality of an old busybody; second, that love, as the speaker puts it, "no season knows, nor clime, / Nor hours, days, months, which are the rags of time"; third, that the speaker's love affair is so important to the universe that kings and princes simply copy it, that the world is literally contained within their bedroom. Of course, each of these assertions simply describes figuratively a state of feeling—to the wakeful lover; the rising sun does seem like an intruder, irrelevant to the operations of love; to the man in love, the bedroom can seem to enclose all the matters in the world. The inspiration of this poem is to pretend that each of these subjective states of feeling is an objective truth.

Accordingly, Donne endows his speaker with language implying that what goes on in his head is primary over the world outside it; for instance, in the second stanza, the speaker tells the sun that it is not so powerful, since the speaker can cause an eclipse simply by closing his eyes. This kind of heedless, joyful arrogance is perfectly tuned to the consciousness of a new lover, and the speaker appropriately claims to have all the world's riches in his bed (India, he says, is not where the sun left it; it is in bed with him). The speaker captures the essence of his feeling in the final stanza, when, after taking pity on the sun and deciding to ease the burdens of his old age, he declares "Shine here to us, and thou art everywhere."

A Valediction for Bidding Mourning

Summary

The speaker explains that he is forced to spend time apart from his lover, but before he leaves, he tells her that their farewell should not be the occasion for mourning and sorrow. In the same way that virtuous men die mildly and without complaint, he says, so they should leave without "tear-floods" and "sigh-tempests," for to publicly announce their feelings in such a way would profane their love. The speaker says that when the earth moves, it brings "harms and fears," but when the spheres experience "trepidation," though the impact is greater, it is also innocent. The love of "dull sublunary lovers" cannot survive separation, but it removes that which constitutes the love itself; but the love he shares with his beloved is so refined and "Inter-assured of the mind" that they need not worry about missing "eyes, lips, and hands." Though he must go, their souls are still one, and, therefore, they are not enduring a breach, they are experiencing an "expansion"; in the same way that gold can be stretched by beating it "to aery thinness," the soul they share will simply stretch to take in all the space between them. If their souls are separate, he says, they are like the feet of a compassHis lover's soul is the fixed foot in the centre, and his is the foot that moves around it. The firmness of the centre foot makes the circlc that the outer foot draws perfect"Thy firmness makes my circle just, / And makes me end, where I begun."

The nine stanzas of this Valediction are quite simple compared to many of Donne's poems, which utilize strange metrical patterns overlaid jarringly on regular rhyme schemes. Here, each four-line stanza is quite unadorned, with an ABAB rhyme scheme and an iambic tetrameter meter.

Analysis

"A Valedictionforbidding Mourning" is one of Donne's most famous and simplest poems and also probably his most direct statement of his ideal of spiritual love. For all his erotic carnality in poems, such as "The Flea," Donne professed a devotion to a kind of spiritual love that transcended the merely physical. Here, anticipating a physical separation from his beloved, he invokes the nature of that spiritual love to ward off the "tear-floods" and "sigh-tempests" that might otherwise attend on their farewell. The poem is essentially a sequence of metaphors and comparisons, each describing a way of looking at their separation that will help them to avoid the mourning forbidden by the poem's title.

First, the speaker says that their farewell should be as mild as the uncomplaining deaths of virtuous men, for to weep would be "profanation of our joys." Next, the speaker compares harmful "Moving of th' earth" to innocent "trepidation of the spheres," equating the first with "dull sublunary lovers' love" and the second with their love, "Inter-assured of the mind." Like the rumbling earth, the dull sublunary (sublunary meaning literally beneath the moon and also subject to the moon) lovers are all physical, unable to experience separation without losing the sensation that comprises and sustains their love. But the spiritual lovers "Care less, eyes, lips, and hands to miss," because, like the trepidation (vibration) of the spheres (the concentric globes that surrounded the earth in ancient astronomy), their love is not wholly physical. Also, like the trepidation of the spheres, their movement will not have the harmful consequences of an earthquake.

The speaker then declares that, since the lovers' two souls are one, his departure will simply expand the area of their unified soul, rather than cause a rift between them. If, however, their souls are "two" instead of "one", they are as the feet of a drafter's compass, connected, with the centre foot fixing the orbit of the outer foot and helping it to describe a perfect circle. The compass (the instrument used for drawing circles) is one of Donne's most famous metaphors, and it is the perfect image to encapsulate the values of Donne's spiritual love, which is balanced, symmetrical, intellectual, serious, and beautiful in its polished simplicity.

Like many of Donne's love poems (including "The Sun Rising" and "The Canonization"), "A Valedictionforbidding Mourning" creates a dichotomy between the common love of the everyday world and the uncommon love of the speaker. Here, the speaker claims that to tell "the laity," or the common people, of his love would be to profane its sacred nature, and he is clearly contemptuous of the dull sublunary love of other lovers. The effect of this dichotomy is to create a kind of emotional aristocracy that is similar in form to the political aristocracy with which Donne has had painfully bad luck throughout his life and which he commented upon in poems, such as "The Canonization"This emotional aristocracy is similar in form to the political one but utterly opposed to it in spirit. Few in number are the emotional aristocrats who have access to the spiritual love of the spheres and the compass; throughout all of Donne's writing, the membership of this elite never includes more than the speaker and his lover—or at the most, the speaker, his lover, and the reader of the poem, who is called upon to sympathize with Donne's romantic plight.

Divine Meditation 10

Summary

The speaker tells Death that it should not feel proud, for though some have called it "mighty and dreadful," it is not. Those whom Death thinks it kills do not truly die, nor, the speaker says, "can'st thou kill me." Rest and sleep are like little copies of Death, and they are pleasurable; thus, the speaker reasons, Death itself must be even more so—indeed, it is the best men who go soonest to Death, to rest their bones and enjoy the delivery of their souls. Death, the speaker claims, is a slave to "fate, chance, kings, and desperate men," and is forced to dwell with war, poison, and sickness. The speaker says that poppies and magic charms can make men sleep as well as, or better than, Death's stroke, so why should Death swell with pride? Death is merely a short sleep, after which the dead awake into eternal life, where Death shall no longer existDeath itself will die.

This simple sonnet follows an ABBAABBACDCDEE rhyme scheme and is written in a loose iambic pentameter. In its structural division of its subject, it is a Petrarcan sonnet rather than a Shakespearean one, with an octet establishing the poem's tension, and the subsequent sestet resolving it.

Commentary: This rather uncomplicated poem is probably Donne's most famous and most anthologized; "Death be not proud" seems to be, for some reason, the most famous phrase in Donne. The sonnet takes the oblique reasoning and topsy-turvy symbolism of Donne's metaphysical love poems and applies them to a religious theme, treating the personified figure of Death as someone not worthy of awe or terror but of contempt. Donne charts a line of reasoning that explores a different idea in each quatrain. First, Death is not powerful or mighty because he does not kill those he thinks he kills; second, the experience of being dead must be more pleasurable than rest and sleep, which are pleasurable, pale copies of death, and the best people die most readily to hurry to their "soul's delivery" ("delivery," a childbearing pun, introduces the idea that the death of the body is a birth for the soul).

In the third quatrain, the speaker mocks Death's positionIt is inferior to drugs and potions, a slave to fate, chance, kings, and desperate men (each of which deals out death), and lives in the gutter with poison and sickness. In the couplet, the speaker rounds out the idea of the poem, by saying that, if the afterlife is eternal, then upon the moment a person dies, it is really Death that dies to that person and not vice-versa, for that person will never again be subject to Death. This final idea represents the classic metaphysical moment, in which an established idea is turned completely on its head by a seemingly innocuous line of reasoning—the idea that Death could die is startling and counterintuitive but completely sensible in light of Donne's reasoning. Of course, even in the seventeenth century the idea would not have seemed as startling as many of Donne's other metaphysical conceits—it is an idea that appears not only in Shakespeare ("And death once dead, there's no more dying then") but also in the Bible itself ("The last enemy that shall be destroyed is death," from I Corinthians).

Divine Meditation 14

Summary

The speaker asks the "three-personed God" to "batter" his heart, for as yet God only knocks politely, breathes, shines, and seeks to mend. The speaker says that to rise and stand, he needs God to overthrow him and bend his force to break, blow, and burn him, and to make him new. Like a town that has been captured by the enemy, which seeks unsuccessfully to admit the army of its allies and friends, the speaker works to admit God into his heart, but Reason, like God's viceroy, has been captured by the enemy and proves "weak or untrue." Yet the speaker says that he loves God dearly and wants to be loved in return, but he is like a maiden who is betrothed to God's enemy. The speaker asks God to "divorce, untie, or break that knot again," to take him prisoner; for until he is God's prisoner, he says, he will never be free, and he will never be chaste until God ravishes him.

This simple sonnet follows an ABBAABBACDDCEE rhyme scheme and is written in a loose iambic pentameter. In its structural division, it is a Petrarchan sonnet rather than a Shakespearean one, with an octet followed by a sestet.

Analysis

This poem is an appeal to God, pleading with Him not for mercy or clemency or benevolent aid but for a violent, almost brutal overmastering; thus, it implores God to perform actions that would usually be considered extremely sinful—from battering the speaker to actually raping him, which, he says in the final line, is the only way he will ever be chaste. The poem's metaphors (the speaker's heart as a captured town, the speaker as a maiden betrothed to God's enemy) work with its extraordinary series of violent and powerful verbs (batter, o'erthrow, bend, break, blow, burn, divorce, untie, break, take, imprison, enthrall, ravish) to create the image of God as an overwhelming, violent conqueror. The bizarre nature of the speaker's plea finds its apotheosis in the paradoxical final couplet, in which the speaker claims that only if God takes him prisoner can he be free, and only if God ravishes him can he be chaste.

As is amply illustrated by the contrast between Donne's religious lyrics and his metaphysical love poems, Donne is a poet deeply divided between religious spirituality and a kind of carnal lust for life. Many of his best poems, including "Batter my heart, three-personed God," mix the discourse of the spiritual and the physical or of the holy and the secular. In this case, the speaker achieves that mix by claiming that he can only overcome sin and achieve spiritual purity if he is forced by God in the most physical, violent, and carnal terms imaginable.

"Hymn to God, my God, in my Sickness"

Summary

The speaker says that since he will soon die and come to "that holy room" where he will be made into the music of God as sung by a choir of saints, he tunes "the instrument" now and thinks what he will do when the final moment comes. He likens his doctors to cosmographers and himself to a map, lying flat on the bed to be shown "that this is my south-west discovery / *Per fretum febris*, by these straits to die." He rejoices, for in those straits he sees his "west," his death, whose currents "yield return to none," yet which will not harm him. West and east meet and join in all flat maps (the speaker says again that he is a flat map), and in the same way, death is one with the resurrection.

The speaker asks whether his home is the Pacific Sea, or the eastern riches, or Jerusalem. He lists the straights of Anyan, Magellan, and Gibraltar, and says that only straits can offer access to paradise, whether it lies "where Japhet dwelt, or Cham, or Shem." The speaker says that "Paradise and Calvary, / Christ's Cross, and Adam's tree" stood in the same place. He asks God to look and to note that both Adams (Christ being the second Adam) are unified in him; as the first Adam's sweat surrounds his face, he says, may the second Adam's blood embrace his soul. He asks God to receive him wrapped in the purple of Christ, and, "by these his thorns," to give him Christ's other crown. As he preached the word of God to others' souls, he says, let this be his sermon to his own soul"Therefore that he may raise the Lord throws down."

Like many of Donne's religious poems, the "Hymn to God my God" is formally somewhat simpler than many of his metaphysical secular poems. Each of the six five-line stanzas follows an ABABB rhyme scheme, and the poem is metered throughout in iambic pentameter.

Commentary

Scholars are divided over the question of whether this poem was written on Donne's deathbed in 1630 or during the life-threatening fever he contracted in 1623. In either case, the "Hymn to God my God" was certainly written at a time when Donne believed he was likely to die. This beautiful, lyrical, and complicated poem represents his mind's attempt to summarize itself, and his attempt to offer, as he says, a sermon to his soul. In the first stanza, the speaker looks forward to the time when he will be in "that holy room" where he will be made into God's music—an extraordinary image—with His choir of saints. In preparation for that time, he says, he will "tune the instrument" (his soul) by writing this poem.

The next several stanzas, devoted to the striking image of Donne's body as a map looked over by his navigator-doctors, develop an elaborate geographical symbolism with which to explain his condition. He is entering, he says, his "south-west discovery"—the south being, traditionally, the region of heat (or fever) and the west being the site of the sunset and, thus, in this poem, the region of death. (A key to this geographical symbolism can be found in A.J. Smith's concise notation in the Penguin Classics edition of Donne's *Complete English Poems.*) The speaker says that his discovery is made *Per fretum febris*, or by the strait of fever, and that he will die "by these straits."

Donne employs an elaborate pun on the idea of "straits," a word that denotes the narrow passages of water that connect oceans, yet which also refers to grim personal difficulties (as in "dire straights")Donne's personal struggles with his illness are like the straits that will connect him to the paradise of the Pacific Sea, Jerusalem, and the eastern riches; no matter where one is in the world—in the region of Japhet, Cham, or Shem—such treasures can only be reached through straits. (Japhet, Cham, and Shem were the sons of Noah, who divided the world between them after the ark came to restJaphet lived in Europe, Cham lived in Africa, and Shem lived in Asia.)

Essentially, all of this word play and allusion is merely another way of saying that Donne expects his fever to lead him to heaven (even on his deathbed, his mind delighted in spinning metaphysical complexities). The speaker says that on maps, west and east are one—if one travels far enough in either direction, one ends up on the other side of the map—and, therefore, his death in the "west" will lead to his "eastern" resurrection.

He then shifts to a dramatically different set of images, claiming that Christ's Cross and Adam's tree stood physically on the same place, and that by the same token, both the characteristics of Adam (sin and toil) and of Christ (resurrection and purity) are present in Donne himselfThe phrase "Look Lord, and find both Adams met in me" is Donne's most perfect statement of the contrary strains of spirituality and carnality that run through his poems and ran through his life. As the sweat of the first Adam (who was cursed to work after expulsion from Eden) surrounds his face in his fever, he hopes the blood of Christ, the second Adam, will embrace and purify his soul.

Donne concludes by charting his actual entry into heaven, saying that he hopes to be received by God wrapped in the purple garment of Christ—purple with blood and with triumph—and to obtain his crown. As his final poetic act, he writes a sermon for his own soul, just as he preached sermons to the souls of others during his years as a priest. The Lord, he says, throws down that he may raise up; Donne, thrown down by the fever, will be lifted up to heaven, where his soul, having been "tuned" now on Earth, may be used to make the music of God.

Chapter 10

Study Questions

Q Write a critical essay on Donne's poem ?

Or

Q. Write Practical Criticism of John Donne's "Song" and "Go and Catch a Falling Star..."

This poem chiefly concerns the lack of constancy in women. The tone taken is one of gentle cynicism, and mocking. Donne asks the reader to do the impossible, which he compares with finding a constant woman, thus insinuating that such a woman does not exist. The title, "Song", leads us to expect certain thingsa lyrical element to the words, and a musical rhythm, which are fulfilled by this neatly crafted poem. It is also very ambiguous, not hinting at the subject matter of the poem. The stanzas are slightly longer than might be expected, nine lines each, but this allows for the more complex and abstract ideas, which are archetypal of metaphysical poetry. The first stanza is the most forceful, employing the imperative to achieve a sense of command, and implying that he is talking to one specific person. The second stanza begins conditionally, "if", and continues to be directed towards the apparent listener by the repeated use of the second person singular, "thou". Both are heavy in exotic imagery, which the final stanza is completely devoid of, and the final stanza also takes on a far more conversational, monosyllabic tone.

The first sentence is a command"Go and catch a falling star", and an impossible one, for how can one catch a star? The word "falling" suggests a gradual deterioration, rather than fallen which would be irretrievable, there is a sense that there is a chance, but it is narrow. It is interesting that Donne is using the conventionally romantic image of a star in defiance of such a traditional idea as monogamy. It could also be linked to the fourth line which references the devil, as Lucifer was a fallen angel, and the stars are often symbolic of Angels and heaven, this devil imagery perhaps is an early suggestion of the duplicity of women. Donne builds on this idea of the impossible in the second line, "Get with child a mandrake root", there is much superstition surrounding the mandrake plant, it is said to scream when pulled from the ground, and it "resembles the human form, sometimes the female form and sometimes the male, according to whether the roots are twofold or threefold".

This could again be linked to the devil who has "cleft" feet, which also resemble the fork-rooted plant through the idea of division and multiplicity. This in turn is suggestive of the inconstancy of women, suggesting their doubled relationships. Further fantastical imagery is that of the "mermaids singing". Mermaids could be seen as important in this poem as they appear to be women above the waist but are not beneath, and this could therefore suggest that women can be deceptive creatures. There is also the idea of them luring men to a watery death, it has been said that this links to the experience of Odysseus in "The Odyssey", although he encountered the sirens who dwelt on an island, not in the sea.

Donne uses the word "stinging" to describe envy, finally coming to the point of the poem overtly. The word sting suggests something, which is inflicted by some external force, it shifts any blame away from the subject of the envy. It is a piquant image, suggesting intensity of feeling. There is also a slightly bitter undertone caused by the constant use of hard consonants such as "go", "get", "teach" and "tell". Then the poem seems to slow down very quickly in the final refrain, seeming to echo the sound of the wind, the speaker wonders how honesty can be gained, and we can presume that this refers to honesty in the sense of being chaste. It is necessary to point out that although "wind" does not seem as if it should rhyme with "find" and "mind", it was pronounced as such at the time, as is often seen in Shakespeare. In fact it was rather a familiar rhyme to use, quite boring in fact, which combined with the monosyllabic beat of these last few lines, seems to mirror his boredom with women.

The second stanza is full of convoluted images and hyperbole; it is as if Donne is mocking the idea of a love poem in itself. "Ride ten thousand days and nights, / Till age snow white hairs on thee," seems to echo the professions of love made by the other poets of his time, and yet he is using these images against the idea of love and monogamy. It is interesting that Donne takes the commonly used hyphenated adjective of "snow-white" and uses it as a subjunctive verb; he is making the image fairytale like, suggesting perhaps how unlikely it would be for a woman to be faithful. Donne also uses the paradoxical idea of things "invisible to see" which further emphasises this idea. Again the suggestion of time implicit in the line is surely a reference to other love poets and their impossible promises to women, to love them forever and a day etc. In this part of the poem it seems as if he is challenging the reader to find evidence contrary to his opinion, asserting that it simply does not exist"Thou, when thou return'st, wilt tell me...[that nowhere]...Lives a woman true, and fair". What is odd is that here Donne seems to be saying that it is only beautiful women who will be unfaithful; does this mean that the ugly women will be? The repeated "thou" is accusing, it seems as though the listener is in fact such a woman, beautiful and inconstant. The tone at the end of this stanza is far more personal, and the syntax more difficult; this is perhaps an indication of personal feeling, of his mistrust.

The final stanza begins in a sardonic manner, "if thou findst one, let me know", he appears to be expressing the opinion that a woman of character and beauty is implausible. It is comparatively colloquial, there being no images to speak of and the words are less poetic, and less apparently organised than in the previous two stanzas. It seems dismissive of women, it all seems to be a waste of time, he is saying that even if you do find the woman I'm looking for, it will take only the time of you writing a letter for her to be unfaithful to "two, or three" other men. The monosyllabic style of these lines accentuates the sense of boredom and irritation, as does the nay rhyme used for the final triplet.

However this rhyme does add to the phonological quality of the poem, as the simplicity is perhaps more songlike than the rest of the poem. The regular rhyme and meter of the poem also help to create this feeling. There is a very tight verse structure, which consists of a sestet of ABAB rhyme preceding the rhyming triplet in each stanza. The triplet shows an insistence of opinion, it emphasises the points being made but also creates a lilting rhythm to the end of each verse, like the refrain to a song. The two very short lines immediately precede a far longer one, thus creating contrast, which mirrors the contrasting images in the poem.

For example, there is the heavenly image of a "falling star" adjacent to the earth bound image of the "mandrake root", then there follows the lovely image of the "mermaids singing" with the ugly apparition of the devil It would seem that light and dark are being paralleled, and it is strange imagery to use when describing love and constancy. This is continued into the second stanza where in the third line there is the contrast between day and night, which continues to express images of lightness and darkness as in the first stanza. Significant also is the idea of a "pilgrimage", this seems to tie in with the other religious elements in the poem and suggests sacrifice and religious Puritanism, but this serious image is immediately followed by a light hearted quip, "Yet do not, I would not go, / Though at next door we might meet...". This seems to mock the seriousness of love in other poems, he seems cynical about women, but not in a way which could be construed as misogynistic.

It seems that the poem is rebuking one lady in particular as it appears to be directed specifically, and yet it is rhetoric; no answer seems to be expected. It could be said therefore that this poem is predominantly light and mocking in tone, but with an undercurrent of cynicism. This is reflected in the contrasting pairs of images such as light and dark, and of the ugly and the beautiful; and it seems that in the main, those images also relate in some way to religion. It is typical of Donne to use such mixed images and to relate love to religion, and this is evident in the poem.

Q. Comment on Donne's love – poetry ?

Or

Q. Comment on Donne as love poet ?

Or

Q. Comment on songs and sonnets of John Donne ?

Donne's *Songs and Sonnets* do not describe a single unchanging view of love; they express a wide variety of emotions and attitudes, as if Donne himself were trying to define his experience of love through his poetry. Love can be an experience of the body, the soul, or both; it can be a religious experience, or merely a sensual one, and it can give rise to emotions ranging from ecstasy to despair. Taking any one poem in isolation will give us a limited view of Donne's attitude to love, but treating each poem as part of a totality of experience, represented by all the *Songs and Sonnets,* it gives us an insight into the complex range of experiences that can be grouped under the single heading 'Love'.

In 'To his Mistris Going to Bed' we see how highly Donne can praise sensual pleasure. He addresses the woman as:

Oh my America, my new found lande,
My kingdome, safeliest when with one man man'd,
My myne of precious stones, my Empiree

The images are of physical, material wealth, and anyone reading this poem alone would think Donne's interest in women was limited to the sexual level. He describes sex in terms of a religious experience; the woman is an 'Angel', she provides 'A heaven like Mahomet's Paradise', and the bed is 'loves hallow'd temple'. But although erotic, this is not a love poem; nowhere does he say that he loves the woman, or that sex is part of a deeper relationship.

In *The Extasie* Donne conveys a very different and more complex attitude to erotic pleasure, when it is just one part of the experience of love.

This Extasie doth unperplex
(We said) and tell us what we love,
Wee see by this, it was not sexe,

Wee see, we saw not what did move...
Love's mysteries in soules doe grow,
But yet the body is his booke.

The body and the soul are distinct, but related aspects of the totality of love. The uniting of souls is the purest and highest form of love, but this can only be attained through the uniting of bodies.

Soe soule into the soule may flow,
Though it to body first repaire.

This focus on the soul leads Donne to express a condescending attitude towards physical love in this poem which is in marked contrast to the attitude he expressed in *To his Mistris Going to Bed.*

But O alas, so long, so farre
Our bodies why doe wee forbeare?
They're ours, the though they're not wee. Wee are
Th'intelligences, they the spheare.

But in reading Donne one soon learns that an attitude expressed in one poem is not to be taken as absolute and exclusive. One of Donne's characteristics is that he freely contradicts himself from one poem to another. The title of this poem, *The Extasie,* implies that love is a religious experience, just as the diction of *To his Mistris Going to Bed* conveyed sex as a religious experience. The religious metaphors give a hyperbolic intensity to his imagery, but the ideas expressed in *The Extasie* are firmly rooted in the scientific theories of his day.

Donne's view that spiritual love can be attained through physical love ties in with the contemporary theory of the 'chain of being'. Angels, presumably, could experience a totally spiritual love, unadulterated by the physical. But man, being part divine and part animal, can only reach the spiritual level through the sensual.

So must pure lovers soules descend
T'affections, and to faculties,
That sense may reach and apprehend,
Else a great Prince in prison lies.

The inherent superiority of the spiritual level, and the part love can play in refining man's nature towards the spiritual, is expressed in these lines:

If any, so by love refin'd,
That he soules language understood,
And by good love were grown all minde

The scientific framework of Donne's view of love is also seen here:

But as all severall soules containe
Mixture of things, they know not what,
Love, these mixt soules, doth mixe againe,
And makes both one, each this and that.

Just as the four elements, earth, air, fire, and water were supposed to combine to form new substances, so two souls mix to form a new unity. The strength and durability of this new unit is dependent upon how well the elements of the two souls are balanced, as we see from these lines from *The Good-Morrow*:

What ever dyes, was not mixt equally;
It our two loves be one, or, thou and I
Love so alike, that none doe slacken, none can die.

A good example of this state, where two lovers' souls cannot be separated, even when they are physically far apart, is seen in *A Valedictionforbidding mourning*:

If they be two, they are two so
As stiffe twin encompasses are two,
Thy soule the fixt foot, makes no show
To move, but doth, if th'other doe.

The idea of two coming together to form one is very important in Donne's view of love. When a couple find perfect love together they become all-sufficient to one another, forming a world of their own, which has no need of the outside world. This idea is expressed in these lines from *The Sunne Rising*:

She'is all States, and all Princes, I,
Nothing else is.
Shine here to us, and thou art everywhere;
This bed thy centre is, these walls, thy spheare.
And again it in The Good-Morrow:

For love, all love of other sights controules,
And makes one little roome, an everywhere.

For Donne love transcends all worldly values. As we see in *The Canonization,* values such as wealth and glory have no place in the world of love.

With wealth your state, your minde with Arts improve,
Take you a course, get you a place,
Observe his honour, or his grace,
Or the Kings reall, or his stamped face
Contemplate; what you will, approve,
So you will let me love.

Like love itself, the women to whom Donne's verses are addressed are usually praised in hyperbolic terms. In *The Sunne Rising* her eyes shine brighter than the sun. And in *The Dreame* she is praised as a being above the level of angels.

Yet I thought thee
(For thou lov'st truth) an Angell, at first sight,
But when I saw thou saw'st my heart,
And knew'st my thoughts, beyond an Angels art,
When thou knew'st what I dreamt, when thou knew'st when
Excess of joy would wake me, and cam'st then,
I do confesse, it could not chuse but bee
Profane, to thinke thee any thing but thee.

This reverence for woman sometimes leads Donne close to adopting the traditional attitude of the courtly lover, who suffers through being in love with a woman, usually already married, who scorns him. An example of this kind of love is suggested by the references to the symptoms of love in *The Canonization*:

Alas, alas, who's injur'd by my love?
What merchant ships have my sighs drown'd?
Who saies my teares have overflow'd his ground?
When did my colds a forward spring remove?
When did the heats which my veines fill
Adde one man to the plaguie Bill?

The courtly love ideal, however, is in conflict with Donne's ideal of two well-matched and well-balanced lovers whose souls unite to form one. In the poem *Loves Deitie* he expresses his contempt for the courtly ideal, which he sees as a corruption of the true nature of love.

I cannot thinke that hee, who then lov'd most,
Sunke so low, as to love one which did scorne,
... It cannot bee
Love, till I love her, that loves mee.

In fact Donne is unusual, if not unique, for his era in that courtly love hardly appears in his poetry at all. Courtly love seems to depend on the lover being unsuccessful, whereas Donne rejoices in success at every level. And the courtly love poet always expresses the same experience of love, the range of situations and emotions dealt with being very limited. In contrast Donne expresses an enormously wide range of feelings in his Songs and Sonnets, all relating to the experience of love, but varying from the heights of ecstasy to the depths of despair. This variety of feeling lends Donne's poetry much of its impact, for we seem to be reading an individual's personal experience of love, and not just a poet's contribution to a long-standing tradition of poetic love.

We have seen how in *The Extasie* Donne describes love as a sublime union of two souls. This, perhaps is the highest form of love, but by no means the only one. *The Dreame* expresses a passionate mood of a more down-to-earth nature.

Enter these armes, for since thou thoughtst it best,
Not to dreame all my dreame, let's do the rest.

The Sunne Rising expresses the reckless pride and satisfaction felt by the lover in bed with his mistress.

Busie old foole, unruly Sunne,
Why dost thou thus,
Through windowes, and through curtaines call on us?

In *The Flea* Donne adopts a cynical and rather flippant tone towards his woman, using his wit to try to belittle and overcome her moral arguments, in favour of immediate pleasure.

Marke but this flea, and marke in this,
How little that which thou deny'st me is

For Donne, love can lead to suffering and disillusionment as well as to ecstasy. *A Nocturnall upon S. Lucie's day, Being the shortest day* is an extremely powerful evocation of the suffering caused by the death of a loved one, an experience which takes him beyond suffering to a state of absolute nothingness.

... Yea plants, yea stones detest
And love; All, all some properties invest;
If I an ordinary nothing were,
As shadow, 'a light, and body must be here.
But I am none;

In *Twicknam Garden* Donne expresses extremes of disillusionment, his view of love here being totally opposed to his view in *The Extasie*:

The spider love, which transubstantiates all,
And can convert Manna to gall,

And his view of woman is totally opposed to the view expressed in most of his love poems:

Nor can you more judge womans thought by teares,
Than by her shadow, her what she weares.
O perverse sexe, where none is true but shee,
Who's therefore true, because her truth kills mee.

Perhaps the most extreme anti-love poem of Donne's, and certainly the most un-courtly, is *The Apparition*. The bitterness expressed here is so intense that it is surely a hate poem; it opens:

When by thy scorne, O murdress, I am dead,

And continues with the lover threatening to haunt his mistress after his death.

Finally we ought to consider whether Donne's poetry expresses real love at all, or whether, as some critics suggest, he was merely a talented poet using his wit and ingenuity to create clever poems. Johnson said of the Metaphysical poets'Their courtship was void of fondness and their lamentation of sorrow.' He did not feel that Donne's poetry moved the affections, or that Donne had necessarily felt the emotions in order to write the poems.

Donne's poems are extraordinarily witty and ingenious, but this does not exclude the possibility that they also contain strong emotion. Donne's poems are quite capable of stirring the emotions, and no matter how clever his conceits, or revolutionary his thought, his poems would not work without a seed of genuine feeling at their centre.

Q. Write a critical note on Donne's "The Flea".

The Norton Anthology of English Literature defines the "conceits" of poetics as metaphors that are intricately woven into the verse, often used to express satire, puns, or deeper meanings within the poem, and to display the poet's own cunning with words. The conceits of John Donne are said to "leap continually in a restless orbit from the personal to the cosmic and back again." The outward nature of Donne's poem The Flea appears to be a love poem; dedication from a male suitor to his lady of honour, who refuses to yield to his lustful desires. A closer look at the poem reveals that this suitor is actually arguing a point to his ladythat the loss of innocence does not constitute a loss of honour.

The poet begins his argument by condemning the act of intercourse as a shameful sin. He also belittles it, claiming that if the same effects can be realized within the body of a tiny flea, then the act itself cannot hold tremendous importance. In any case, the act is out of the question in the realm of reality, since the two people in the poem do not appear to be married, so sexual union can only be committed symbolically.

The argument then shifts to a different position, where the flea suddenly becomes the entire world of the lovers; the symbolic becomes reality. The act of intercourse loses its importance as the subject in question, and now the loss of all innocence is addressed. There is obviously some action taken by the poet's mistress between the second and third stanzas, as the next segment seems to be a judgment on those actions. The woman has killed the mysterious flea, casting away her innocence and proving his argument for passion through the use of her own words.

The poet asks his mistress to notice only this flea, to forget everything else as he delivers his argument. The flea has bitten them both, and their bloods mix within its body. The attention paid to the qualities of blood may be noted here and later in the poem (when the woman suddenly gains a stature of royalty [purpling her nail]). This mixing of bloods is somewhat of an insult to the lady, if she is of royal blood and he is not. The description of the swelling of the insect with "one blood made of two" is suggestive of surrogate pregnancy, a perversion of motherhood. Such an allusion is definitely not a pleasant nor natural one, and it would be natural for the lady to kill the flea out of disgust after hearing these lines. The word "suck" in this context would be equivalent to the experience of passion or lust, which leads to the loss of innocence. The man admits that the flea sucked him first, so he has lost his innocence, but he still finds himself honorable, so here he bases his own point of view.

The flea becomes ultimately a symbol of the world in which the lovers' desires are realized, "this marriage bed and marriage temple is." Marriage and consummation is a past issue, since within the flea their blood is already mingled and the "child" of their union grows. The flea is now the realm of marriage, all-encompassing the lovers and excluding any parents or patriarchal sanction. The walls of this realm are jet black, indicating that something sinister or evil is to occur here. This could be a reference to the illicit marriage, or the forbidden mixing of royal and common blood, or perhaps only the impiety of the poet's comparison that loss of innocence should be so trivial as the life of a flea. The lady's significance is reduced to that of a black widow spider at this point, where the poet says she is apt to kill him after this consummation of a non-existent marriage. With this metaphor of the spider, who is also jet in colour, the object of the man's love is reduced to the position of the flea. If the flea is pregnant with their blood-child, then she (the lady) may as well be pregnant too. Now that this tie has been established between the blood of the woman and the flea, if the woman were to kill the flea, it would be a form of suicide. So to kill this flea, the woman would have to commit murder (of the symbolic marriage realm and the child within), suicide (killing of her own blood), and sacrilege (which suicide is). Apparently the woman kills the flea anyway, since the death of the flea and her own corruption is addressed next.

By killing the flea whom the poet has given such strange

attributes, the woman squashes the symbolic world the man has constructed and brought them both back to reality. By murdering the "innocent" flea, the lady has "purpled her nail," a colour assigned to the clothing of royalty. She now becomes a monarch (a pun; she is an autonomous ruler and an insect, the butterfly), gaining her position through the death of the flea. She has committed the sins that destroy the union of their blood, so she triumphs. She says that neither of them are any worse for the loss of blood caused by the pest, which the poet confirms to be the truth. This comment suggests that the lady has just admitted her loss of innocence by implying that the flea really didn't do anything to deserve death. The poet finalizes his argument for his cause by granting that the death of the flea is really of no consequence, as are her fears for her honour. Her honour will not waste when she gives in to him.

The hopeful suitor that addresses his honorable lady in "The Flea" argues ingeniously throughout the verses, shifting the limits of a tiny insect to entire world encompassing the couple. He recognizes sexual relationships out of marriage as a sin, and as a shameful act even when legitimate. Thus the act could only be committed symbolically, within the body of a flea. If such a union of the suitor and his lady can be realized in the flea, then let the flea become the entire world, so that their love can be a reality. As the poet relates his vision of their love in a clandestine world, the lady denies him by smashing the flea. Her reasons may be that she is a noble and he is not, so the suggestion that they mix blood is highly insulting, or that the entire subject he is discussing is not modest enough for a maiden. Upon her smashing of his poetic world of marriage and love, the man assures her that what she has done is of no consequence. He compares her fear for her honour to the importance of the now dead flea, which is nothing.

Q. Compare *To His Mistris Going to Bed* by John Donne, & *The Elegy* by A.D. Hope ?

Or

Q. Write a critical note on Donne's *To His Mistris Going to Bed* ?

Well known to the world of poetry are the works of John

Donne. His seduction poems are enhanced yet softened by the many conceits employed, resulting in an effect of dazzling persuasiveness for any prospective lover. Donne's poem "To His Mistris Going to Bed" (Elegy XIX) is a prime example of his sleek literary tongue in action, and one of the two poems to be discussed here.

Lesser known and even further obscured by his deviation from the more popular poetic themes of Australia are the satirical works of A.D. Hope. Hope's infatuation with experiencing "true nature" through sexuality, a concept more European than Australian, lured him towards more classical references, which we shall explore in "The Elegy." A common thread of belief ties these two poets and these elegies, subtly wound throughout the verses in metaphors but nevertheless present.

The structural similarities between "The Elegy" and Elegy XIX are obviousrhyming couplets in perfect iambic pentameter, with the former poem displaying slightly more alliteration than the latter. As the first poet, temporally speaking, Donne appears to have chosen his rhyme scheme and meter not only for this one poem, but for the majority of the poems in his "Elegies." The choice of rhyming couplets in iambic pentameter produces a smoothly flowing line that carries its metrical inertia into the next line, with the promise of an expected end rhyme.

The end rhymes repeat only seldom, with the exception of lines 28-34 of Elegy XIX. The strong "e" sound that ends all six lines is suggestive of glee, and the building up of the same rhyme in three successive couplets gives us an effect of mounting excitement. This effect is appropriate within the location of the poem, when the speaker is viewing his lady unclothed but for a mere "white lynnen," hoping to divest her of that soon enough. Both poets initiate their line with an imperative directed towards a woman (Donne"Come, Madam, come," and Hope"Madam, no more!") and end with their attention turned toward the man (Donne's naked man and Hope's "Captain"). By beginning each poem in such a way, we expect the speaker to be male, and intimate nature of the requests soon to follow indicate that the speaker and his lady are alone.

The endings of each poem are similar; Donne's speaker is bared and ready to share body and soul, according to the processes bodies undergo during sexual union as described in "The Extasie," and Hope's "warrior lover" contemplates the reinvigoration of his crusading manhood, which seems to have a life of its own. Hope's diction is noticeably more modern than Donne's, easily justified by the four century gap between the two poets. Hope does appear to position his work as a companion piece to Donne's Elegy XIX, as it follows the above mentioned structure well, but it is unlikely that he would attempt to match his diction to the former poet's. Language unnatural to a poet would cause too many problems to criticize here, but examples include misinterpretations of metaphors and unintended double meanings of older vocabulary. Of course, mere structural similarities could not link two poems together as companion poems without note of the poem's contents, which we shall scrutinize next.

Donne's elegy is addressed to a lady who has not yet slept with him (or the speaker, if we wish to distance the poet from the poem). This is implied by his excited reaction to her body as a zone of new discovery in lines 27-30, and the way he addresses the lady directly as "you" from lines 1-24 and "thee" after line 25. The difference between these two words exists in several foreign languages, for example, the German "du" and "Sie" (thee) have quite different meanings regarding the respect of the speaker to the subject.

The speaker has taken on more embellished diction to suit his rising classical and theological conceits within the last half of the poem. If we can accept that the lady of Donne's choice did remove her last garment and submit to the speaker (quite easy to accept considering how far she has gone!), then Hope's elegy picks up right after the act with, "Madam, no more!" Considering the favoritism Hope lends to satire, he suggests that the persuasive speaker of Donne's has overwhelmed his lover with so much passion that he himself is overwhelmed by her. Whereas Donne indulges only in a sexual pun ("foe.../

...fight") within the first five lines of the poem, Hope proceeds to apply a few classical metaphors in the same space, with Venus representing the lady and Mars the man. Venus ties both poems together through conceits, which we will consider presently.

Donne is fairly straight-forward in the first half of Elegy XIX, discussing each article of clothing and what is revealed as it is stripped away, with an amusing "Angel" metaphor employed in lines 20-24, whose "heaven" sets his "flesh upright." At this point, the speaker's excitement is clearly growing, and his metaphors become increasingly elaborate as he marvels over his lady's body; she is a new land of discovery, a living earth. Of course, what Donne poem would be without a paradox"To enter in these bonds, is to be free."

Lines 33-34 make references to death ("souls unbodied"), which refer to the climax the speaker anticipates, mirrored in Hope's poem, line 70. Donne uses the classical conceit of Atalanta, over which much controversy has arisen about whether the poet made a mistake (it was a man who threw the balls that she stopped for), the balls are actually breasts, or the reference was an intentional reversal of gender. I shall approach this conceit from the last angle, though I am in the minority according to most resources; in the heightening tension of the moment, the speaker is willing to twist entire myths just to compliment his lady.

The troublesome balls of Atalanta become a neat tie with Hope's poem, being golden apples. Venus, also known as the Greek Aphrodite, was the winner of the golden apple awarded by Paris. Both poems have this object in common directly, as well as two fixed contests - one of speed, the other of beauty. A theological conceit follows immediately after the classical, describing women as "mystick books," that will only reveal themselves by choice. An interesting juxtaposition of the speaker who asks, "What needest thou have more covering than a man," and "books gay coverings" presents a curious metaphor. If he is trying to replace the book covering, perhaps he feels he is imparted with more "grace" by being the cover on such a sacred tome. It seems that he has no interest in anything but physical appearance of the woman when compared to a picture. The speaker finalizes his persuasive metaphors with a simile, comparing himself to a "Midwife," a relationship any woman would recognize as ultimately intimate. Another questionable meaning appears in line 45-46, "cast all, yea, this white lynnen hence, | Here is no pennance, much less innocence."

The problem arises from two different versions of line 46; my original text contains the Helen Gardner version of the line, but another exists as the following, "There is no pennance due to innocence." The Gardner version translates into a request to remove the white clothing simply because it is inappropriate - the woman is not innocent or penitent in this situation. The second version implies that the act about to be committed is so pure that no penance is needed, hence the white cloth isn't needed either. Judging by the arguments presented in other seduction poems of Donne's, such as "The Flea," I am partial to the second version and its interpretation. It assigns Donne a strongly libertine view of sexuality, which is in accord with my view of Donne. Unfortunately for the casual reader, Hope is not as easy to label by the reading of just one poem, so I endeavored to do a bit of research into his poetic motivations.

It is most helpful to understand Hope's tendency towards dualism when examining "The Elegy," since the poem employs it in many ways. This excerpt from John Docker's "Australian Cultural Elites":

"Although more confused and inconsistent, Hope's concepts of society, art, and nature are...basically dualistic and European- centered. In Hope's metaphysic, on one side are the "eternal" forces of the imagination, sexuality, and the natural universe; on the other side is the "active life", inferior because enmeshed in the "temporal light of practical interests"

The second side mentioned by Docker is largely the subject of "The Elegy," interspersed with a continuous battle conceit, within which the lady and the speaker are the foes mentioned in Donne's poem. The speaker of Hope's poem explains the practical uses of the body, which was most likely engaged in the "eternal" type of activity moments before.

Unlike Donne, Hope has extended his battle metaphors far past a few lines - they nearly control the poem. The speaker appears to have himself under control until line 41, an imaginable moment in which lust is rekindled by mere looks, which starts a chain reaction of land-related conceits in lines 47-70, similar to Donne's "my America!" Yet now the speaker has already "known" his lady intimately, so the land metaphors have different meaning. Indeed, the woman is living earth, but the idea is less a poetic conceit than a basic belief of Hope's ideology. Hope's notion of woman is similar to that of a Mother Earth figure, with which the act of procreation is the closest man can get with his real order in the natural universe; in effect, he is an active part of creation.

The only way that Hope can achieve discovery of eternal nature is through women and sexuality, so it can never be far from his mind. Because Hope's idea of women is entirely procreative, he finds little interest in their intellect and great appeal in their physicalness, their "earthy" side. Hope's land metaphor begins with the lines, "While now the marching stars invest the sky.And the wide lands beneath surrendered lie," designating the woman within the conceit (for she is the land) as passive, whereas he is perhaps the marching stars, active and above her. It is little wonder he calls his phallus a "Captain," for it is the tool with which he seeks to renew himself with nature.

The ever-pervasive battle metaphor demonstrates Hope's own ideology in a paradoxical epic-microcosmic proportion; his mind is the Commander, presiding over "soldiers of the heart," sexual organs as "chief commanders," the eyes "bright vedettes". Naturally, the victory will be his when he successfully impregnates his lover.

Recalling Donne's theological conceit of women as sacred books, we can now see a stronger connection to Hope's poem based on his dualistic ideology of women. Books are opened like gateways, the reader hoping to find some kind of order which he can experience by poring over it. Hopè and Donne seem to have the same idea in mind; Hope wishes to experience conscious participation in natural order, while Donne may feel something similar to "The Extasie," a pouring forth of souls into one bond of joined freedom. In either case, the gateways to nature can only be discovered through nakedness and union. We can apply this reversed motivation to the land conceit in Donne's poem as well - he states in line 32, "Then where my hand is set, my seal shall be." Though we can surmise that the "seal" is reference to territorial designation via sexual union by example of Donne's Elegy VII, "Natures Lay Ideot" ("Must I alas | ...Chafe wax for others seales?"), we can also interpret this word another way. As Hope wishes to facilitate a conception every time he engages in sex, the "seal" could well be the imprint he leaves on the world - he prints himself in his children and his poetry.

Hope has clearly read Donne's Elegy XIX, and attempted to fashion his own elegy as a companion, "after-the-fact" piece. If the two poems were joined together under one name, the meanings of the conceits may will differ depending on which author was chosen. The extensive use of the battle metaphor by Hope may suit Donne, or perhaps it is too excessive for his style. If Donne's editor refused to print "To His Mistris Going to Bed," then it would have taken another few centuries before Hope's poem could be acceptable. Hope has shown both sides of his dualistic view of nature in "The Elegy," demonstrating his skill with conceit in both modes. Donne displays his persuasive pen once more, touching on classical and theological conceits in the height of passionate moments. Just as Hope ties in his metaphors with Donne's, the observant reader can retrace Hope's steps back to Donne and make a fair comparison of motivations. Whether the poems are taken together or separately, both poets manage to leave their "seal" in literary history.

Q. Write a critical note on Donne and Metaphor in A Valediction Forbidding Mourning ?

In his poem *A ValedictionForbidding Mourning (Valediction),* John Donne relates, in verse, his insights on the human condition of love and its relationship to the soul through the conceit of drawing compasses.

Donne brings the reader a separation of body and soul in

his first stanzaAs virtuous men pass mildly away, And whisper to their souls to go, Whilst some of their sad friends do say. The breath goes now, and some say, No;

This seems to say that the soul is not a part of the body, and it is only combined with the body until death, when it "goes". The use of the word "whisper" suggests that the soul and body can communicate with one another as separate entities. Furthermore, the word "virtuous" implies that "unvirtuous" men may not be able to whisper to their souls. Fortunately for the speaker, he seems to be a virtuous man, so this certainly applies. The separation of body and soul is an essential concept to the poem as it progresses, and it must be accepted for his entire argument to work. Donne explicates this in later stanzas. The fact that the "friends" disagree on this separation of body and soul requires more explanation, but perhaps Donne is acknowledging that people do not generally agree with his assumptions.

Donne describes the two souls of the lovers being intermixed, and the bodies as separate. Starting at line 21, this becomes a motif that continues throughout the poem"Our two souls therefore, which are one, / Though I must go, endure not yet / A breach, but an expansion..." Even death cannot separate Donne's lovers because the soul, separate from the body (as alluded to in the opening stanza) is the receptacle of love, and it does not die. Instead of complete separation, the speaker describes what happens as he "goes" as an "expansion". The expansion is explained by his analogy of compasses, but the mixing is made by his comparisons to liquid beginning at line 5.

Donne makes use of the metaphor here to simplify his vision of "the soul" as something that can be melted, melted from what, he does not say, nevertheless, the reader can visualize a liquid, and he makes use of this. His use of the word silent suggests that unlike liquids, which make sound when moved, the soul makes no noise, and is something more like direct sublimation into vapour. The liquid metaphor yields images of flow and mixing; one might perceive a solution of two different substances, oil and water for instance; although they have not become one at the most elemental level, they can be held in the same container and would be very difficult to separate completely. Furthermore, the silence indicates that the souls do not use speech, like "sigh-tempests", line 6, to make their love known. This apparently conflicts with the opening stanza where the soul can communicate with speech, but Donne infers that while the body may speak to the soul, two souls do not need speech to demonstrate magnificent love.

The metaphors of earthquakes, line 9, and celestial spheres, line 11, add to the readerís understanding of the lovers' relationship by adding specific details about the magnitude of the love. The "moving of thí Earth" and "trepidation of the spheres" show great dimension and force of an extraordinary nature, almost beyond the human understanding. Donne uses these to explain how two different and gigantic events can either bring "harms and fears", or "innocence", which add to the theme of silent mixing. If celestial spheres (the largest structures imaginable) can shake with "innocence", then the souls may likewise share their love in silence, without the tumultuous rumblings of earthquakes, which "men" try to interpret. The contrast between the magnitude of earthquakes and celestial trepidation is likened to the love between two bodies and two souls. The souls, of course, are "greater far" in their capacity to love silently than the bodies.

While the early language of the poem relates loverís souls as one, the possibility of separated bodies, yet a single *mixed* soul, is described:

If they be two, they are two so
As stiff twin compasses are two;
Thy soul, the fixed root, makes no show
To move, but doth, if thí other do.
And though it in the centre sit,
Yet when the other far doth roam,
It leans and hearkens after it,
And grows erect, as that comes home.

The conclusion of the poem is that the soul, or "fixed root" can never be separated like the bodies. Furthermore, while the loverís bodies are separated by great distance, they will be like the compass in that the points are wide, but the handle joins them. By using the bodies as the tenor, and a compass as the vehicle for his conceit, Donne argues that the loversí bodies are physically separated, but the two are joined by the soul, or "fixed root". The distance, therefore, is insignificant since they are only spread out and not broken offóthere is still a firm connection between them. Donne uses the entire length of *Valediction* to make his point, which is carefully constructed like a geometric proof.

He first asserts that when men pass away, the soul separates. Once the assumption is made that the soul is separate from the body, he tells us that the soul is mixed like a silent liquid, but that the silence does not make it any less magnificent. Finally, having made these assertions, the compass is used to illustrate the concept. The summation of the argument is that, having accepted the previous statements, his love should not worry about his impending journey:

Such wilt thou be to me, who must,
Like thí other foot, obliquely run;
Thy firmness make my circle just,
And makes me end where I begun.

The speaker states that he is like the "other foot" and must go away, but his strong love will only cause the soul, or fixed root, to lean a bit, like the handle of a compass when drawing large circles. It is precisely the strength, or "firmness" of *her* love that makes the comparison perfect, so that he comes full circle to return like the other leg of a stiff compass.

Two definitions of metaphor:

- Metaphor *(From Greek, "to carry across")*A comparison that likens two different things by identifying one as the other.

In mathematical symbols, a metaphor would require an equal sign, asserting that A=B, as in "That strange flower, the sun," a line from Wallace Stevensí "Gubbinal" that equates the sun with a "strange flower." Unlike a simile, metaphor does not use linking words ("like," "as," "such as") to indicate similarity between two otherwise different things. Metaphor, however, is also the general term for any comparison, including simile, metaphor, conceit, and analogy. In his column in *Natural History*, Stephen Jay Gould writes:

One day, as I sat at an alfresco lunch spot enjoying a view of the Acropolis, a small truck pulled up to the curb and blocked the Parthenon. I was annoyed at first, but later wonderfully amused as I watched the moving men deliver some furniture to the neighboring house. Their van said *Metaphora*. Of course, I realized. *Phor* is the verb for "carrying." And *Meta* is a prefix meaning "change of place, order, condition, or nature." A moving truck helps you change the order of something by carrying it from one spot to anotheróand is surely a metaphor.... A metaphor carries you from one object (which may be difficult to understand) to another (which may be more accessible and therefore helpful, by analogy, in grasping the original concern).

Metaphors, as Gould asserts, are "carriers" which help readers make "imaginative leaps." But it is the poet who must be the moving man, covering that distance, transporting the goods. I.A. Richards invented the terms *tenor* and *vehicle* to denote the two parts of a metaphor. The *tenor* is the literal subject; the *vehicle* is the figurative connection, the likeness, the thing that is compared to the subject or the carrierólike the moving van Steven Jay Gould saw in Greece. For example, the first stanza of Robert Lowellís "For the Union Dead," contains a metaphor "a Sahara of snow"; the tenor is snow, while the vehicle is the Sahara desert. The terms can apply to similes as well. In Robert Burnsí line, "O my luveís like a red rose," the tenor is "my love" and the vehicle is "a red rose."

When a metaphor is extended and elaborated (like the image of "twin compasses" John Donne presents through twelve lines of "A ValedictionForbidding Mourning"), it is a conceit. (Drury, 158-159)

- Metaphor *(Greek "transference")*:... is a trope, or figurative expression, in which a word or phrase is shifted from its normal uses to a context where it evokes new meanings. When the ordinary meaning of a word is at odds with the context, we tend to seek relevant features of the word and the situation that will reveal the intended meaning. If there is a conceptual or material connection between the word and what it denotesó*e.g.* using cause for effect ("I read Shakespeare," meaning his works) or part for whole ("give me a hand," meaning physical help)óthe figure usually has another name (in these examples, metonymy and synedoche respectively). To understand manuscripts, one must find meanings nor predetermined by language, logic, or experience. In the terminology of traditional rhetoric, these figures are "tropes of a word," appearing in a literal context; in "tropes of a sentence," the entire context is figurative, as in allegory, fable, and (according to some) irony.

Q. Write a critical note on Donne's 'The Sun Rising' ?

Aske for those Kings whom thou saw'st yesterday,
And thou shalt heare, All here in one bed lay.

When Donne's speaker suggests to the sun, here at the conclusion of the second stanza of "The Sunne Rising," that he and his lady are a compaction of all royalty, he supplies a true crux for his entire argument. In the first stanza, he has divided all living things into two categories—lovers and nonlovers—and he has implied that even the physical laws of the universe must give place to those of persons caught up in the larger universe of passion. In the third stanza, he will go on to claim that nothing else is, surely the ultimate argument for the priority of any state of being.

In the first stanza the persona has mentioned royaltythe court huntsmen, as reluctant to arise as late schoolboys and sour prentices, must be alerted that the king wishes to ride. That king, then, along with his attendants, falls into the classification of nonlover. The ones in this bed, however, are special kings. They are paradigmatic, and among them they have emptied the material world of significant kingship. I believe that these second-stanza kings are types of the kings or magi who sought and found the Christ child at Bethlehem.

As early as the time of Tertullian (145-22-0), the magi were thought of as kings, most probably because they were seen as the principals in the fulfillment of the prophecy in Psalms 71:10, "Reges Tharsis et insulae munera offerent, reges Arabum et Saba dona adducent." Tertullian comments that in the East the magi were generally regarded as kings (Against Marcion 3.13). Romanesque and Gothic sculptors and painters produced many cycles of episodes in the lives of these saint-kings. In the West they are depicted consistently as kings, not magi, wearing crowns rather than the Phrygian caps given them by artists of the East.

A favourite incident shows the angel warning them by night that they must not return to Herod but go immediately to their own countries. Invariably the three lie together in one bed, under a common coverlet, wearing their crowns, with the angel appearing above them. On a capital at the cathedral of St.-Lazare in Autun, which Donne may have seen, Gislebertus carved the angel awakening one of the kings and pointing above to the star. On the west facade of the cathedral of Notre-Dame at Amiens, an anonymous sculptor has fashioned a three-king programme in a series of quatrefoils. In one they lie sleeping, about to be warned by the angel. This image Donne certainly saw repeatedly in the course of his stay in Amiens in 1611-1612. Or perhaps he had noticed the window in Canterbury Cathedral, where the kings enjoy their last moment of sleep before being told of Herod's chicanery.

The biblical kings, not unlike Donne's metaphorical ones, have seen the Word made flesh. They operate according to a set of divine instructions nicely corresponding to the transcendent vision of the persona addressing the sun. They surpass the earthly politics of King Herod, just as the lovers do the mundane activity of the hunting king. And medieval sculptors and painters well knew, despite the sweet ingenuousness of the Eastern kings bundling together, that they afford an amusing picture. Donne's speaker likewise, though passionately earnest, strikes a droll note in his initial words ("Busie old foole, unruly Sunne"). This complex tonality varies but never falters. Donne's seriocomic trope of kings in one bed pleases us in something of the same way that the biblical kings have instructed and delighted centuries of viewers.

Q. Explain Donne's Holy Sonnet XIV.

Batter my heart, three person'd God; for, you
As yet but knocke, breathe, shine, and seeke to mend;
That I may rise, and stand, o'erthrow me, 'and bend
Your force, to breake, blowe, burn and make me new.
I, like an usurpt towne, t'another due,
Labour to 'admit you, but Oh, to no end,
Reason your viceroy in me, me should defend,
But is captiv'd, and proves weake or untrue,
Yet dearely'I love you, and would be lov'd faine,
But am betroth'd unto your enemy,
Divorce me, 'untie, or breake that knot againe
Take me to you, imprison me, for I
Except you 'enthrall me, never shall be free,
Nor ever chaste, except you ravish me.

The analogous language of romantic passion ("I am my Beloved's and my Beloved is mine") and intellectual paradox ("Whoever will lose his life for my sake will find it" has always seemed natural to those seeking to understand and speak of spiritual mysteries. Even so, John Donne's image of the Divine Rape in the "Holy Sonnet XIV," by which the victim becomes, or remains, chaste is at first startling; we are not accustomed to such spiritual intensity. Previous explications have attempted to downplay this figure; for example, Thomas J. Steele, SJ, maintains that the "sexual meaning" is "a secondary meaning" and "probably not meant to be explicitly affirmed." Moreover, George Knox writes that the poem does not "require our imagining literally the relation between man and God in heterosexual terms" and that "the traditions of Christian mysticism allow such symbolism of ravishment...." However, even granting that the sexual imagery is not intended to be taken literally, but rather symbolically, we still must question Knox, as does John E. Parish"One must infer that in Knox's opinion such symbolism shares nothing with metaphor in its effect on the imagination".

In spite of the shocking character of the poem's imagery,

the "Holy Sonnet XIV" seems coherent, its language apt; it is metrically jagged, yet traditional; its imagery is anthropomorphic, yet pious. If one may be permitted a commonplace, the poem is certainly a poem of paradoxes, as has been explored more fully in its many explications in these pages (articles appearing in 1953, 1954, 1965, 1967, and 1969, as well as in those mentioned above). However, most of these explications seem to focus on the intensity of religious ardor expressed by Donne's expansion of the boundaries of metaphorical usage within the poem. I will address more directly this metaphorical usage as it relates to Donne's experimentation with metrical freedom within the strictures of traditional sonnet form, as a further inroad to the poem's theme.

Both of these characteristics—the sinewy elasticity of meter and the intellectual contortion of metaphorical conceit—are attributes of the "metaphysical" style of poetry of which Donne is the preeminent representative. These attributes caused the critics of metaphysical poetry to label it the "strong-lined" style. It is, however, difficult to imagine Donne's passionate outpouring being expressed in any other way, since the poet uses the irregularities imposed on the iambic pentameter model to reinforce his unusual, striking imagery.

The poem follows the standard sonnet model of three quatrains, each with separate but related image, and concluding couplet. The first quatrain presents the poet in prayerful pleading to God to "o'erthrow" and "break" him, like some sort of tinker's creation; the second presents the poet as a town "usurpt" from God, its rightful lord; the third presents the poet as a woman who loves God, her suitor, but is engaged to his enemy.

In these quatrains, Donne takes the position that reason, though the highest faculty and God's "viceroy" in humanity, is incomplete and flawed, and requires the enlightenment brought about by the intimate revelation of the divine being. The poet, as a fallen human, is "betroth'd" unto God's "enemy," and therefore pleads for God to progressively "break that knot" of attachment to the enemy, "imprison" the poet, "enthrall" him (or her, since the soul is typically feminine in Elizabethan poetry) into freedom, and finally, in the most daring of the paradoxical juxtapositions, "ravish" the poet into the condition of spiritual chastity. The tinker's object is broken and remade, the town is taken, and the love affair is irresistibly consummated, even as the paradox of virtue and passion is glowingly resolved.

So the strategy of the poem appears to be that of approaching a dangerous, blasphemous anthropomorphism in the heat of devotion, but deflecting that danger, just in time, by the equation of sensual passion to spiritual virtue; for the concluding couplet declares that true freedom comes when one is imprisoned by God, and that purity of heart comes with God's ravishment (sexual assault, with the double meaning of "ravish" as "to win the heart of" someone). By the poem's conclusion, the conceit of the rape which ensures chastity no longer skirts blasphemy. In fact, in Donne's hands, it even becomes orthodox, an ideal of devotion worthy of emulation.

This resolution of discordant imagery, this stillness after the petitioner storm, is reflected in the poem's metrical pattern as well. Nominally iambic pentameter, as befits a sonnet, the first twelve lines (with the exceptions of lines 3 and 11) are full of irregularities. For instance, the first line opens with a trochee on the violent "Batter my heart," the trochee reinforcing the idea of the crashing blow and response for which the poet prays. This verb also foreshadows the daring imagery to comethe hardened heart is battered ("heart" also being Elizabethan slang for the vagina), even as the tinker's artifact is battered, even as an entry is forced through the closed city gates (through which the poet labors to admit the attacker), even as, finally, a sexual entry is forced.

As the poet grapples with these daring but compressed and contorted images, the poem's meter contorts in response. Several lines have repeated strokes of accent, with two lines having as many as three accents in a row (a far remove from the iambic model:

Line 2As yet but knocke, breathe, shine, and seeke to mend;

- Bend /Your force, to reake, blowe, burn and make me new.
- I, like an usurpt town, t'another due,
- Labour to admit you, but oh,to no end (or an alternate readingLaor to admit you, but oh, to no end),
- Reason your vicroy in me, me should defend,
- But is captiv'd, and proves weake or untrue,
- Yet dearely I love you, and would be lov'd faine...

The violence of these repeated strokes of accent mimics the violence of the poet's attempts to cope with the implications of his central conceit, the divine violation. The reader will note also that the irregularities of Donne's meter would be even greater were it not for the enforced splicing (in the original Elizabethan English) of several words. For instance, the normal iambic pattern of line 3 would also be irregular were it not for the pronunciation of "me' and" as "m' and" or "mand." The same holds true for the iamb "captiv'd" of line 8, in which the accent is shifted to the second syllable of the word; for the iambs "Yet dearely I love" of line 9, in which "dearely'I" becomes "dearl'I" or "dear-lie" ("Yet dear-lie love"); for the iambs "Divorce me,'untie" of line 11, in which "me,' untie" becomes "m'untie"; and for the iamb "you'enthrall" of line 13, which becomes "y'enthfall."

Yet Donne uses this last example for his own purposes as well, tor the jarring metrical irregularity of the previous quatrains is suddenly transformed into pure iambic pentameter for the final couplet:

Except you enthrall me, never shall be free,
Nor ever chaste, except you ravish me.

The iambic meter here reflects the peace found as the poem finds its spiritual resolution, not necessarily its intellectual solution. The tension still exists, but in a poised state of equilibrium. "Beautifully calculated," as critic William Kerrigan puts it, "the final line... presents the word 'chaste' before 'ravish me,' relaxing anxieties an instant before the revelation that focuses them." The divine assault is now seen fully as a spiritual act. That which is humanly imperfect and even exploitative becomes divinely perfect and fulfilling. The rape preserves, rather than destroys, chastity. God builds up as he tears down, possesses as he frees, is as honorable as passionate—that is, in him all paradoxes find their supra-rational resolution, resolution not only presented in the imagery of the closing couplet, but reflected in the sudden tranquillity of the completely regular iambic pentameter.

Thus Donne links content to form throughout the "Holy Sonnet XIV." His aesthetic presentation of the relationships "implicit in the ancient theological conceit of the righteous soul's marriage to God" is therefore doubly moving.

Q. Examine the Use of Conceits in "The Flea"?

The "conceits" of poetics are metaphors that are intricately woven into the verse, often used to express satire, puns, or deeper meanings within the poem, and to display the poet's own cunning with words. The conceits of John Donne are said to "leap continually in a restless orbit from the personal to the cosmic and back again."

The outward nature of Donne's poem "The Flea" appears to be a love poem; a dedication from a male suitor to his lady of honour, who refuses to yield to his lustful desires. A closer look at the poem reveals that this suitor is actually arguing a point to his ladythat the loss of innocence does not constitute a loss of honour. The poet begins his argument by condemning the act of intercourse as a shameful sin. He also belittles it, claiming that if the same effects can be realized within the body of a tiny flea, then the act itself cannot hold tremendous importance. In any case, the act is out of the question in the realm of reality, since the two people in the poem do not appear to be married, so sexual union can only be committed symbolically.

The argument then shifts to a different position, where the flea suddenly becomes the entire world of the lovers; the symbolic becomes reality. The act of intercourse loses its importance as the subject in question, and now the loss of all innocence is addressed. There is obviously some action taken by the poet's mistress between the second and third stanzas, as the next segment seems to be a judgment on those actions.

The woman has killed the mysterious flea, casting away her innocence and proving his argument for passion through the use of her own words. The poet asks his mistress to notice only this flea, to forget everything else as he delivers his argument. The flea has bitten them both, and their bloods mix within its body. The attention paid to the qualities of blood may be noted here and later in the poem (when the woman suddenly gains a stature of royalty [purpling her nail]).

This mixing of bloods is somewhat of an insult to the lady, if she is of royal blood and he is not. The description of the swelling of the insect with "one blood made of two" is suggestive of surrogate pregnancy, a perversion of motherhood. Such an allusion is definitely not a pleasant or natural one, and it would be natural for the lady to kill the flea out of disgust after hearing these lines. The word "suck" in this context would be equivalent to the experience of passion or lust, which leads to the loss of innocence. The man admits that the flea sucked him first, so he has lost his innocence, but he still finds himself honourable, so here he bases his own point of view.

The flea becomes ultimately a symbol of the world in which the lovers' desires are realized, "this our marriage bed and marriage temple is." Marriage and consummation is a past issue, since within the flea their blood is already mingled and the "child" of their union grows. The flea is now the realm of marriage, all-encompassing the lovers and excluding any parents or patriarchal sanction. The walls of this realm are jet black, indicating that something sinister or evil is to occur here. This could be a reference to the illicit marriage, or the forbidden mixing of royal and common blood, or perhaps only the impiety of the poet's comparison that loss of innocence should be so trivial as the life of a flea.

The lady's significance is reduced to that of a black widow spider at this point, where the poet says she is apt to kill him after this consummation of a non-existent marriage. With this metaphor of the spider, which is also jet in colour, the object of the man's love is reduced to the position of the flea. If the flea is pregnant with their blood-child, then she (the lady) may as well be pregnant too. Now that this tie has been established between the blood of the woman and the flea, if the woman were to kill the flea, it would be a form of suicide. So to kill this flea, the woman would have to commit murder (of the symbolic marriage realm and the child within), suicide (killing of her own blood), and sacrilege (which suicide is). Apparently the woman kills the flea anyway, since the death of the flea and her own corruption is addressed next.

By killing the flea that the poet has given such strange attributes, the woman squashes the symbolic world the man has constructed and brought them both back to reality. By murdering the "innocent" flea, the lady has "purpled her nail," a colour assigned to the clothing of royalty. She now becomes a monarch (a pun; she is a autonomous ruler and an insect, the butterfly), gaining her position through the death of the flea. She has committed the sins that destroy the union of their blood, so she triumphs. She says that neither of them is any worse for the loss of blood caused by the pest, which the poet confirms to be the truth. This comment suggests that the lady has just admitted her loss of innocence by implying.

Q. Write a critical note on Donne's Holy Sonnet XIV

Batter my heart, three person'd God; for, you
As yet but knocke, breathe, shine, and seeke to mend;
That I may rise, and stand, o'erthrow me, 'and bend
Your force, to breake, blowe, burn and make me new.
I, like an usurpt towne, t'another due,
Labour to 'admit you, but Oh, to no end,
Reason your viceroy in me, me should defend,
But is captiv'd, and proves weake or untrue,
Yet dearely'I love you, and would be lov'd faine,
But am betroth'd unto your enemy,
Divorce me, 'untie, or breake that knot againe
Take me to you, imprison me, for I
Except you 'enthrall me, never shall be free,
Nor ever chaste, except you ravish me.

The analogous language of romantic passion ("I am my Beloved's and my Beloved is mine") and intellectual paradox ("Whoever will lose his life for my sake will find it") has always seemed natural to those seeking to understand and speak of spiritual mysteries. Even so, John Donne's image of the Divine Rape in the "Holy Sonnet XIV," by which the victim becomes, or remains, chaste is at first startling; we are not accustomed to such spiritual intensity. Previous explications have attempted to downplay this figure; for example, Thomas J. Steele, SJ, maintains that the "sexual meaning" is "a secondary meaning" and "probably not meant to be explicitly affirmed." Moreover, George Knox writes that the poem does not "require our imagining literally the relation between man and God in heterosexual terms" and that "the traditions of Christian mysticism allow such symbolism of ravishment...." However, even granting that the sexual imagery is not intended to be taken literally, but rather symbolically, we still must question Knox, as does John E. Parish"One must infer that in Knox's opinion such symbolism shares nothing with metaphor in its effect on the imagination"

In spite of the shocking character of the poem's imagery, the "Holy Sonnet XIV" seems coherent, its language apt; it is metrically jagged, yet traditional; its imagery is anthropomorphic, yet pious. If one may be permitted a commonplace, the poem is certainly a poem of paradoxes, as has been explored more fully in its many explications in these pages (articles appearing in 1953, 1954, 1965, 1967, and 1969, as well as in those mentioned above). However, most of these explications seem to focus on the intensity of religious ardor expressed by Donne's expansion of the boundaries of metaphorical usage within the poem. I will address more directly this metaphorical usage as it relates to Donne's experimentation with metrical freedom within the strictures of traditional sonnet form, as a further inroad to the poem's theme.

Both of these characteristics—the sinewy elasticity of meter and the intellectual contortion of metaphorical conceit—are attributes of the "metaphysical" style of poetry of which Donne is the preeminent representative. These attributes caused the critics of metaphysical poetry to label it the "strong-lined" style. It is, however, difficult to imagine Donne's passionate outpouring being expressed in any other way, since the poet uses the irregularities imposed on the iambic pentameter model to reinforce his unusual, striking imagery.

The poem follows the standard sonnet model of three quatrains, each with separate but related image, and concluding couplet. The first quatrain presents the poet in prayerful pleading to God to "o'erthrow" and "break" him, like some sort of tinker's creation; the second presents the poet as a town "usurpt" from God, its rightful lord; the third presents the poet as a woman who loves God, her suitor, but is engaged to his enemy. In these quatrains, Donne takes the position that reason, though the highest faculty and God's "viceroy" in humanity, is incomplete and flawed, and requires the enlightenment brought about by the intimate revelation of the divine being.

The poet, as a fallen human, is "betroth'd" unto God's "enemy," and therefore pleads for God to progressively "break that knot" of attachment to the enemy, "imprison" the poet, "enthrall" him (or her, since the soul is typically feminine in Elizabethan poetry) into freedom, and finally, in the most daring of the paradoxical juxtapositions, "ravish" the poet into the condition of spiritual chastity. The tinker's object is broken and remade, the town is taken, the love affair is irresistibly consummated, even as the paradox of virtue and passion is glowingly resolved.

So the strategy of the poem appears to be that of approaching a dangerous, blasphemous anthropomorphism in the heat of devotion, but deflecting that danger, just in time, by the equation of sensual passion to spiritual virtue; for the concluding couplet declares that true freedom comes when one is imprisoned by God, and that purity of heart comes with God's ravishment (sexual assault, with the double meaning of "ravish" as "to win the heart of" someone). By the poem's conclusion, the conceit of the rape which ensures chastity no longer skirts blasphemy. In fact, in Donne's hands, it even becomes orthodox, an ideal of devotion worthy of emulation.

This resolution of discordant imagery, this stillness after the petitionary storm, is reflected in the poem's metrical pattern as well. Nominally iambic pentameter, as befits a sonnet, the first twelve lines (with the exceptions of lines 3 and 11) are full of irregularities. For instance, the first line opens with a trochee on the violent "Batter my heart," the trochee reinforcing the idea of the crashing blow and response for which the poet prays. This verb also foreshadows the daring imagery to comethe hardened heart is battered ("heart" also being Elizabethan slang for the vagina), even as the tinker's artifact is battered, even as an entry is forced through the closed city gates (through which the poet labors to admit the attacker), even as, finally, a sexual entry is forced.

As the poet grapples with these daring but compressed and contorted images, the poem's meter contorts in response. Several lines have repeated strokes of accent, with two lines having as many as three accents in a row (a far remove from the iambic model: Line 2As yet but knocke, breathe, shine, and seeke to mend;

- Bend /Your force, to reake, blowe, burn and make me new.
- Like an usurpt town, t'another due,
- Labour to admit you, but oh,to no end (or an alternate readingLaor to admit you, but oh, to no end),
- Reason your vicroy in me, me should defend,
- But is captiv'd, and proves weake or untrue,
- Yet dearely I love you, and would be lov'd faine...

The violence of these repeated strokes of accent mimics the violence of the poet's attempts to cope with the implications of his central conceit, the divine violation. The reader will note also that the irregularities of Donne's meter would be even greater were it not for the enforced splicing (in the original Elizabethan English) of several words. For instance, the normal iambic pattern of line 3 would also be irregular were it not for the pronunciation of "me' and" as "m' and" or "mand." The same holds true for the iamb "captiv'd" of line 8, in which the accent is shifted to the second syllable of the word; for the iambs "Yet dearely I love" of line 9, in which "dearely'I" becomes "dearl'I" or "dear-lie" ("Yet dear-lie love"); for the iambs "Divorce me,'untie" of line 11, in which "me,' untie" becomes "m'untie"; and for the iamb "you'enthrall" of line 13, which becomes "y'enthfall."

Yet Donne uses this last example for his own purposes as well, for the jarring metrical irregularity of the previous quatrains is suddenly transformed into pure iambic pentameter for the final couplet:

Except you enthrall me, never shall be free,
Nor ever chaste, except you ravish me.

The iambic meter here reflects the peace found as the poem finds its spiritual resolution, not necessarily its intellectual solution. The tension still exists, but in a poised state of equilibrium. "Beautifully calculated," as critic William Kerrigan puts it, "the final line... presents the word 'chaste' before 'ravish me,' relaxing anxieties an instant before the revelation that focuses them."The divine assault is now seen fully as a spiritual act. That which is humanly imperfect and even exploitative becomes divinely perfect and fulfilling. The rape preserves, rather than destroys, chastity. God builds up as he tears down, possesses as he frees, is as honorable as passionate—that is, in him all paradoxes find their supra-rational resolution, resolution not only presented in the imagery of the closing couplet, but reflected in the sudden tranquility of the completely regular iambic pentameter.

Thus Donne links content to form throughout the "Holy Sonnet XIV." His aesthetic presentation of the relationships "implicit in the ancient theological conceit of the righteous soul's marriage to God" is therefore doubly moving.

Q. Write a critical note on Holy Sonnet 18.

Show me, dear Christ, thy spouse so bright and clear.
What! is it she which on the other shore
Goes richly painted? or which, robbed and tore,
Laments and mourns in Germany and here?
Sleeps she a thousand, then peeps up one year?
Is she self-truth, and errs? now new, now outwore?
Doth she, and did she, and shall she evermore
On one, on seven, or on no hill appear?
Dwells she with us, or like adventuring knights

First travel we to seek, and then make love?
Betray, kind husband, they spouse to our sights,
And let mine amorous soul court thy mild dove,
Who is most true and pleasing to thee then
When she is embraced and open to most men.

Donne's Holy Sonnets are well described as "a personal record of a brilliant mind struggling towards God". Sonnet 18 reveals the speaker's anguish over the fragmentation of the Church visible and his perplexity over the identity of the true Church. Lines 7-8 ask, "Doth she, and did she, and shall she evermore / On one, on seven, or on no hill appear?". At which place, the speaker inquires, dwells Christ's true "spouse"? The seven hills clearly allude to the Church of Rome, and "no hill" is generally understood as a reference to the Church of England with its see at Canterbury. Donne's mention of "one... hill," however, is problematic. Critics are divided over whether it alludes to Geneva, the centre of Calvinism, with its old city positioned on a hill, or Mount Moriah, the traditional site of Solomon's Temple, in the Holy Land. Grandsen , Louthian , and Warnke , for example, all hold the former opinion, while Carey , Gardner , and Shawcross contend the latter. The editors of The Norton Anthology of English Literature perhaps put the problem best"It is a crux, not easy of solution"

The poem's final image of the Church as a promiscuous wife "embraced and open to most men" , as well as the puzzling mention of one hill, finds antecedents in Christ's conversation with the Samaritan woman in John's Gospel. Recognizing the intertextuality of this New Testament passage with the poem not only resolves the "crux" mentioned by the Norton editors, but unlocks a significant reading of the poem.

In John, chapter 4 (King James Version), the woman of Samaria contends with Jesus, as a Jew, over the true place of worship"Our fathers worshipped in this mountain, and ye say, that in Jerusalem is the place where men ought to worship". Jesus' response revolutionizes the question"Woman, believe me, the hour cometh, when ye shall neither in this mountain, nor yet at Jerusalem, worship the Father". The mountain to which both Jesus and the woman refer is Gerizim, sacred to the Samaritans, who had diverged from Orthodox Judaism during the Babylonian exile. Insisting on their exclusively proper places of worship, Jews and Samaritans anathematized one another, Moriah in Jerusalem being Judaism's holy mount. Predicting the approach of an age when the seat of worship will be located only in the human heart, Jesus explains, "the hour cometh, and now is, when the true worshippers shall worship the Father in spirit and in truth; for the Father seeketh such to worship him".

With reference to our poem it is essential to recognize that St. John's image is of Christ in propria persona courting his true bride. The key features of this episode follow those of the Old Testament betrothal type-scene, which, as Robert Alter outlines must take place with the future bridegroom, or his surrogate, having journeyed to a foreign land. There he encounters a girl... or girls at a well. Someone, either the man or the girl, then draws water from the well; afterward, the girl or girls rush to bring home the news of the stranger's arrival (the verbs "hurry" and "run" are given recurrent emphasis at this junction of the type-scene); finally, a betrothal is concluded between the stranger and the girl...

The two most famous Old Testament versions of the betrothal type-scene are those of Isaac and Rebekah and Jacob and Rachel. Donne would likely have noted in them typological foreshadowing of Jesus' encounter with the Samaritan woman, particularly since the well in John is "Jacob's well" and the Samaritan woman pointedly challenges Jesus, "Art thou greater than our father Jacob, which gave us the well, and drank thereof himself... ?".

When Jesus discerns that the woman, in contrast to her typological predecessors Rachel and Rebekah, has "had five husbands; and he whom thou now hast is not thy husband," she, flustered, initiates debate on the true place of worship. Following the exchange already outlined, the woman departs, astonished, to tell her countrymen, many of whom also "believed on him [Jesus] for the saying of that woman". The entire episode therefore presents the spiritual acceptance of an outcast nation into true worship through the agency of

Christ. The heavenly bridegroom courts his promiscuous bride, who urgently goes out and embraces other men"The woman then left her waterpot, and went her way into the city, and saith to the men, Come, see a man, which told me all things that ever I didis not this the Christ?".

The Samaritans learn that with the advent of Messiah, true worship is no longer tied to a geographical location, but rather to a disposition of the heart. By thinking in terms of geography and tradition rather than spiritual attitude, the poem's speaker errs comparably to the Samaritan woman protesting that Mount Gerizim is the true place of worship. Is the true Church, he asks, "she which on the other shore / Goes richly painted? Or which, robbed and tore, / Laments and mourns in Germany and here?" (lines 2-4). The source of his perplexity is that he wishes to see that which is invisible, invisible because no longer localized, though the traditions of Christendom erroneously attempt to make it so. Christ's true spouse, comprehending all traditions of the visible church without being bound to any, is therefore "open to most men".

An undated letter to his friend Sir Henry Goodyer provides probably the best insight into Donne's ecclesiastical catholicity"I never fettered nor imprisoned the word religion, not straightening it friarly `ad Religiones factitias' (as the Romans call well their orders of religion) nor immuring it in a Rome, a Wittenburg or a Geneva" (Gosse 226). "Christianity," he adds, "which being too spiritual to be seen by us, doth take an apparent body of good life and works." True worship, to Donne, as established in Jesus' words to the Samaritan woman, is an invisible act of the spirit that can only tenuously be recognized in its external manifestations. The true "spouse so bright and clear," paradoxically, can only be seen by those mortals to whom the "kind husband" will "betray" the sight of her. When envisioned thus, she may appear on Gerizim, on Moriah, on the hill of old Geneva, and wherever true worship occurs.

Q. Explain Donne's eighth elegy "The Comparison".

Donne's eighth elegy, "The Comparison," is generally understood as an exercise in contrasting hyperbole, a poem in which the superlative beauty of the speaker's mistress is contrasted with the superlative ugliness of the addressee's mistress. It is true that the poem is constructed as a set of contrasting passages, but I believe that the end of the poem alters our understanding of just what was being contrasted. The elegy has what amounts to a punch line, but we have missed Donne's joke. The poem builds to a surprise, humorous ending in which what had previously seemed to be two different mistresses is revealed to be in fact a single woman.

Editors and critics typically, and understandably, treat the poem as though it compares two different women. Grierson and Gardner both speak of the poem as involving a contrast between the speaker's mistress and that of his "enemy" (74,121). John Carey says that the poem is one in which the speaker's "own girl's perfections are contrasted with the filthy deformities of another's". Similarly, Arthur Marotti speaks of the poem as contrasting the "antagonist's mistress" with "the speaker and his mistress".

Only Achsah Guibbory considers that "perhaps the two mistresses described in the poem are not different women but rather a single woman seen in two ways". The speaker's and the addressee's mistress are, I believe, undoubtedly the same woman; indeed, the very point of the poem is to compel in readers a belated recognition that the speaker and the addressee love the same woman.

As a first indication that only one woman is being discussed, consider some otherwise puzzling aspects of the dramatic situation depicted in the poem. If the addressee is so unfortunate in his mistress and the speaker so happy with his own, what motivates this venomous outpouring? Why does the speaker not simply go enjoy his mistress and leave the poor addressee in his miserable state? The speaker, of course, might be gloating, but the tone seems too aggressive for mere gloating; Marotti is on to something when he speaks of the addressee as an "antagonist." But what offense can the addressee have committed against the speaker by loving a loathsome mistress? More particularly, what motivates the speaker's insistence that the addressee "leave" his mistress?

What sense does it make to say "I have a wonderful mistress, and I will not stop harassing you until you leave your horrible one"?

The reason for the speaker's peculiar emotional investment in the romantic affairs of his addressee, I believe, becomes clear late in the poem when we discover that what had seemed like a contrast between two women is actually a description of one woman as the speaker sees her from two contrasting states of mind. When he believes she is involved with him exclusively, she seems ideal; when he considers that she is also involved with his addressee, he finds her loathsome.

The pronouns in the closing couplet are what reveal that only one woman is being discussed. In the penultimate line of the poem, the speaker commands the addressee to break off with his mistress by telling him to "leave her." But throughout the poem, the pronoun her has, with only one exception, been used to refer to the mistress of the speaker (lines 5, 15, 24, 28, 38). When he speaks of the addressee's mistress, he uses the word thy (7,19,25,32,34,39). In fact, after the phrase "my Mistris" in line 4, the word her serves as the speaker's sole means of indicating that he is talking about his own mistress. When at the close of the poem he tells his interlocutor to leave "her," the pattern of pronoun reference established earlier in the poem prompts us to realise that it is the speaker's own mistress whom he wants the addressee to leave.

The one time that her is used to refer to the mistress of the addressee comes in line 14, when the speaker refers to the skin of the addressee's mistress as "her skinne." This lone use of "her" in reference to the addressee's mistress serves to intimate the surprise ending, for it is confusingly followed by a line in which the pronoun "her" is used again, but this time in reference to the speaker's mistress"And like vile lying stones in saffrond tinne / Or warts, or wheales, they hang upon her [i.e., your mistress's] skinne. / Round as the world's her [i.e., my mistress's] head". Line 15 will initially sound like a continuation of the abuse in 13 and 14, so that at this stage of the poem, it is only by a deliberate effort that we supply different referents for the two hers. The penultimate line, then, strongly suggests that the addressee's mistress is the same woman that the speaker loves, an identification that is subtly underscored by the pronoun in the final line"she." The word she had not previously been used in the poem to refer to either mistress; it has been reserved for this moment, when the reader realizes that a single woman has been the object of both the idealization and the vilification in the poem.

With the dramatic, belated reversal, the elegy resembles some of Donne's other poems that are constructed almost as versified jokes. For example, the ending of "SongGo and Catch a Falling Star" operates almost like a punch line, resolving the tension carefully built up through the previous four verses. And "Woman's Constancy" similarly closes with an abrupt and humorous reversal.

By missing the punch line of "The Comparison," we also miss some of the poem's significance. Read as I am suggesting, the elegy is more than just an exercise in contrasting hyperbole; it becomes a psychological study of the effects of faithfulness on desirability.

Q. Write a critical note on Donne's Ecstasy ?

As 'twixt two equal armies, Fate
Suspends uncertain victory,
Our souls, (which to advance their state,
Were gone out), hung 'twixt her, and me.
And whilst our souls negotiate there,
We like sepulchral statues lay;
All day, the same our postures were,
And we said nothing, all the day.

The "equal armies" analogy in the fourth and fifth stanzas of "The Ecstasy" is crucial, for it introduces the relationship between body and soul that dominates the rest of the poem. Moreover, as Helen Gardner has shown, the analogy is Donne's own, something he finds "for himself and not in his source," Leone Ebreo's Dialoghi d'Amore . Yet if this analogy is important to our understanding of the poem, it also is ambiguous-so ambiguous, in fact, that critics have been unable to agree even on such a basic matter as which figures in the simile Donne means to compare. Yvor Winters claims that

Donne is likening the disembodied souls to two equal armies; Arthur Marotti counters that "[t]he bodies are the combatting armies, the souls the individual negotiators". What links these competing views-and those of many other explicators of the analogy-is the assumption that Donne means the comparison to be clear, and that its ambiguity is therefore unintentional, the result either of conceptual confusion or of sloppy writing.

It seems a better strategy, given Donne's characteristic "high standard of metaphorical precision" (Stein II), to assume that Donne means what he says, that the analogy makes multiple connections among its different figures, and that the resulting ambiguity somehow serves Donne's design for the poem. For if we read the analogy as Donne wrote it, and not as we, for the sake of clarity, would like to rewrite it, we are forced to acknowledge the validity, the striking aptness, of all the connections that it implies. As Winters suggests, the analogy does link battling armies with motionless souls, but it also relates "her and me" to "equal armies" and "our souls" to "uncertain victory." The lovers, this second reading implies, are like two armies in that something conditional and beyond their control hangs between themboth pairs are objects of the preposition "'twixt."

The souls, linked in negotiations, hovering between the lovers' bodies, resemble an undecided contest that Fate dangles between two well matched armies. Yet a third reading links Fate and the lovers' souls. The connection here does at first seem, in Gardner's words, "purely verbal", a coupling produced by tortured syntax'As fate suspends uncertain victory between two equal armies, our souls hung between her and me." But Fate and the souls are indeed related, for they all are active agents, the only figures in the first five stanzas not presented as purely passive—a point I will return to presently. The analogy, then, contains multiple comparisons, each well home out by both the grammar and sense of the section. It is impossible to determine a single definitive reading, for all are equally legitimate. To admit this is not to deconstruct the poem, but to read its words faithfully. Compounding this confusion is Donne's shifting description of the differences between the lovers' bodies and souls. Marotti has argued that "the fifth stanza contradicts the clear suggestions of the previous four as it brings physical (erotic) activity to a standstill".

Erotic undertones abound in the first four stanzas, but hand-holding and sweating hardly qualify as erotic, or even especially physical, activity. The lovers lie motionless and silent. In the first twenty lines, they are the subject of exactly three verbs; and these, "sat," "lay," and "said," only further emphasize their passivity.

To this static setting the analogy introduces the souls as active participants in the ecstatic experience. Like aggressive armies, they "Were gone out" "to advance their state," to "negotiate" a settlement to their implied impasse. Later in the poem, however, the contrast between passive bodies and active souls undergoes a reversal; the bodies become necessary actors in human experience, the agents through which the lovers first gain knowledge of each other:

We owe them thanks, because they thus,
Did us, to us, at first convey,
Yielded their forces, sense, to us,
Nor are dross to us, but allay.

This shift resembles another reversal originating in the analogy, one in which the locus of the lovers' identity moves from their bodies to their souls. The analogy reveals that the speaker's consciousness is grounded firmly in the body. "Whilst our souls negotiate" he says, "we"-the lovers' bodies-"like sepulchral statues lay." And when he says that the couple's souls "hung 'twixt her, and me," "her" and "me" clearly refer to the physical husks that are reclining on the ground. In the analogy, then, the first-person pronouns strongly suggest that the lovers' selves reside in their bodies. Toward the end of the poem, however, the speaker contradicts his earlier statements:

But O alas, so long, so far
Our bodies why do we forbear!
They are ours, though they are not we....

"We" now clearly refers to the lovers' souls; the bodies

are their possessions. The poem has reversed its former positionwhereas it first led us to think of the lovers' bodies as their true selves, it now suggests exactly the opposite.

This ambiguity is crucial to "The Ecstasy," for it is Donne's way of eliding the customary distinction between body and soul, and hence of tightening "That subtle knot, which makes us man" . By creating multiple connections among its parts, by defining "we" first as the body, then as the soul, the analogy suggests that any division between the speaker's physical and spiritual selves is insignificant or illusory. This vision of human beings as mysteriously and wonderfully indivisible must have been profoundly important to Donne, who cherished the Christian doctrine of the body's resurrection and felt deeply troubled by the prospect of a soul's being eternally severed from its physical frame.

Q. Write a critical note on Donne's to his Mistress Going to Bed.

Full nakedness, all joyes are due to thee.
As soules unbodied, bodies uncloth'd must bee
To taste whole joyes.

Despite extensive commentary on the eroticism of Donne's To His Mistress Going to Bed, apparently unnoted is a quite bawdy pun in these lines. Helen Gardner's commentary paraphrases lines 34-35 as follows"As souls must cast off the body to taste the fullness of joy, so bodies must cast off their clothes." She then refers to Aquinas, citing the argument that the "full reward of the blessed is after death and that in this life they have only a foretaste of bliss." A. J. Smith comments on these lines that "just as souls must divest themselves of their bodies before they can enjoy total bliss, so the bodies must shed their clothes." Other editors and critics make similar assertions, primarily emphasizing the audacious analogy of soul and body and the implication of experiencing total, "whole joyes" through physical nakedness.

Surely, however, Donne is punning on "whole" as the female "hole" revealed by nakedness. This is very much in the vein of the bawdy conversation among Benvolio, Romeo, and Mercutio in Romeo and Juliet. Mercutio speaks of the idiot wishing to hide his "bable" in a "hole" and then speaks of his own coming "to the whole depth of my tale," with sexual puns on "whole" and "tale". This implication is reinforced by the further bawdy meaning of "taste" as to enjoy a woman sexually. Pertinent examples, again from Shakespeare, are found in Posthumus's "If you can make it apparent / that you have tasted her in bed" (Cymbeline 2.4.57-58) and in Othello's "I had been happy, if the general camp / Pioneers and all, had tasted her sweet body" (Othello 3.3.345-46).

The likelihood that Donne is making such a pun on "whole" is supported by his own bawdy statement in Love's Progress"Men to such Gods [Cupid and Pluto] their sacrificing coales / did not in Altars lay, but pits and holes" (lines 31-32). Then, in line 36 he says, "we love the Centrique part," that is, the vagina, the "hole."

Chapter 11

Critical Essays

The Religious Poetry of John Donne

With the probable exception of "The Cross," for which no precise date can be suggested, and which is more a verse-letter than a divine poem, the earliest of Donne's Divine Poems appears to be *La Corona. La Corona* is a single poem, made up of seven linked sonnets, each of which celebrates not so much an event in the life of Christ as a mystery of faith. Those brought up in a different tradition might well wonder why Donne should devote one sonnet of his seven to the Finding in the Temple, and omit all reference to the events of the Ministry, except for a brief reference to miracles. The emphasis on the beginning and close of the life of Christ is characteristic of mediaeval art, whether we think of a series of windows like those at Fairford, or of the mediaeval dramatic cycles. It was dictated by the desire to present with simplicity the Christian scheme of man's redemption.

The popular devotional equivalent of this emphasis upon the plan of salvation was the meditation on the Fifteen Mysteries of the Rosary, and reference to them explains at once why Donne would find it natural to pass directly from the Finding in the Temple to the events of Holy Week. Habits of prayer, like other early habits, can survive modifications of a man's intellectual position. It is doubtful whether Donne felt there was anything particularly Catholic in concentrating on the Mysteries of the Faith, or in addressing his second and third sonnets to the Blessed Virgin, or in apostrophizing St. Joseph in his fourth; but it is also doubtful whether anyone who had been brought up as a Protestant would have done so. *La Corona* has been undervalued as a poem by comparison with the *Holy Sonnets,* because the difference of intention behind the two sets of sonnets has not been recognized. The *La Corona* sonnets are inspired by liturgical prayer and praise—oral prayer; not by private meditation and the tradition of mental prayer.

They echo the language of collects and office hymns, which expound the doctrines of the Catholic Faith, recalling the events from which those doctrines are derived, but not attempting to picture them in detail. Instead of the scene of the maiden alone in her room at Nazareth, there is a theological paradox"Thy Makers maker, and thy Fathers mother." The scandal of the Cross is presented not by a vivid picture of its actual ignominy and agony, but by the thought that here the Lord of Fate suffered a fate at the hand of his creatures.

The petitions with which the last three poems end, though couched in the singular, are petitions which any man might pray. Each is the appropriate response to the mystery propounded. It is not surprising to find that the first sonnet of the set is a weaving together of phrases from the Advent Offices in the Breviary, and that the second draws on the Hours of the Blessed Virgin. As always happens with Donne, direct dependence on sources weakens as he proceeds. But the impulse with which he began *La Corona* is clearly visible in the first two sonnets.

His "crowne of prayer and praise" was to be woven from the prayers and praises of the Church. It is possible that he chose to use the sonnet, a form he had used before this only for epistles, because he wished to write formally and impersonallyto create an offering of beauty and dignity. *La Corona* is perhaps no more than a religious exercise, but it is an accomplished one.

The sonnets are packed with meaning, with striking and memorable expressions of the commonplaces of Christian belief. The last line of each, repeated as the first line of the next, is both a fine climax and a fine opening. Unlike the majority of Elizabethan sonneteers, Donne has chosen the more difficult form of the sonnet. He follows Sidney in limiting the rhymes of the octave to two, and employs Sidney's most favored arrangement of those rhymes in two closed quatrains. He alternates between two arrangements of the rhymes of the sestet. His seventh sonnet presented a problem; if it contrasted with his sixth, it would be the same as his first. He chose the lesser evil, and repeated the form of the sixth sonnet in the seventh, in order to make the last lead round again to the first and form a circle.

"A Litany," which is probably the next important divine poem, is less successful than *La Corona,* but more interesting. Donne has cast his "meditation in verse" into the formal mould of a litany. On the other hand, he has employed a stanza of his own invention. The contrast between the simple traditional outline of the poem and the intricacies of the separate stanzas is the formal expression of the poem's ambiguity. It appears impersonal, but is, in fact, highly personal. It tells us much, though indirectly, of its author's mind at the time when it was written, not least because it is in some ways uncharacteristic of him. It has the special interest of poems which are the product of a period of transition, when in the process of reshaping a personality some elements are stressed to the exclusion of others.

"A Litany" is remarkable for a quality that is rare in Donne's poetry, though it is often found in his letters and sermonssobriety. Although it is the wittiest of the Divine Poems, startling in paradox, precise in antithesis, and packed with allusions, its intellectual ingenuity and verbal audacity are employed to define an ideal of moderation in all things. Sir Herbert Grierson called it "wire-drawn and tormented." "Wire-drawn" it may be called with justice; it analyzes temptations with scrupulosity, and shows a wary sense of the distinctions that divide the tainted from the innocent act or motive. But "tormented" seems less just, even if we confine the word to the style. The ideal which is aspired to is simplicity of motive, "evennesse" of piety, and a keeping of "meane waies." Something of this ideal is already realized in the deliberate care with which the aspiration is expressed. At first sight the poem may appear overingenious. On further acquaintance it comes to seem not so much ingenious as exact; less witty, and wiser. We know from Donne's letter to Goodyer, in which he refers to its composition, that "A Litany" was written during an illness and in a mood of dejection [see letter dated 1609]. The "low devout melancholie" of *La Corona* has deepened into a sin from which Donne prays to be delivered in the first verse.... It is a casuist's poem and shows traces both of the current debate on the Oath of Allegiance and of Donne's personal searching of conscience in his years of failure, when he was still hoping for worldly success and, if Walton is right, had already been offered and had rejected advancement in the Church.

Donne, who was "subtle to plague himself," must have been conscious of the contrast between his relatives, who for conscience' sake had chosen exile, imprisonment or death, and himself. He had conformed to the Established Church and was using his powers in its defence, and had even been offered a means of maintenance in its ministry. The rather exaggerated stress in "A Litany" on the compatibility of the service of God with "this worlds sweet" may reflect his need, at this time, to assure himself that the way that appears easier is not, for that reason, necessarily wrong. Intransigence may even, he hints, be a form of self-indulgence, an easy way out of the strain of conflicting duties:

For Oh, to some Not to be Martyrs, is martyrdom.

But if this seems an over subtle explanation, there is another reason why Donne should at this period pray more strongly to be delivered from contempt of the world than from overvaluing it. The temptation to despise what one has not obtained and to cry, because one has been unsuccessful, "the world's not worth my care" is strong to ambitious natures. It must have been strong to Donne who had by nature both the melancholy and the scorn of the satirist. If we remember the circumstances of his life at Mitcham—his anxiety for his wife whom he had brought to poverty and for the future of his growing family, his inability to find secure employment and his broken health—the petitions of "A Litany" gain in meaning. We see the passionate and hyperbolical Donne, the proud and irritable young man of the Satires and Elegies, attempting to school himself to patience, not rejecting with scorn a world that has disappointed him, but praying that he may accept what life brings in a religious spirit. His declarations that happiness may exist in courts, and that the earth is not our prison, show an affinity with the contemporary movement in France, which Bremond described under the name of "l'humanisme devot."

They also contrast most interestingly with the pessimism of some Jacobean writers, particularly Webster, with whom Donne is often compared. The dying Antonio's cry, "And let my Sonne, flie the Courts of Princess," and Vittoria's last words, "O happy they that never saw the Court," only sum up the constant Senecan despising of the world in Webster's two greatest plays. "A Litany" has none of this cynicism. It is, whatever else we may say of it, a singularly unbitter poem, although it was written at a bitter time. In many ways it is the most Anglican of the Divine Poems and continually anticipates Donne's leading ideas as a preacher. Although we may see in his restoration of the saints, whom Cranmer had banished from the Litany, a further sign of his loyalty to "the ancient ways," his own praise of his poem in his letter to Goodyer makes the typical Anglican claim of avoiding both excess and defect:

> That by which it will deserve best acceptation, is, That neither the Roman Church need call it defective, because it abhors not the particular mention of the blessed Triumphers in heaven; nor the Reformed can discreetly accuse it, of attributing more then a rectified devotion ought to doe.

We may also see in the whole poem a habit of mind which has been shaped by the practice of systematic self-examination, and thinks more in terms of particular sins and failings than in terms of general and total unworthiness; but the particular sins which Donne prays to be delivered from are not the traditional sins. There is no trace of the old classifications under which the conscience can be examinedsins against God and sins against my neighbour, or the seven deadly sins and their branches. Instead the sins in "A Litany" can all be referred back to two general philosophic conceptionsthe conception of virtue as the mean between two extremes, and the related conception of virtue as the proper use of all the faculties. Donne anticipates here that ideal of "reasonable piety" which is so familiar later in the century in the manuals of the Caroline divines. The resolute rejection of otherworldliness, the antimystical bias of the poem, the concentration on "a daily beauty" and the sanctification of ordinary life, with the consequent ignoring of any conception of sanctity as something extraordinary and heroic, the exaltation of the undramatic virtues of patience, discretion, and a sobre cheerfulness—all these things are characteristic of Anglican piety in the seventeenth century and after.

In comparison with the Roman Catholic books of devotion, which they frequently drew upon and adapted, the Anglican manuals seem to some tastes rather dry, with their stress on edification and "practical piety" and the "duties of daily life." "A Litany" has something of this dryness. It has neither the warmth of mediaeval religious devotion, nor the exalted note of the Counter-Reformation. It reflects the intellectuality which Anglicanism derived from its break with mediaeval tradition and its return to the patristic ages.

But in spite of its many felicities in thought and expression, its beauty of temper, its interest in what it tells us of Donne's mind, and its historical interest as an early expression by a writer of genius of a piety characteristic of the Church of England, "A Litany" cannot be regarded as a wholly successful poem. It is an elaborate private prayer, rather incongruously cast into a liturgical form. Donne's letter to Goodyer shows he was aware of the discrepancy between such a "divine and publique" name and his "own little thoughts." He attempted to defend himself by the examples of two Latin litanies which he had found "amongst ancient annals."

The defence is not a very cogent one. The litanies he refers to, although written by individuals, are genuine litanies, suitable for general use. Donne's poem could hardly be prayed by anyone but himself. Although he preserves the structure of a litany (Invocations, Deprecations, Obsecrations, and Intercessions), he does not preserve the most important formal element in a litany, the unvarying responses in each section. His opening invocations to the Persons of the Trinity have each a particular petition in place of the repeated "Miserere nobis." He is, of course, debarred by his membership of a Reformed Church from using the response "Ora pro nobis"; instead he exercises his ingenuity in finding suitable petitions for each group of saints to make, or for us to make as we remember them. There is some awkwardness in this "rectified devotion," which, accepting that the saints pray for men, avoids direct requests for their suffrages while suggesting fitting subjects for their intercessions; and the absence of any response makes these stanzas formally unsatisfactory.

With the Deprecations, Obsecrations, and Intercessions, he makes use of the responses "Libera nos" and "Audi nos"; but he treats them as refrains to be modified according to each stanza, as he had loved to adapt and twist refrains in his love-poetry. In one place he goes so far as to invert his response, and beg the Lord not to hear. One may sympathize with Donne's desire to find a form for his meditation; but the incompatibility between the material of the poem and the chosen form is too great. The form has had to be too much twisted to fit the material, and the material has been moulded to the form rather than expressed by it.

Most critics have agreed in regarding *La Corona* and "A Litany" as inferior to the *Holy Sonnets*, which give an immediate impression of spontaneity. Their superiority has been ascribed to their having been written ten years later, and their vehemence and anguished intensity have been connected with a deepening of Donne's religious experience after the death of his wife. There can be no question of their poetic greatness, or of their difference from *La Corona* and "A Litany"; but I do not believe that greatness or that difference to be due to the reasons which are usually given. The accepted date rests on an assumption which the textual history of the sonnets does not supportthe assumption that the three *Holy Sonnets* which the Westmoreland manuscript alone preserves were written at the same time as the other sixteen. These three sonnets are, as Sir Herbert Grierson called all the *Holy Sonnets*, "separate ejaculations"; but the other sixteen fall into clearly recognizable sets of sonnets on familiar themes for meditation. They are as traditional in their way as *La Corona* and "A Litany" is, and as the three Hymns are not. The Hymns are truly occasional; each arises out of a particular situation and a personal mood. But in theme and treatment the *Holy Sonnets*, if we ignore the three Westmoreland sonnets, depend on a long-established form of religious exercisenot oral prayer, but the simplest method of mental prayer, meditation.

To say this is not to impugn their originality or their power. Donne has used the tradition of meditation in his own way; and it suits his genius as a poet far better than do the more formal ways of prayer he drew upon in *La Corona* and "A Litany." Yet although, with the possible exception of the Hymns, the *Holy Sonnets* are his greatest divine poems, I do not myself feel that they spring from a deeper religious experience than that which lies behind "A Litany." The evidence which points to a date in 1609 does not seem to me to conflict with their character as religious poems; on the contrary it accords rather better with it than does the hitherto accepted date.

Many readers have felt a discrepancy between the *Holy Sonnets* and the picture which Walton gives of Donne's later years, and between the *Holy Sonnets* and the sermons and Hymns. There is a note of exaggeration in them. This is apparent, not only in the violence of such a colloquy as "Batter my heart," but also in the strained note of such lines as these:

But who am I, that dare dispute with thee?
O God, Oh! of thine onely worthy blood,
And my teares, make a heavenly Lethean flood,
And drowne in it my sinnes blacke memorie.

That thou remember them, some claime as debt, I thinke it mercy, if thou wilt forget.

At first sight the closing couplet seems the expression of a deep humility; but it cannot be compared for depth of religious feeling with the "Hymn to God the Father," where, however great the sin is, the mercy of God is implied to be the greater....

The almost histrionic note of the *Holy Sonnets* may be attributed partly to the meditation's deliberate stimulation of emotion; it is the special danger of this exercise that, in stimulating feeling, it may falsify it, and over dramatize the spiritual life. But Donne's choice of subjects and his whole-hearted use of the method are symptoms of a condition of mind very different from the mood of *La Corona* or even from the conflicts which can be felt behind "A Litany." The meditation on sin and on judgment is strong medicine; the mere fact that his mind turned to it suggests some sickness in the soul. The "low devout melancholie" of *La Corona*, the "dejection" of "A Litany" are replaced by something darker.

In both his preparatory prayers Donne uses a more terrible word, despair. The note of anguish is unmistakable. The image of a soul in meditation which the *Holy Sonnets* present is an image of a soul working out of its salvation in fear and trembling. The two poles between which it oscillates are faith in the mercy of God in Christ, and a sense of personal unworthiness that is very near to despair. The flaws in their spiritual temper are a part of their peculiar power. No other religious poems make us feel so acutely the predicament of the natural man called to be the spiritual man. None present more vividly man's recognition of the gulf that divides him from God and the effort of faith to lay hold on the miracle by which Christianity declares that the gulf has been bridged.

Donne's art in writing them was to seem "to use no art at all." His language has the ring of a living voice, admonishing his own soul, expostulating with his Maker, defying Death, or pouring itself out in supplication. He creates, as much as in some of the *Songs and Sonnets*, the illusion of a present experience, throwing his stress on such words as "now" and "here" and "this." And, as often there, he gives an extreme emphasis to the personal pronouns:

Take mee to you, imprison mee, for I
Except you'enthrall mee, never shall be free,
Nor ever chast, except you ravish mee.

The plain unadorned speech, with its idiomatic turns, its rapid questions, its exclamatory Oh's and Ah's, wrests the movement of the sonnet to its own movement. The line is weighted with heavy monosyllables, or lengthened by heavy secondary stresses, which demand the same emphasis as the main stress takes. It may be stretched out to

All whom warre, dearth, age, argues, tyrannies,

after it has been contracted to

From death, you numberlesse infinities.

Many lines can be reduced to ten syllables only by a more drastic use of elision than Donne allowed himself elsewhere, except in the Satires; and others, if we are to trust the best manuscripts, are a syllable short and fill out the line by a pause. This dramatic language has a magic that is unanalyzable-words, movement, and feeling have a unity in which no element outweighs the other.

The effect of completely natural speech is achieved by exploiting to the full the potentialities of the sonnet. The formal distinction of octave and sestet becomes a dramatic contrast. The openings of Donne's sestets are as dramatic as the openings of the sonnets themselvesimpatient as in

Why doth the devill then usurpe in mee?

or gentle as in

Yet grace, if thou repent, thou canst not lacke;

or imploring as in

But let them sleepe, Lord, and mee mourne a space.

Though the *turn* in each of these is different, in all three there is that sudden difference in tension that makes a change dramatic. Donne avoids also the main danger of the couplet endingthat it may seem an afterthought, or an addition, or a mere summary. His final couplets, whether separate or running on from the preceding line, are true rhetorical climaxes, with the weight of the poem behind them. Except for Hopkins, no poet has crammed more into the sonnet than Donne. In spite of all the liberties he takes with his line, he succeeds in the one essential of the sonnethe appears to need exactly fourteen lines to say exactly what he has to say. Donne possibly chose the sonnet form as appropriate for a set of formal meditations, but both in meditation and in the writing of his sonnets he converts traditional material to his own use.

He was not, I believe, aiming at originality, and therefore the originality of the *Holy Sonnets* is the more profound.

With the exception of "The Lamentations of Jeremy," in which Donne, like so many of his contemporaries, but with more success than most, attempted the unrewarding task of paraphrasing the Scriptures, the remainder of the Divine Poems are occasional. The poem "Upon the Annunciation and Passion" is very near in mood and style to *La Corona*. As there, Donne writes with strict objectivity. He contemplates two mysteries which are facets of one supreme mystery, and tries to express what any Christian might feel. On the other hand, "*Good Friday, Riding Westward*" is a highly personal poema free, discursive meditation arising out of a particular situation. The elaborate preliminary conceit of the contrary motions of the heavenly bodies extends itself into astronomical images, until the recollection of the Passion sweeps away all thoughts but penitence. As in some of the finest of the *Songs and Sonnets*, Donne draws out an initial conceit to its limit in order, as it seems, to throw it away when "to brave clearnesse all things are reduc'd." What he first sees as an incongruity—his turning his back on his crucified Savior—he comes to see as perhaps the better posture, and finally as congruous for a sinner. The poem hinges on the sudden apostrophe:

and thou look'st towards mee,
O Saviour, as thou hang'st upon the tree.

After this, discursive meditation contracts itself to penitent prayer. The mounting tension of the poem—from leisurely speculation, through the imagination kindled by "that spectacle of too much weight for mee," to passionate humility—makes it a dramatic monologue. So also does the sense it gives us of a second person present—the silent figure whose eyes the poet feels watching him as he rides away to the west.

"Good Friday" is the last divine poem Donne wrote before his ordination and it points forward to the Hymns. They also arise from particular situations, are free, not formal meditations, and have the same unforced feeling. They are the only lyrics among the Divine Poems, and it is not only in their use of the pun and conceit that they remind us of the *Songs and Sonnets*. They have the spontaneity which *La Corona* and "A Litany" lack, without the overemphasis of the *Holy Sonnets*. In them Donne's imagination has room for play. Each sprang from a moment of crisis. The "Hymn to Christ" was written on the eve of his journey overseas with Doncaster, a journey from which, as his Valediction Sermon shows, he felt he might not return. It is a finer treatment of the subject of the sonnet written after his wife's death in the Westmoreland manuscript. While the sonnet is general and reflective, in the Hymn his imagination is fired by his immediate circumstances and he translates his thoughts into striking and moving symbols. The "Hymn to God the Father" was written, according to Walton, during Donne's grave illness of 1623, and the "Hymn to God my God, in my sickness," whether it should be dated during the same illness or in 1631, was written when he thought himself at the point of death. In both the conclusion is the same"So, in his purple wrapp'd receive mee Lord," and "Sweare by thy selfe."

Donne's earliest poem on religion, the third Satire, ended with the words "God himself to trust," and it is fitting that what is possibly his last divine poem, and certainly one of his best known, should end with the memory of the promise to Abraham, the type of the faithful. For the Divine Poems are poems of faith, not of vision. Donne goes by a road which is not lit by any flashes of ecstasy, and, in the words he had carved on his tomb, "aspicit Eum cujus nomen est Oriens." The absence of ecstasy makes his divine poems so different from his love poems. There is an ecstasy of joy and an ecstasy of grief in his love-poetry; in his divine poetry we are conscious almost always of an effort of will. In the *Holy Sonnets* there is passion and longing, and in the Hymns some of the "modest assurance" which Walton attributed to Donne's last hours, but there is no rapture....

Donne was a man of strong passions, in whom an appetite for life was crossed by a deep distaste for it. He is satirist and elegist at the same period, and even in the same poem. The scorn of the satirist invades the world of amorous elegy; his gayest poems have a note of bitterness, his most passionate lyrics are rarely free from a note of contempt, even if it is only a sardonic aside or illustration. In his love-poetry he set the ecstasy of lovers over against the dull, foolish, or sordid business of the world, or exalted one member of her sex by depreciating all the rest, or, in revulsion from the "queasie pain of being belov'd and loving," turned on his partner with savagery or mockery. But he was also a man of strong and loyal affectionsa good son, a devoted husband, a loving father, and a warm and constant friend.

From the beginning there is this other side to Donne. In moral and psychological terms, Donne's problem was to come to terms with a world which alternately enthralled and disgusted him, to be the master and not the slave of his temperament. Like Wordsworth in his middle years, he came to long for "a repose that ever is the same." He did not look to religion for an ecstasy of the spirit which would efface the memory of the ecstasy of the flesh; but for an "evennesse" of piety which would preserve him from despair.

In the boldest of the *Holy Sonnets* it is in order that he may "rise and stand" that he prays to be overthrown, and in order that he may be ever chaste that he prays God to ravish him. The struggles and conflicts to which the Divine Poems witness did not lead to the secret heights and depths of the contemplative life, but to the public life of duty and charity which Walton describes. That Donne had to wrestle to the end is clear. Like Dr. Johnson, with whom, in his natural melancholy and as a practical moralist, he has much in common, he remained burdened by the consciousness of his sins and aware of his need for mercy at the judgment.

Donne's divine poems are the product of conflict between his will and his temperament. They lack, therefore, the greatness of his love-poetry, whose power lies in its "unchartered freedom"in the energy of will with which he explores and expresses the range of his temperament. In his love-poetry he is not concerned with what he ought or ought not to feel, but with the expression of feeling itself. Passion is there its own justification, and so is disgust, or hatred or grief.

In his divine poetry feeling and thought are judged by the standard of what a Christian should feel or think. As a love poet he seems to owe nothing to what any other man in love had ever felt or said before him; his language is all his own. As a divine poet he cannot escape using the language of the Bible, and of hymns and prayers, or remembering the words of Christian writers.

Christianity is a revealed religion, contained in the Scriptures and the experience of Christian souls; the Christian poet cannot voyage alone. The truths of Donne's love-poetry are truths of the imagination, which freely transmutes personal experience. They are his own discoveries. The truths of revelation are the accepted basis of his religious poetry, and imagination has here another task. It is, to some extent, fettered. Donne anticipated Johnson's criticism of "poetical devotion," and was perhaps his own best critic, when he wrote to Sir Robert Carr, apologizing for his poem on Hamilton:

> You know my uttermost when it was best, and even then I did best when I had least truth for my subjects. In this present case there is so much truth as it defeats all Poetry.... If you had commanded mee to have waited on his body to Scotland and preached there, I would have embraced the obligation with more alacrity.

But although the Divine Poems are not the record of discoveries, but of struggles to appropriate a truth which has been revealed, that truth does not "defeat all Poetry," but gives us a poetry whose intensity is a moral intensity. Some religious poetry, Herbert's perhaps, can be regarded as a species of love-poetry; but Donne's is not of that kind. The image of Christ as Lover appears in only two of his poems—both written soon after the death of his wife. The image which dominates his divine poetry is the image of Christ as Savior, the victor over sin and death. The strength with which his imagination presents this figure is the measure of his need, and that need is the subject of the finest of his religious poems.

Criticism by Terry G. Sherwood

[Sherwood is a Canadian educator and literary essayist.

In his *Fulfilling the CircleA Study of John Donne's Thought* (1984), he stressed that "there can be no absolute separation between the importance of epistemological and psychological principles for Donne and his personal consciousness that infuses his works. That these principles are manifested in writings clearly enlivened by Donne's own experience simply adds convincing evidence of their importance in his thought.

And the fact that these writings define the experience of consciousness according to shaping metaphysical forces makes them characteristic of Donne's thought in general." In the following excerpt from this work, Sherwood examines *Deaths Duell* as "the final part added to a consistent whole"a work that completes a lifelong cycle involving "Donne's own person as a factor in his works."]

The event of *Deaths Duell* was remarkable even by the standards of Donne's day. He had been appointed to preach on 'his old constant day, the first *Friday* in *Lent,* ' at Whitehall before the king. Though wasted by illness, Donne 'passionately denied' the requests of concerned friends that he not preach. His text was Psalm 68:20'*And unto God the Lord belong the issues of death. i.e. from death.*' Isaak Walton captures a very special drama'Many that then saw his tears, and heard his faint and hollow voice, professing they thought Text prophetically chosen, and that Dr. Donne *had preach't his own funeral Sermon.* ' But it is not just the drama of a wasted, dying man who embodies his own words about death that is remarkable.

Even more so is that the event of Donne's delivery and the sermon itself, taken together, represent a coherent and fulfilling conclusion to his life and thought.The vivid sight of the dying man could have made the sermon itself anticlimactic if not for its own powerful effects. A forceful statement of omnipresent mortality and vivid images of putrefaction and vermiculate relentlessly aggravate fear of death. Donne's dying body becomes only the most immediate example of the principle of mortality and of the inevitability of material decay and putrefaction.... And the portrayal of the crucified Christ that concludes the sermon remains amongst the most powerful statements in Donne's religious prose.

To say that the sermon itself was not anticlimactic is not to say that it can have the same power for us as for the actual audience. Both the dying man and the artifact would have been important. Even for a spellbinder like Donne, his presence in the pulpit then would have been a rare moment; and in his very self-conscious staging of it can be found much of the intended effect on his audience. Walton's account of Donne's final days—his return from Essex to deliver the sermon, the delivery itself before the king and the Whitehall audience, his order that a life-size burial effigy be drawn prematurely, his contemplation of that drawing as his 'hourly object'—reveals parts of a whole.

There is a consciousness of the interrelationship between his own person, the artifacts embodying or expressing it, and the communal Body including both person and artifacts. Familiar assumptions here reach back to Donne's beginnings. His abiding sense of the body as a legitimate medium of truth and of the human need to read it... were revealed in the conception of the body as a 'book' as early as the love poetry in *'To his Mistris Going to Bed'* and *'The Exstasie'* and later in the verse letter *'To Sir Edward Herbert, at Julyers.'* The body's experience must be understood and known by an attentive reason. Likewise, we find the assumption that artifacts are surrogate bodies necessary for expressing truth. Such diverse works as *'The Canonization,' 'The Relique,' The Anniversaries,* the verse letters, and the *Devotions* reveal this assumption.

Walton's nervous estimate of Donne's order for the burial effigy as showing 'a desire of glory or commendation... rooted in the very nature of man' is not the only interpretation that can be given of Donne's motives. In the *Devotions* Donne assumes that his own diseased body has significance for other members of the participating Body. This significance is embodied in the literary artifact, which must be considered rationally by members of Donne's audience just as Donne must consider the events of his immediate experience. In *Deaths Duell* Donne's own person is not explicitly expressed in the artifact, but it would have been tangibly present. As members of the same Body as Donne, his auditors could have participated, in a very immediate way, in the significance of his dying body....At bottom is operating the elemental bodily consciousness that... [is] one key factor in Donne's epistemology and psychology and which, in *Deaths Duell*, provokes the fear of physical death and dissolution of bodily identity. The imminence of Donne's own death would exacerbate that fear in members of his audience.

The fearful appeal to this bodily consciousness is answered by the climactic image of the crucified Christ, with its assurance that through identification with death itself, in the pattern of Christ's suffering death, fear can be transformed into hope. Only through conformity to Christ that bends man's will to God's through penitentially crucifying sin, in humility, obedience, and patience, can one escape the fear of death. Donne's assurance of his own resurrection from sin through conformity to Christ in the *Devotions* and Walton's account of his joyful assurance of salvation during the days before his death suggest that Donne would have viewed his own wasted body as an example of penitential conformity to Christ's suffering death. Thus, the vivid image of the dying man is fulfilled in the vivid depiction of the suffering God as its pattern.

The audience is invited, implicitly, to participate in Donne as one exemplary member of the Body and, explicitly, to conform to the suffering and death of Christ the Head. In accordance with his Lenten purposes, '*Crucifying* of that *sinne* that governes thee' to achieve conformity, Donne pulls tight the strings of bodily consciousness with his image of the suffering incarnate Word'There wee leave you in that *blessed dependancy*, to *hang* upon *him* that *hangs* upon the *Crosse*, there *bath* in his *teares*, there *suck* at his *woundes*, and *lye downe in peace* in his *grave*, till hee vouchsafe you a *resurrection*, and an *ascension* into that *Kingdome*, which hee hath *purchas'd for you*, with the *inestimable price* of his *incorruptible blood*. Amen.' Only this palpable image of Christ can change bodily fears into hope through acceptance of the body's own necessary death and resurrection.

Donne keeps our attention on Christ's bodily suffering as,

increasingly, the sermon, like the development of Donne's own thought, converges on the Cross. Divine love inspires Christ's freely given love: *Many waters quench not love,* Christ's tryed many; He was *Baptized* out of his *love,* and his love determined not there; He wept over *Jerusalem* out his love, and his love determined not there; He *mingled blood* with *water* in his *agony* and that determined not his love; hee *wept pure blood,* all his blood at all his eyes, at all his pores, in his *flagellation* and *thornes (to the Lord our God belong'd the issues of blood)* and these *expressed,* but these did *not quench his love.*

Love of Christ, in return, inspires penitential conformity in body and tripartite soul, thereby converting the forces of annihilation and recreating man the damaged goal of Creation. In the suffering of the Cross that pays sin's debt, God shows to man the pattern in body and soul that mortifies sin. Donne's emphasis upon the humanity of the Word, his very palpable physical and psychological suffering, brings the specifically human together with the larger metaphysical power of the Word. In the explicit conformity built on love, humility, obedience, patience, and acceptance of suffering and death, being is recreated. And Donne, in offering his own accomplished suffering to the audience, exemplifies this recreation for others, thereby, like Paul, fulfilling the suffering of Christ in his own flesh for the Body's sake.

Consistent with his earlier works, Donne stresses that this meeting of the personal and metaphysical occurs in time. Donne ends *Deaths Duell* at the end of his own circle with yet another meditation on time that places importance on the given moment. In the sermon the movement from fear to conformity with Christ, from death of the body to the resurrection of hope, recreates time. The sermon's initial weight on the omnipresence of death points to the negativity of fallen time'We celebrate our owne funeralls with cryes, even at our own birth, as though our *threescore and ten years life* were spent in our mothers labour, and our circle made up in the first point thereof.' Similarly, the progression of fallen time is crippled and reversed'That which we call life, is but *Hebdomada mortium, a week of deaths,* seaven dayes, seaven periods of our life spent in dying, *a dying seaven times over*, and there is an end. *Our birth dyes* in *infancy*, and our *infancy* dyes in *youth*, and *youth*, and the rest dye in *age*, and *age* also dyes, and *determines all.*'

Against the degeneration of time through death, Donne, fittingly himself a dying man nearing his own last day, offers the model of Christ's last day. Gradually, the sermon conforms time itself to Christ, thereby re-informing time according to the Incarnate Word:

Take in the *whole day* from the *houre* that *Christ received* the *passeover* upon *Thursday, unto* the *houre* in which hee *dyed* the *next day*. Make *this* present *day* in thy *devotion*, and consider what *hee did*, and remember what *you have done*. Before hee *instituted and celebrated* the *Sacrament*, (which was *after* the *eating of the passeover*) hee proceeded to that *act* of *humility*, to *wash his disciples feete*, even, *Peters, who* for a while *resisted* him; In thy *preparation* to the holy and blessed *Sacrament*, hast thou with a sincere *humility* sought a *reconciliation* with all the *world*, even with those that have been *averse* from it, and *refused* that *reconciliation* from thee? If so (and not else) thou hast spent that *first part* of this his *last day* in a *conformity* with him.

The day of Donne's sermon and the day before Christ's death are both special days. For Donne, it is his last sermon before an expected and welcome death, a point close to the Omega of his circle of time. For Christ, it is the period of a single day immediately before his Crucifixion, likewise a point close to the Omega of his exemplary circle. The auditors, like Donne and Christ, must face the continuing possibility that each day may end their circles. Each day is a '*criticall* day' that must be regarded as potentially man's last to be brought into conformity with Christ's last day.

Donne's visible conformity to Christ's pattern will dilate this particular moment in the respective lives of his listeners. Thus, *Deaths Duell* speaks to the immediate moment, to both individuals and to the communal Body, applying these special days of Donne and Christ. As in the *Devotions* Donne is speaking to members of the Body, the Church, invoking the image of Christ the Head; and he is speaking to members of the Body, the Kingdom, here in the presence of its regal Heart.

All members hear the same pattern for fulfilling time. As elsewhere in Donne's works, time is fulfilled within the human soul. The reference points are psychological and epistemological; and the guiding conformity to Christ, which is so crucial in Donne's theology of participation, works within a larger conformity of the tripartite human soul to the tripartite God, In the *divisio* in preparation for 'these three considerations' of the three meanings of *exitus mortis* that make up the sermon, Donne establishes parallels to the three Persons of the Trinity:

In all these three lines then, we shall looke upon these words; *First*, as the *God* of *power*, the *Almighty Father* rescues his servants from the jawes of death*And then*, as the *God* of *mercy*, the glorious *Sonne* rescued us, by taking upon himself this *issue of deathAnd then* betweene these two, as the *God of comfort*, the *Holy Ghost* rescues us from all discomfort by his blessed impressions before hand, that what manner of death soever be ordained for us, yet this *exitus mortis* shall be *introitus in vitam* our *issue in death*, shall be an *entrance into everlasting life*. Similarly, the sermon works on all members of the tripartite Image in the human soulon the reason in the frequent request that the auditors consider the matter of the sermon, especially the experience of Christ; on the will in the stimulation of love for Christ's loving sacrifice; and on the memory in the request that believers remember their own sinful actions in comparison with Christ's example. The recreation of time requires attentive efforts by the entire soul.

In the *Devotions* reason considers each moment in time according to the principles informing it. The same assumption in *Deaths Duell* makes conformity to Christ dependent on the soul's keen rational awareness. The audience is asked to consider the significance of moments in Christ's 'day' ending with his death. 'Make *this* present *day* that *day* in thy *devotion*, To consider what *hee did*, and remember what *you have done*. Donne repeatedly points to the importance of considering the matter of the sermon, 'to consider with mee how to *this God the Lord belong'd the issues of death*, explicitly sharpening the audience's rational attention. Implicitly, the audience is also being asked to consider the dying preacher standing before them, just as they are asked to consider his diseased body in the *Devotions*. The dramatic force of the given moment in Donne's works develops in these later works into a full- blown sense of temporal events as a form of communication from God to man, to be understood and known. When Donne speaks of God as Logos, who necessarily proceeds logically, for whom a minute in time is a 'syllogisme' he is emphasizing the rational dimension in that communication. The audience in *Deaths Duell* must consider not only Donne's spoken words, but also his presence in the pulpit as a form of temporal communication from God. This is necessarily the domain of reason's same bright attention emphasized throughout Donne's works as the condition for fulfilling temporal life. Reason must also attentively arbitrate the will's experience in love and examine anew what memory comprehends.

That Donne would expect the members of his audience to consider not only his words but also he as part of the same event [brings us to a crucial matter in understanding Donne's works] namely, Donne's own person as a factor in his works. The complexities of Donne's nature have set off varied and, at times, conflicting responses. Clearly, Donne was unsettled as a young man; it is nonetheless possible to determine those elements which dominate his essential nature even at that time. Merritt Hughes's clear warning against 'kidnapping' Donne in our own modern preconceptions still exhorts us to see Donne as he wished to be seen. Behind the restlessness and the chafing in Donne there was a yearning for constancy.... In Donne's restatement of Paul's joyous fulfillment of Christ suffering in his own flesh for the Body's sake, Donne expressed a Calling that, in the received forms of his Faith, fulfilled his yearning for constancy.

Walton's chronicle of Donne's final days, an account which his modern counterpart R. C. Bald regards as unexceptionable, suggests that Donne's faith was fulfilled in his death. But death does not compromise his abiding sense that the Body of Christ, the physical and spiritual community that contributes to the constancy of Donne's mature being, would continue to span heaven and earth after his death. Though Donne himself was spiraling closer to his circular God, whose mercy ever moved perpendicularly above the believer, he recognized even in his last acts the responsibility to other participating members. Donne's relationship to the community was not always so resolved, and his life on the circumference of his temporal circle was not always so fulfilled. In the third satire there is the incomplete search for a 'true religion,' the injunction to 'doubt wisely' in a progress spiraling upward ('about must goe') to Truth on a 'huge' hill. In *'A Valedictionforbidding Mourning,'* its calmness a marked contrast to other love poems of Donne, is expressed the conviction that mutual love bonded by spiritual union can make an individual, private circle just.

And in *'Good Friday, 1613. Riding Westward'* he affirms the need for affliction to turn his sinful soul in its circular, westward movement back to its eastern origin, in conformity with the suffering Christ. However, in Donne's maturity, in his priestly Calling, he did achieve a personal assurance and constancy that fulfilled life along the circumference of his circle. In his assurance of his conformity with Christ, he offered his bodily presence to fulfill Christ's suffering for the sake of the communal Body. And in his literary works he embodied his sense of the epistemological and psychological immediacies that make up that conformity.

To conclude, it is in the two major artifacts in his last remains, the sermon *Deaths Duell* and the death effigy in St Paul's, that we can find the final measure of the Calling that fulfilled his life. The sermon, although it now lacks the startling ambience centered in the dying man, still leaves its deep imprint on readers in the way it emboldens the problems of mortality and time. The death effigy likewise leaves its imprint, with its composed face accepting the inevitability of death. Donne would have appreciated time's witty justification of his personal value for the Body; the marble effigy remains, but the original building was destroyed by fire. Many modern readers would say that both the sermon and the effigy, like his other literary works, have outlasted the system of belief that inspired Donne. Yet it is not too fanciful to suggest—and we can perhaps appreciate this irony better than Donne—that his artifacts still inform a kind of Body in so far as they unite us in asking that we know and feel the large forces that shape us. That Donne's own works accomplish this successfully, often in the most immediate ways, make them a coherent and understandable achievement that can be said to help fulfill life on the circumference of time's circle.

The Plot Of Donne's Anniversaries

"What draws the reader to the novel," Walter Benjamin once wrote, "is the hope of warming his shivering life with a death he reads about." Such, too, is one appeal of John Donne's Anniversaries, which promise to warm their cold readers with the radiance of Elizabeth Drury's death. Moreover, though the poems are far from novelistic, a teleological principle informs them which can properly be called plot, defined by Peter Brooks as "the internal logic of the discourse of mortality." In "A Funerall Elegie," first printed with An Anatomy of the World in 1611, Donne himself represents the girl's truncated life as though it were a story in a book:

He which not knowing her sad History,
Should come to reade the booke of destiny,
How faire and chast, humble and high shee'ad beene,
Much promis'd, much perform'd, at not fifteene,
And measuring future things, by things before,
Should turne the leafe to reade, and read no more,
Would thinke that eyther destiny mistooke,
Or that some leafes were tome out of the booke.

"Life story" is an easy metaphor, but taking it seriously is harder. In the Anniversaries Donne takes it so, which means that his telling of Elizabeth Drury's "sad History" may be read first neither as typology nor as exhortation but as a plot. Her life, as rendered in these poems, reveals a principle of order, though incompletely realized, and energy of procession, though imperfectly discharged. Her mourners become readers of narrative, and Donne's readers become mourners, driven to find a proper end for her story. They keep turning the pages.

Most interpretations of the Anniversaries—whether religious, symbolic, generic, or rhetorical—relate the two poems to each other in ultimately no teleological ways. It is often assumed that the two installments constitute one whole poem, but that wholeness is usually taken to be defined by what Barbara Lewalski has called Donne's "coherent symbolic meaning and method as well as... careful logical articulation." As a result of this assumption, interpreters specialize the poems in order to view them all at once.

According to Paul Parrish, for example, the poems in their "complementary nature" are like a diptych. Ruth Fox claims that Donne "does not anatomize... in order that he may then leave the first process and move to progression"; instead, she contends, the two Anniversaries enact "concurrent processes" that "depend on and comment on each other" (p. 533). It could be said that claims for synchronic awareness of the two elegies derive from the necessary circularity of hermeneutics and not from the poems themselves. A teleological reading, by contrast, looks for that narrative wholeness which gives the Anniversaries a relation like that between desire and satisfaction, a movement through tension to pleasure.

In a controversial essay of 1970, Carol M. Sicherman suggested that "the two parts of the poem relate to each other as draft to revision, as problem to tentative solution," a solution in which crystallize "the ultimate insights which unify the entire bipartite poem." She aimed to uncover these insights by reading the Anniversaries" for themselves alone" (p. 127), an attempt to which historical scholars naturally objected. But a narrative or teleological reading of the poems does not have to repeat Sicherman's New Critical claims. In fact, it much more logically entails two other beliefsfirst, that the Anniversaries are not timeless at all but bound to time; second, that their course may hold much ambivalence and disunity. Because reading the poems for their logic of mortality need not rest on New Critical assumptions, it can, twenty;years later, reassert a psychological and consecutive way of interpreting the poems.

This approach, if it does nothing else, respects the

publication history of the poems. "A man... who died at thirty-five will appear to remembrance at every point in his life as a man who dies at the age of thirty-five," Benjamin writes, because "the 'meaning' of his life is revealed only in his death" (pp. 100-101). The remark bears poignantly, of course, on Elizabeth Drury, who died in December 1610 at "not fifteene" ("A Funerall Elegie," line 86), but it also illuminates the publication of the Anniversaries.

Soon after the girl's death, perhaps encouraged by his sister, who had known her, Donne wrote "A Funerall Elegie" and presented it to her parents, noble mourners but also prospective patrons. In return, the Drurys asked him to compose a Latin epitaph for their daughter's monument and, late in 1611, to accompany them to France. Donne complied with both requests, but before he left England in November, he also wrote and got into print the text which we call The First Anniversarie. It was his first published poem. As far as a public audience was concerned, however, no text by that name existed until some months later.

An Anatomy of the World, the short form of Donne's original title, became The First Anniversarie only when it was reprinted together with a new poem, which he had written in France, called The Second Anniversarie or Of the Progres of the Soule.Thus, without changing a line, the 1612 volume turned An Anatomy into a previously nonexistent work. The meaning or real name of the poem could thenceforward be revealed in its relation of sequence as closure with The Second Anniversarie. Circumstances of the publication strengthened the temporal dimension of both poems, inviting readers to interpret the Anniversaries, now first and second, by appealing to codes of succession or narrative.

I

If the Anniversaries have a plot, one should be able to describe its shape and the agents or "characters" that carry it out. Broadly speaking, Donne arranges his agents in the familiar triangle of the morality plays, where a central figure wavers between good and bad influences. Here that figure is not Elizabeth Drury but Donne himself as narrator and surrogate hero. The girl (even if she represents "the Idea of a Woman," as Donne reportedly said to Ben Jonson stands on one side of him as both the goal and the model for his quest. On the other stands the world, both as scene and as antagonist.

This triangle is oriented, in turn, toward a fictive audience, those implied readers to whom the Anniversaries are addressed—fictive because it does not coincide with either Donne's coterie of 1611-1612 or his new public readership. By definition, its members are prepared to measure the girl's worth and participate in Donne's poetic action. By doing so, he says in The First Anniversarie, they can become "new creatures" and "weedlesse Paradises" (lines 76, 82). In The Second Anniversarie, this fictive audience is reduced by the anima mea topos to a single "insatiate" soul (line 45), but its relation to the narrative remains constant.

The audience is thus closely tied to the working out of Donne's narrative drives. "The ambitious hero," according to Brooks, "stands as a figure of the reader's efforts to construct meanings in ever-larger wholes, to totalize his experience of human existence in time, to grasp past, present, and future in a significant shape" (p. 39).In the Anniversaries, Donne stands in for Drury's readers and mourners, attempting to "make up that booke" of her life, totalizing its movement by "filling up" the "blanks" ("A Funerall Elegie," lines 101-109).

Because the story Donne tells is abstract or allegorical rather than mimetic, certain qualities need to be recognized in its agents. First, abstract narratives, as Angus Fletcher has shown, permit part and whole to exchange attributes. Consequently, the agents of these poems, like many of Spenser's characters, combine restricted natures with elaborated characterizing detail. For example, whether we conceive of the world as a trifle, cripple, monster, ghost, or cinder, Donne restricts its essence to the worst thing imaginable. Likewise, Elizabeth Drury's character is elaborated as queen, balm, alchemist, magnet, compass, harmony, paradise, and demiurge, but her characteristics all signify perfect virtue and power. This synonymy is held in common by the flanking agents of the Anniversaries. The second quality of abstract narratives makes Donne's own character somewhat different from the others, however. The logic of the narrative drives him, as Spenser's chivalric heroes are driven, to search for an idea and an identity. Moreover, this obsessive process is full of conflict. Fletcher (pp. 85-88) argues that most allegorical heroes are divided agents, not only pursuing their quest but also generating from within their helpers and opponents. So Donne here plots to split and project himself in ways that can be specified. As soon as the Anniversaries begin, the dynamic just described comes into play. Donne starts with a classic narrative gesture, a "when" clause, which specifies the moment of this action:

When that rich soule which to her Heaven is gone,
Whom all they celebrate, who know they' have one,
(For who is sure he hath a soule, unlesse
It see, and Judge, and follow worthinesse,
And by Deedes praise it? He who doth not this,
May lodge an In-mate soule, but 'tis not his.)
When that Queene ended here her progresse time,'
And, as t'her standing house, to heaven did clymbe,
Where, loth to make the Saints attend her long,
Shee's now a part both of the Quire, and Song,
This world, in that great earth-quake languished;
For in a common Bath of teares it bled,.
Which drew the strongest vitall spirits out:
But succour'd then with a perplexed doubt,
Whether the world did loose or gaine in this,
(Because since now no other way there is
But goodnes, to see her, whom all would see,
All must endevour to be good as shee,)
This great consumption to a fever turn'd,
And so the world had fits; it joy'd, it mournd. (lines 1-20)

Elaboration of characterizing detail is easy to observe here, as is Donne's nearly obsessive concentration. Also at work in these opening lines, however, is the splitting typical of an abstract hero. Ambivalence appears in small details. With good reason, for instance, Fox has called the syntax of these lines "diabolical" (p. 535). Donne weaves ten subordinate clauses into the first sentence, not even counting the tortuous, three-clause parenthesis in lines 3-6. The second sentence of the poem is another compound-complex arrangement with a difficult parenthesis of its own. A New Critic might have argued that such hypo taxis can control focus and embody mature, perhaps even "ultimate" insight. By placing subordinate clauses around a central element, a poet can defy the onward rush of normal predication and, Janus-like, appear almost omniscient. But these clauses that begin The First Anniversarie, encountered one after another, suggest little control or certainty. Instead, Donne's syntax isolates and fragments the lines of his inception. Its two predications, "this world... languished" and "this consumption... turn'd," are overwhelmed by the elements they are supposed to control.

Like syntax, imagery works against itself in this beginning. Donne's subordinate clauses, for example, associate the girl's death with images of wealth, royalty, and celestial song. In the first independent clause, however, the same event is a "great earthquake" and a bloodbath (lines 11-12). What should one make of this contrast? According to Fox, Donne opens in confusion in order to warn the reader that "the poems exist as denials of straightforward development of ideas" (p. 535). If Donne's beginning is fully "diabolical," however, its contradictory syntax and imagery can be read less as metadiscursive signals than as tokens of emotional disturbance that must be worked through.

Caught between mourning and mirth, the speaker is "succour'd... with a perplexed doubt" (line 14). His mind is trapped in what interpreters have called "deadly oscillation" (Martz, p. 40) or "inner strife" and "spiritual vacillations" (Sicherman, p. 128). Thus, from the start of the Anniversaries, one process wavers between two competing metaphors. Although his thoughts do not fit together, the speaker tries, as Samuel Johnson saw, to yoke them by violent syntax. Here, however, the psychology of violence is, in fact, its own story. In other words, such incongruity is less an aporia than a type of anacolouthon, which is "both a vice and a device to demonstrate emotion." What fails as syntax may succeed as plotting. The problem of this inception is repeated throughout The First Anniversarie, as Donne, by continuing to wrench together incommensurate attitudes, generates the "middle" that narrative requires. In the satiric passages which actually dissect the old world, he seems willing to disrupt traditional orders. For example, Donne claims with some relish that "in length is man, / Contracted to an inch, who was a span" (lines 135-36), just as the earth's face, once imagined in "round proportion" (line 285) is now seen to be disfigured by "warts, and pock-holes" (line 300).

These apparent devaluations of the world are crossed by other gestures, however. Donne cannot really do away with worldly orders by simply manipulating scale. When he says that an adult is really only a pigmy or that the rondure of the earth is really all scabs and pits, he implicitly invokes the normal scales of anatomy and geometry. Thus the heralded anatomy does not ever dismember the world's body. Instead, it enacts a series of displacements where, counter to the normally anagogical path of Christian allegory, the objects of satire slip backward in being. This process can best be described as katagogy, a leading downward.

Taking the satiric portions of The First Anniversarie as downward-tending allegory brings them into line with what happens in the other portions of the poem. Thus when he speaks of Elizabeth Drury, Donne reverses the exponential series and raises his claims for her to the highest imaginable power. For example, a most familiar couplet asserts that "new Philosophy cals all in doubt, / The Element of fire is quite put out" (lines 205-206). Soon after, however, Donne claims that "Ayre, and Fire but thicke grosse bodies were, / And liveliest stones but drowsie, 'and pale to her" (lines 367-68). Martz originally complained that Donne barely connects his praise of the dead child with his anatomy of the world; this complaint was not strong enough, however. The halves of the poem are not merely tangential to each other but powerfully contradictory. Having given this ambivalent structure of feeling to his Anniversaries for Elizabeth Drury, Donne must continue to generate an onward impulse for her history. This necessity draws attention to those places where, in their narrative "middle," the poems shift between satire and encomium. W.M. Lebans has claimed that Donne's way of turning from "meditative insight" or "ecstatic contemplation" to the inescapable fact of death always "surprises and impresses with a sense of control." Whether consciously or not, in these turns Donne never simply juxtaposes Elizabeth Drury and the world but always asserts some logical or metaphorical relation between them. Moreover, he finds a distinctive way of making these turns in each Anniversarie.

Some lines on the colorlessness of the world may illustrate how Donne moves between satire and encomium in The First Anniversarie:

Sight is the noblest sense of any one,
Yet sight hath onely colour to feed on,
And colour is decaydsummers robe growes
Duskie, and like an oft dyed garment showes.
Our blushing redde, which us'd in cheekes to spred,
Is inward sunke, and onely'our soules are redde.
Perchance the world might have recovered,
If she whom we lament had not beene dead:
But shee, in whom all white, and redde, and blue
(Beauties ingredients) voluntary grew,
As in an unvext Paradise...
Shee, shee is dead; shee's dead. (lines 353-69)

Here the turn comes in a conditional clauseif Elizabeth Drury had not died, the world might have regained its original colors. Yet like the opening sentences of the poem, this subjunctive, contrary-to-tact clause crosses itself with its own contradictionsif the girl had not died (but she did), the world might have recovered (but it has not). In The First Anniversarie, we find this structure of feeling almost every time Donne moves between the dead child and the world. On the plane of grammar, these subjunctive turns. advance and reiterate the central conflict.

In The Second Anniversarie, Donne manages his turns somewhat differently. For example, in another passage about colors, Donne describes the flight of the dead girl's soul through the elemental and planetary spheres of the universe. Along its path, the soul (like Milton's Raphael) resolutely declines to settle disputes in theoretical astronomy. Instead, "ere shee can consider how shee went," the soul "At once is at, and through the Firmament" (lines 205-206). Donne continues:

And as these stars were but so many beades
Strunge on one string, speed undistinguish'd leades
Her through these spheares, as through the beades, a string,
Whose quicke succession makes it still one thing:
As doth the Pith, which, least our Bodies slacke,
Strings fast the little bones of necke, and backe;
So by the soule doth death string Heaven and Earth,
For when our soule enjoyes this her third birth,
(Creation gave her one, a second, grace,)
Heaven is as neare, and present to her face,
As colours are, and objects, in a roome
Where darknesse was before, when Tapers come. (lines 207-18)

The ancient figure of plot as a soul (or, here, as a soul of string or pith) conjoins narrative and personal continuity. Having reasserted that identity in vivid detail, Donne is ready to turn from praise to exhortation:

This must, my soule, thy long-short Progresse bee;
To'advance these thoughts, remember then, that shee,
Shee, whose faire body no such prison was,
But that a soule might well be pleas'd to passe
An Age in her...
Shee, shee, thus richly,'and largely hous'd, is gone.

"To'advance these thoughts"this way of moving between clauses, typical of The Second Anniversarie, makes a new narrative gesture. The turnings of The First Anniversarie, as I have suggested, imply a subjunctive, conditional structure of feeling that is symptomatic of inner division. Now, though, Donne begins to use fortiori reasoningif Elizabeth Drury can relinquish her body to death, surely, he reasons, he can part with his own "small lump of flesh" (line 164). Although this sort of turn is also conditional and thus permits conflict to be implied (one can imagine a number of rebuttals to almost any a fortiori conclusion), the feeling here is far less troubled than before. Donne's images of praise and condemnation do not move closer together as we approach the end of the Anniversaries, but he does change the trajectory of his crossings between them. To explain this difference, we must return to the notion of plot, considering the unusual dynamic of these poems.

II

I have suggested that Donne, much like many allegorical heroes, acts out the duality of his aversion and desire. Before turning to the end of this action, I would like to introduce as possibly fruitful analogies three similar abstract plots. In the Bible, and not just in its overt narratives, plot often unfolds from inward division. The Psalms, for example, often act out dual impulses to preserve and destroy. The duality is strongly marked in the phrases of exile that are so familiar from the Authorized Version"If I forget thee, O Jerusalem, let my right hand forget her cunning.

If I do not remember thee, let my tongue cleave to the roof of my mouth" (Psalm 137:5-6). The imagination of revenge in the same psalm is no less strong, however, for the community taunts the "daughter of Babylon" with murderous wishes"Happy shall he be that taketh and dasheth thy little ones against the stones" (verses 8-9). Thus both hatred and longing generate little conditional narratives here. The Epistle to the Romans provides a more complex example of duality.

Paul first uses a favourite topic of the Psalms, claiming to "delight in the law of God after the inward man." But then, interiorizing the Psalmist's exile, he defers redemption even as he imagines it"I see another law in my members, warring against the law of my mind, and bringing me into captivity to the law of sin which is in my members."

This new captivity causes Paul to cry, "O wretched man that I am! who shall deliver me from the body of this death?" (Romans 7:18-24). I take a final analogy from Plato's Republic, where, in Book 4, Socrates tells a story about a certain Leontius, who one day happened upon the corpses of some executed criminals. According to Socrates, Leontius "felt a desire to see them, and also a dread and abhorrence of them." From this minimal conflict, something like Donne's in the Anniversaries, an ambiguous action unfolds. "For a time," Plato writes, Leontius "struggled and covered his eyes, but at length the desire got the better of him; and forcing them open, he ran up to the dead bodies, saying, 'Look, ye wretches, take your fill of this fair sight'."

These examples act out conflicts in two different ways. The Psalmist keeps his affective objects, Jerusalem and Babylon, entirely distinct and recognizes no subterranean passage between them. Also confronted with the logic of mortality, however, both Paul and Leontius are caught between contradictory impulses—to look or not to look at the corpses, to delight in the law of God or in "all manner of concupiscence" (Romans 7:8). Neither two nor one, their single natures have double names. In the context of the Republic, the story of Leontius illustrates such inward divisions, coming as part of Plato's analysis of human psychology. It shows why reason and desire, the two chief faculties of the soul, require a third entity, spirit, to shuttle between them.

If Donne, too, moves between aversion and desire in the Anniversaries, then it is fair to ask which of these narratives his resembles. At first, the dualities of the Anatomy and the Progres seem most like the Psalmist's decisive oppositions. The "Idea of a Woman" and the anatomy of a dying world appear to remain distinct and unbridgeable in the poems, like Jerusalem and Babylon. As long as Donne keeps his objects of desire and aversion apart, he may hate the world and love Elizabeth Drury at once, and with equanimity. As I have suggested, however, the Anniversaries, once in motion, in fact bring these poles of value into conflict. Just as Leontius both wants and abhors the pleasure of seeing the corpses, so, by predicating two things at once, Donne both allows and represses a desire to speak death. In each case, the repressed wishes crowd to the surface of speech or action. Leontius defends against contradiction by personifying his eyes, casting on them his undesirable desire. But the wish, projected, remains his. Nor can Donne escape any better the antithetical pull of his desires, enacted at the level of syntax. He may inwardly delight in the holy death of Elizabeth Drury, but, like Paul, he feels a different principle at work in his members. The narrative premise of the Anniversaries is thus Donne's attempt to maneuver among his contrary impulses toward the world in its systems and scales.

The life these systems constitute, with humanity at its centre, is vital and beautiful. In turn, however, worldly life is sinful and dying. As it dies, humanity is being decentered. In both parts of the Anniversaries, Donne would like to join and not to join in this paradoxical world-structure. What gets him over this conflict—and thus what gives the poems as narrative an ending—is finally a change in his defensive strategies.

In The First Anniversarie, as I have suggested, Donne is torn between wishes and finds a defence against ambivalence or, in theological terms, against temptation, by splitting the world into objects of desire and aversion. Following the Psalmist's way, he then "kills" the world symbolically by saying, "the world is dead," attacking the signifier to hurt the signified. But this defence against ambivalence is insufficiently complex. Donne's original wish in the Anniversaries is not simply that the world may die. It is rather"May what is evil in me die so that what is good may live." In The First Anniversarie, however, this original wish never comes out straight. It emerges instead as the claim that Elizabeth Drury's death has slain the world.

True, Donne really believes that the girl survives both in Heaven and in the register of fame. This comfort summons its antithesis, however. It may be granted that the good is not really dead, but neither then is the world. Joseph Hall (or whoever wrote the introductory poem called "To the Praise of the Dead, and the Anatomy") pertinently asked Donne, "How can I consent the world is dead / While this muse lives?" (lines 7-8). How, indeed? As some have argued, The First Anniversarie fails, if it is considered as an attempt to resolve Donne's inward distress. This beginning cannot, in fact, break the spell of the world on Donne's narrative. Instead, he uses the very tropes in his blessings that he rejects in his curses. It can mean little to call Elizabeth Drury a beautiful queen if royalty is dead and beauty with it. Such opposites contaminate one another in the beginning of the girl's story and supply the psychodynamism of those curious transitions, with their contrary-to-fact grammar, in The First Anniversarie.

Although many have felt that The Second Anniversarie is more successful than the first, Donne begins it by repeating his old defenses against doubleness or example, in the opening lines, which endeavor to explain why Donne has survived a year since Elizabeth Drury's death, a group of similes repeats vividly his attempt to kill the world. One, reminiscent of the story of Leontius, likens the world's movements to the last twitchings of a decapitated corpse:

His eies will twinckle, and his tongue will roll,
As though he beckned, and cal'd backe his Soul,
He graspes his hands, and he puls up his feet,
And seemes to reach, and to step forth to meet
His soule. (lines 13-17)

Such men's final confessions were one origin of the novel and of its warmth for the shivering survivors, grimly noted by Benjamin. But these bodily movements of the condemned, Donne says, are motiveless signification; like this man,. the world dies in dumb futility. Imperatives throughout The Second Anniversarie particularize that death. "Thinke thy selfe laboring now with broken breath," Donne insists, "Thinke thy selfe parch'd with fevers violence," "Thinke that thou hearst thy knell" or "'Thinke that thy body rots" (lines 90, 96, 99, 115).

But as the Anniversaries move toward their end, there is a subtle change in Donne's defensive strategy. Before, he repressed worldly desire by saying that the world is dead. Now he meets the same desire for the world with an injunction"Think thyself dead," that is, "remember that you must die." A clear difference separates this strategy from the former. To say that the world is dead is unconsciously to literalize a metaphor. It is wish-fulfillment. By thinking himself dead, however, Donne becomes conscious of the metaphorical gesture required of one who would assume a dead man's perspective. Imagining something certain to happen, his own death, he recognizes at the same time that he is not dead yet. This recognition, in turn, gradually frees energy that had earlier gone into repression. Gone at the end of The Second Anniversarie is the effort to kill the world by vivisection. To the last, Donne still questions whether health, beauty, and honour can have lasting meaning, but he does not vainly try to define life out of existence. Thus a kind of freedom eventuates from the logic of mortality in the Anniversaries, the central figure of this plot no longer squandering but sublimating his desires.

Two final points of contrast between the first and second installment may further define the curve of Donne's plotting. The first contrast concerns illness and memory. In The First Anniversarie, Donne imagines that once she gets free of "the carcasse of the old world," Elizabeth Drury will create "a new world" and populate it with "new creatures" (line 76), his fictive audience, who will in turn extend the girl's virtue by imitation. Remembering Elizabeth Drury is not sufficient to prevent illness, however. Donne admits that "though to be thus Elemented, arme / These Creatures, from home-borne intrinsique harme" (lines 79-80), no small gain,

Yet, because outward stormes the strongest breake,
And strength it selfe by confidence growes weake,
This new world may be safer, being told
The dangers and diseases of the old. (lines 85-88)

Elizabeth Drury's creatures assure themselves of health by rehearsing the symptoms of "venemous sinne," transmitted to humankind by "some lorraine Serpent" (lines 83-84).

As Freud knew, however, repeating is not remembering, especially when illness is alienated, attributed to someone else, an old world. The Second Anniversarie breaks the compulsion to repeat not by further rehearsal but by a deliberate and paradoxical forgetfulness: Forget this world, and scarse thinke of it so,

As of old cloaths, cast off a yeare agoe.
To be thus stupid is Alacrity;
Men thus lethargique have best Memory. (lines 61-64)

Closing the abstract motion of the poems, Donne finally

abandons his defence against wanting and not wanting the world. In the end, remembering and forgetting are extinguished in prophecy.

The idea of the prophetic leads to a final point of contrast between the two Anniversaries. In the first, Donne compares himself with Moses, Elizabeth Drury with the Scripture itself. God gave Moses a song, recorded in Deuteronomy 32 that encapsulated "The Law, the Prophets, and the History" (line 465). The Israelites might otherwise have forgotten their story. Just so, Donne claims, his song can preserve the essence of Elizabeth Drury's story, even though it may be a "matter fit for Chronicle, not verse" (line 460). The Second Anniversarie ends with a similar analogy. Again putting himself into a triangular relationship with God and the dead girl, Donne seeks to define the status of his own voice:

Since his will is, that to posteritee,
Thou shouldst for life, and death, a patterne bee,
And that the world should notice have of this,
The purpose, and th'Autority is his;
Thou art the Proclamation; and I ame
The Trumpet, at whose voice the people came. (lines 523-28)

As Lewalski has shown, in the metaphor of the trumpet Donne claims for himself both the prophetic and the priestly office. Moreover, the lines may recall the unique trumpet blast that announces the theophany of Yahweh and the giving of the Law upon Sinai in Exodus 19.

If these triangles that end the Anniversaries were identical, we might lose confidence in a teleological reading of the poems. But they are not the same. What separates them can be read in a third triad, too easily dismissed, at the very end of The First Anniversarie. There Donne figures not between God and the people but between death and life. Verse, he says, has a "middle nature" between the grave, which "keeps bodies," and heaven, which "keepes soules" (lines 473-74). What verse keeps or "enroules" is "the fame" (line 474). Verse holds out neither certain corruption nor certain bliss but rather something that shuttles between them. So long as its movements are reified and alienated from the versifier, this shuttling may seem untroubled. But Donne's task, and ours when we read the Anniversaries as a plot or discourse of mortality, is precisely to negotiate what is taken as settled in the final biblical analogies of the poems.

"There is therefore now no condemnation to them which are in Christ Jesus, who walk not after the flesh, but after the Spirit" (Romans 8:1). These trumpeting words announce the end of Paul's "life story" of division and ambivalence. In his Anniversaries for Elizabeth Drury, Donne blows a similar blast but accomplishes something else. He imagines the temporal accommodations by which such freedom as Paul describes might be narrated.

Criticism by A. Alvarez

Alvarez is a prominent British critic, editor, poet, and novelist. In his writings of the early 1960s, he campaigned against what he viewed as the excessive gentility of British poetry since World War II, advocating instead poetry of extreme personal, emotional, and political import. In his insistence upon seeing the whole individual, Alvarez stands as a modern Metaphysical, himself a follower of 'the school of Donne.' In the following excerpt, he appropriates and sharpens the thematic focus of one of T. S. Eliot's assessments of Donne, outlining the nature of Donne's poetic realism.]

Donne was not only one of the most supremely intelligent poets in the language, he was also the first Englishman to write verse in a way that reflected the whole complex activity of intelligence. A number of Elizabethan poets embodied the philosophical truths of their period in verse of considerable elegance and power. But Donne created a poetic language of thought, a mode of expression which so took for granted the intellectual tone and preoccupations of his time that it made of them, as it were, the stage on which the intimate give-and-take of personal poetry was played. He was, in short, the first intellectual realist in poetry.

Eliot first made much the same point as early as 1923 in an article that has, to my knowledge, never been reprinted [see excerpt dated 1923].... The difference between the time at which

Eliot wrote this and our own lies in the way in which psychology can now be taken more or less for granted. The complexity and contradictoriness of the emotions are no longer fighting subjects. Instead, the contemporary problem is to write with intelligence that recognizes this complexity and controls it in all its baffling fragmentariness.

Eliot's insights into Donne's originality were largely sidetracked by later critics in their search for a technique to produce certain effects. Hence the inordinate concentration on the 'outlandish conceit', as though the whole of Metaphysical poetry were reducible to a single, rather ostentatious trick of style. I simply want to replace the stress on the element of realism in Donne, the skill by which he created a poetic language in which technique was at the service of a fullness of the intelligence.

Nowadays 'realism' usually means a certain willful harping on the facts of life, an insistence on the short, frank word and the daringly, or drearily, sordid detail. There is, of course, an element of this kind of frankness in Donne's poetry, but, as often as not, it enters when he is most classicalin, say, *'Elegie XIX. Going to Bed'*, where he is being a kind of new English Ovid. The realism I am referring to is, however something more diffused and its effect is distinctly not of grinding the reader's nose into the dirt. On the contrary, the final impression is one of a peculiarly heightened dignity.

This sense of personal dignity is at the centre of Donne's work. At the simplest level, it is his perennial theme:

She'is all States, and all Princes, I,
Nothing else is:

is an extreme but typical way of putting it. This dignity measures his distance from the more conventional Elizabethans... [and] it is at the root of his 'masculine', 'strong' style. More important, it makes for the cohesion of his work, that unity and strength which give his collected poems an importance difficult to pin down in any single one of them. He is, after all, one of the few major poets before this century whose achievement is not summed up in any one really extended work. Yet despite this unity there is considerable variation in his style. The *Elegies,* for example, seem definably younger work than the best *Songs and Sonnets.* This is due to something more than their occasional self-consciousness, which was the young Donne's fatal Cleopatra.

It is a question of technique. The key to Donne's mature style is his use of logicthe more subtle and complex the emotion, the greater the logical pressure. The mature Donne organizes his poems in such a way that each shift of feeling seems to be substantiated logically. In the *Elegies,* however, the emotions are simpler and are sustained in their singleness. He adopts a stance and then develops it dramatically, not logically. So instead of a piece of elaborate human dialectics, he leaves you with a situation presented in the vivid colouring of a more or less single strong feeling.

Even the best of the *Elegies,* in fact, are more uncomplicatedly assertive than most of Donne's other work of the same standard. *'Elegie IV. The Perfume'*, for instance, is perhaps the most inventive of all Donne's poems, but its wit is more ornamental than profoundit has gone into the puns, into the dramatic detail, into maintaining the overriding masculine independence. It is, in short, less analytic than energetic. The only deepening of tone comes at the moment when his masculinity itself is threatened:

Onely, thou bitter sweet, whom I had laid
Next mee, mee traiterously hast betraid...

It may seem odd that the perfume should inspire a couple of lines which are as moving and as moved as anything Donne ever wrote on the theme of the inconstant mistress. But the reason comes a few lines later:

By thee, the greatest staine to mans estate
Falls on us, to be call'd effeminate...

The perfume, in fact, has undermined the whole basis of this and most of the other *Elegies*the almost belligerent masculinity of the young Donne who was 'a great visitor of ladies'. The difference between the *Elegies* and Donne's maturest technique [exemplified by *'A nocturnall upon S. Lucies day, Being the shortest day'*] is large and clear.... This is the only one of Donne's poems which might validly be called 'modern'.

As in *The Waste Land*, the poet is on the rack to define a complex negative state which he apparently cannot fully understand and, what is even more pertinent to Donne's difficulty, which he cannot properly dramatize. The theme is a depression so deep as to verge on annihilation (he wrote, after all, a defence of suicide). And its root, I think, is inaction, or the impossibility of action, as he described it in the famous letter to Goodyer:

Therefore I would fain do something; but that I cannot tell what no wonder is. For to chuse, is to dobut to be no part of any body, is to be nothing.

He tries to force some kind of clearing through this swaddling depression by bringing to bear upon it an extraordinarily tense logic and a great concentration of learning. Each stanza moves forward to its own temporary resolution; the twisted, pausing, in-turning movement clears to make way for a direct but invariably negative statement:

"The worlds whole sap is sunke"

"Compar'd with mee, who am their Epitaph"

"For I am every dead thing"

"... things which are not"

"... made us carcasses"

"But I am None"...

Unlike most of his other lyrics, the logic of the *'Nocturnall'* does not exorcise his troubles. Despite all the dialectic and the learning, despite the invocation of the outside lovers and even, in the third stanza, the invocation of his own more dramatic love poems, he is left with the blank fact of his isolation. Yet although whatever pressure he brings to bear on the situation produces no clear answer, it does help him to achieve some kind of balance. The last lines of the poem—"since this / Both the yeares, and the dayes deep midnight is"— may simply be a restatement of the first—"Tis the yeares midnight, and it is the dayes, *Lucies*"—but they are a restatement with a differencethe difficult, questioning movement of the start has been resolved into a clearer, more measured statement. He finishes, that is, by *accepting* the depression, instead of trying, with all the intellectual ingenuity at his command, to wriggle through it. So the poem ends with his facing the adult necessity of living with grief and depression, instead of giving in to them. Donne's logic and learning, in short, were the prime forces in his emotional maturity *as a poet.*

It is the absence of this quality, incidentally, which marks off Shakespeare's formal verse from Donne's.... Like the *'Nocturnall','Sonnet XCIV'* is also, in its way, a rather modern poemits mode is complex, negative and founded perhaps on the same sexual anger and frustration that produced Othello's "O thou weed / Who art so lovely fair and smell's so sweet / That the sense aches at thee, would thou hadst ne'er been born!" But unlike Donne's, Shakespeare's compression is all in the imagery rather than the argument. Where Donne often begins with a straightforward situation (those famous, or infamous, dramatic openings) and then produces infinitely complicated arguments to justify it, Shakespeare begins with the abstractions and then gives them body....

However far, of course, Donne seems from the usual Elizabethan rhetoric, he did produce rhetoric of his own. He produced it for his rare public performances—the two *Anniversaries,* for example—and it was the rhetoric of the intellectual, abstract and analytic. Hence, Ben Jonson's irritated declaration "That Donne's *Anniversarie* was profane and full of Blasphemies. That he told Mr. Done, if it had been written of ye Virgin Marie it had been something to which he answered that he described the Idea of a Woman and not as she was." In the *First Anniversarie* Donne dissects 'the idea of a woman' in order to produce *An Anatomie of the World,* a theological and political analysis of the state of corruption; that is, he was using the occasion to be deliberately less Donne the poet than Donne the learned wit, author of *Pseudo-Martyr*. The *Second AnniversarieThe Progresse of the Soule,* is less abstract, more dramatic and, seemingly, more deeply felt. It is possible, indeed, that its roots were much more personal than those of the *First Anniversarie*. Donne apparently wrote it well before the date it was due, while he was staying with Sir Robert Drury in Amiens. He had gone abroad unwillingly, full of anxiety for his wife whom he left ill and pregnant. It was at Amiens that he had the terrible dream in which his wife appeared to him with a dead child in her arms. It may be, then, that 'the idea of a woman' was, in this instance, his wife, not Elizabeth Drury. Be that as it may, the dramatic meditation on death and the after-life is closer to the style of Donne the preacher or Donne the author of the *Devotions* than to that of the more analytic theologian of the *First Anniversarie*. In both poems, his public personality is foremost. Their rhetoric is formally and formidably that of the intellectual, the debater.

Yet fundamentally it is the same rhetoric which, on less public occasions, is used to heighten a personal strength and richness. Philosophy, science, logic, divinity, poetry itself are all means of enhancing the dignity of the individual. His realism lies in the richness of the resources he brings to bear upon more or less conventional subjects and his ability to falsify the full range of his response. Donne's achievement was to take a poetry over which the academic theorists were fiercely haggling, and break down the constrictions of mere aesthetic criteria; to take a dialectical form which had become rigid in centuries of scholastic wrangling, and break down its narrow casuistry; to take the sciences in all the imaginative strength of the new discoveries, and bring them all together as protagonists in the inward drama of his own powerful experience. He substantiated less a poetic technique than a form of intelligence which the most talented men of the following generation could use without, at any point, belying their natural gifts outside the realm of poetry. As a result, the style of Donne lasted until, under the imperative stresses of the Civil War, the whole mode of intelligence changed. We are now far enough removed from the tensions that split the seventeenth century to be able to judge Donne's monarchy of wit not as a trick or a fashion but as one of the greatest achievements of the poetic intelligence.

Forget the Hee and Shee"Gender and Play in John Donne.

Donne's ambivalence about self-other relations is well known to readers of Songs and Sonnets. Poised at the brink between leaving and lingering, Donne's speakers navigate the competing urgencies of intimacy and autonomy, what Roy

Roussell has described as "the twin inevitabilities of distance and desire." In fact, we can think of the dilemma as a quadrupled one, over determined by the paradox that staying behind with the beloved entails both the pleasure of contact and the risk of being consumed by that contact, while parting rewards the adventurer with independence but no guarantee of his lover's faithfulness. To strengthen a self made vulnerable by the conflictual demands of this crowded psychical threshold, Donne deploys his linguistic skill—the "masculine perswasive force" so often invoked by critics—in terms that can seem to denigrate the very women for whom the poet professes love and to undermine even the most apparently genuine expressions of devotion.

Yet the threshold is not simply or consistently a space of anxiety in Donne's love poetry, and against the need to safeguard his male identity from threatening contact with women runs a countercurrent of playful transgressiveness where Donne exhibits not only an ability to recognize women's separate identity, but also, at his most explicitly revisionary, a desire to exceed the restrictions of binary gender roles. My goal here is to suggest that Donne frequently depicts self-other dynamics in ways that extend beyond the familiar accounts of his encounters with women (e.g., pleading or arguing with them, curiosity and fear about their difference from—or similarity to—him, worry that he will never fully know them) toward a more radical gesture of testing the boundaries of gendered identity. Overlapping realms of self and other, male and female, appear throughout the Songs and Sonnets, in ways that suggest less a rhetorical (and ultimately aggressive) exchange of positions than an eager dissolution of outlinethe speaker of "The Relique" claims "we lov'd well and faithfully, / Yet knew not what wee lov'd, nor why, / Difference of sex no more wee knew" (lines 23-25); the speaker of "The Dampe" ambiguously exhorts his audience to "Kill mee as Woman, let mee die / As a meere man" (lines 21-22); the lover of "The Undertaking" suggests we "forget the Hee and Shee" (line 20). Even the "expansion" endured by the parting couple of "A ValedictionForbidding Mourning"—who like gold are pounded into an "ayery thinnesse" (lines 23-24)—transforms the distance between them as polarized, gendered selves into a continuum of connectedness, uncovering the paradox of a separation that is also a form of union.

Often, too, when Donne preserves a sense of self in relation to women without feeling annihilated by proximity to another's psyche, the connection is articulated through metaphors of sovereignty that describe both speaker and mistressthe lovers in "The Anniversarie," who "Prince enough in one another bee" (line 14), or in "The Sunne Rising," whom "Princes doe but play".

Donne's manner of blurring boundaries between male and female has typically been regarded as a way of reentrenching conventional gender roles and of suppressing the assertiveness of female sexuality. In her discussion of the elegies, for example, Achsah Guibbory argues that the "effect" of "transferring conventionally `masculine' terms... to the woman is not to question traditional distinctions," but rather acts as a "strategy" designed to expose the essential monstrousness of the female body and "reassert masculine dominance" with a vengeance. Far from transgressing gender difference in any potentially liberatory way, Guibbory contends, Donne's acts of positioning himself as feminine or rendering the female in traditionally masculine terms are ultimately antifemale, motivated both by intense anxiety about the literal fact of a woman's monarchical rule and by a more general worry about women's potential influence over him in psychological or sexual ways. Diana Benet has similarly maintained that the poet is "generally conservative," his elegies depicting sexual transgression in derisive terms that reinforce gender distinctions, making violation a crime to be "guilty" of. It has become something of a commonplace to speak of Donne's coercive "ventriloquizing," as Elizabeth Harvey does in her discussion of "Sapho to Philaenis." Harvey asserts that Donne's identification with Sappho "turns out to be an act of colonization" in which the male poet-speaker overpowers the woman by taking on her voice. Stanley Fish reiterates this notion of Donne as a desperate egotistbecause "Donne occupies every role on his poem's stage," he is "protected" from "the intrusion of any voice he has not ventriloquized." Fish also suggests that Donne's attempts at gender reversal are doomed to collapse "in the face of a fierce and familiar desire to be master of his self" —a fate that Janel Mueller once described, somewhat differently, as Donne's inevitably "gendered consciousness, his identity as a man."

Such discussions of Donne's efforts to consolidate his masculine identity through rhetorical force recall Thomas Laqueur's well-known claim that seventeenth-century conceptions of gender were bound up with a one-sex model of human physiology, in which the anatomical similarity between male and female bodies required elaborate discursive and educational codes to stabilize difference. Following this idea that gender preceded rather than derived from a sexed body, Mark Breitenberg writes that early modern male subjectivity is "inherently anxious," because the body offered no certain ground of identity"humoral psychology comprehends the male body as constantly in need of regulating its dangerous but nonetheless essential fluidity."

"If masculine identity is fundamentally unstable," argues Breitenberg, "then the assertion of gender difference... functions as a way to compensate for the lack of anatomical guarantee of difference." At the core of this struggle between body and discourse is the fact that "male and female seed were not seen as sexually specific," as Anthony Fletcher explains, so that "there was seen to be in everyone some trace at birth of gender doubleness." Breitenberg's claim that early modern male writers "stag[e] masculine loss and vulnerability for the purpose of maintaining control of the performance of one's gendered identity" suggests that the very conceptual ambiguity that allows for Donne's poetic "inversions" of gender might also be what produces, as Harvey and others maintain, a rhetoric of cementing difference.

Yet Donne's recurring articulation of gender as a fluid realm of experience indicates that he was able to construe subjectivity and intimacy alike outside of a patriarchal ideology in which "woman" is first constructed and then regulated as a threatening Other. In an article on the sapphic epistle, Janel Mueller describes Donne's "'what if' imaginings" as the poet's efforts to "[bond] with Sappho across gender difference as a subject of otherwise unimagined or unimaginable possibility," and to "[write] his way beyond the confines of a Renaissance social context." Contrary to the notion of gender play as a carnival of transgressions that always, ultimately, reaffirms power hierarchies, I would agree with Mueller that a "what if" dynamic is at work in a number of Donne's poems. As I hope to show, Donne's courting of liminal experience often registers a disruption in discursively enforced gender identity and thus offers the possibility of both identification with women and recognition of their separateness. By blueprinting Donne's play within the space-between, such familiar tropes as teardrops, maps and globes, windowpanes, and the compass bring into view this ability to resist the static constraints of the pairs (self-other, attachment-loss, male-female) that they themselves contain, as well as the poet's fascination with destabilizing gendered identity in a pleasurable, rather than a strictly policing, manner.

The notion of playing with and in threshold spaces, a central concern of object relations psychoanalysis, allows us to think anew about what might be at stake in a seventeenth-century male writer's figuration of gendered selfhood. D. W. Winnicott's concept of the "potential space" between subjects in which psychical play occurs provides an especially useful model for considering the ways in which Donne manipulates the paradox of an identity always both "male" and not fully male. (Winnicott himself notes that the "intermediate area... appears in full force in the work characteristic of the so-called metaphysical poets.") By definition a borderland activity, to play in Winnicott's sense is to invite the paradox of simultaneity; the field of play is at once illusory and real, solitary and connected. In the dialectic of this "intermediate area" between self and other, the individual's "potential" for creativity and wholeness can be fostered, even as—or perhaps precisely because—the play space imbricates internal psychical reality with the external world.

Winnicott defines play as a coalescence of reliability and intimacy, a psychic activity dependent on the self's trust that the other will neither abandon it nor intrude upon the privacy of its imagination. Anticipated by the "holding" space of nursing, play is intimate and intersubjective, a paradoxical realm in which self and other, interior and exterior, reality and fantasy, autonomy and attachment all coincide. It is the notion of loosening the borders of self in contact with the other—a way of being both "me" and "not-me" at once—that can help us to recognize how a writer like Donne might pose alternatives to his culture's construction of gender.

Winnicott's focus on the care giving "environment" leads to a theory of selfhood in which no individual exists outside of its object relationships"self" emerges from the "relational matrix," a subject's ongoing engagement with real people in the external world as well as with internalized imagos. Because object relations theory does not, then, in Jane Flax's words, "require a fixed or essentialist view of 'human nature,' it becomes a useful method of exploring the representation of self-other relations in Donne's poetry, particularly in view of what Breitenberg calls "the specifically social basis of subjectivity in the early modern period."

A notion of intersubjective "play" founded on mother-infant interaction also accords with recent historical studies of childhood that have contested earlier conclusions about the formality and emotional indifference of parent-child relations in the early modern period.

In an article addressing seventeenth-century attitudes toward infancy and nursing, Patricia Crawford argues that "contemporaries were aware of the close bonding which occurred between mother or nurse and child," and that "maternal love was recognized as a strong bond," a very symbol of "the closest human love." Crawford offers evidence that breast-feeding was believed to provide "comfort" as much as nutrition to babies and to be a source of "pleasure" to infant and woman alike Linda Pollock cites similar evidence that children were "wanted and valued," regarded with "concern and interest" by their parents in the seventeenth century, and she contends that "the closeness of the parent-child bond" was "very much a dyadic one." A further connection between object relations theory and early modern subjectivity derives from the peculiarly indeterminate nature of the body. I would argue that the early modern male infant resided, in effect, in a space of Winnicottian play, always "in-between"—subject to the instability of anatomy as well as to the absence of culturally enforced gender differentiation in the first years of life. To dissolve gender difference in poetic potential spaces—as Donne does—or to rest from the perpetual task of maintaining it is to evince the ambiguity of the body and to call up the psychical doubleness of a male infant's experience of the wholly female domain into which he was born.

As Anthony Fletcher shows, early modern "manhood" was equated with "separation from the mother," signaling an end to the "sexual twinship which began with conception and the concoction of male and female seeds." But rather than insisting that Donne is forever at work to enforce that separation, denying a changeable self or the possibility of full engagement with women who might remind him of the discomfiting possibility of his own inconstancy, we can instead explore the way in which he plays with that very paradox. In this way, Winnicott's central paradigms—holding, play, and potential space—help advance a reading of those poems where Donne's speakers evoke the autochthonous pleasures of relaxing the borders of subjectivity.

Other readers of Donne who make use of psychoanalytic theories of play, most notably Anna K. Nardo in her formidable book, The Ludic Self, have tended to discuss threshold experience as the poet's way of assuaging conflicting fears about separation and engulfment. In Nardo's study, play becomes a mediatory outlook as much as an actual activity, taken up by the adult poet in order to cope with the resurgence of childhood conflicts newly triggered by the turbulent landscape of widespread social change. Describing the witty contradictions of so many of Donne's images and poems, Nardo presents Donne as a self-conscious "player," fully aware of the fragility of the play world his language creates.

In a richly contextualized essay, William Shullenberger draws on both Nardo's and Lagan's discussions of mirroring in the mother-infant dyad, but focuses instead on triangulations in which a third party is invoked to witness acts of lovemaking (and acts of poetry making) so as to guarantee the self's stable identity. But while proposing that the most trusting moments of connectedness between adult lovers "have their experiential basis in the totalizing and exclusive intimacy of mother and child," Shullenberger does not address the possibility that Donne's male speakers get beyond an emphatically male identity. Indeed, they remain stably, steadily male. And while Nardo does assert that "the conflict [Donne] felt so keenly between separation and union" necessarily entails the female other, her descriptions of Donne's play vis-a-vis that other do not connect the intermediate space with a specific interest in transgressing gender or with reconfiguring male-female relations.

Yet it is in such moments of trespass that Donne articulates what may be his most nuanced sense of identity and of gender. Donne's overt linguistic wittiness suggests "play" in a literal sense, but he seems most actively to solicit the dialectic of play when his speakers move beyond the rules of logic and boundary and into intermediate psychical areas where they can enjoy what Winnicott called "rest"—a secure, pleasurable overlap of inner and outer, of self and other. Modern Donne scholarship seems to have moved away from an interest in the poet's "metaphysical" ingenuity and toward accounts of strain and incompletion, particularly in terms of his relation to women. Psycho-analytic readings tend to combine the two perspectives, suggesting that verbal inventiveness masks, exposes, and assuages anxiety all at once. But there is perhaps another way of thinking about gender and emotion in Donne. In what follows, I understand Donne's playfulness to serve less as a public display of his clever intellect, or as a defence against social upheaval, than as a way of rethinking the possibilities of gender and erotic connection. Through the liminality of teardrops, windows, even the transitional act of breathing, Donne creates poetic potential spaces in which speakers enjoy intimacy without threat and—even as they enter into imaginative revision of the contours of their own identity—respect the subjectivity of the women they address.

The opening stanza of "The Flea" provides a compelling example of Donne's play with gender. Here, the male seducer becomes identified with the female seduced through the mutual sucking of the insect:

Marke but this flea, and marke in this,
How little that which thou denys't me is;
It suck'd me first, and now sucks thee,
And in this flea, our two bloods mingled bee;
Thou know'st that this cannot be said
A sinne, nor shame, nor loss of maidenhead,
Yet this enjoys before it wooe,
And pampered swells with one blood made of two
And this, alas, is more than wee would do. (Lines 1-9)

The stanza radically revalues the domineering, "male" sexuality that the poem seems to be urging the woman toward. The speaker takes on the position not of the invasive flea whose behaviour serves as vehicle of his argument, but rather that of the woman herself. He announces that he was "suck'd... first" (line 3), and the ambiguity of "this" in line 5 suggests that what "cannot be said / A sinne, nor shame" is at least on some level the speaker's experience of having been pleasured by that sucking—in addition to, or even superseding, the "mingled" blood that represents a more overtly heterosexualized genital coupling (and thus loss of virginity). Coursing beneath the overt terms of the seduction is a longing to do the passive thing, not just to penetrate but to be "pampered," not simply to suck but to be sucked (with implications both of being nursed and of being "fucked"). And this sucking occurs before seduction and erection, which emphasizes that pleasure can be obtained prior to the more explicitly and conventionally masculine forms of sexual arousal signaled by "wooes" and "pampered swells."

Thus the stanza shifts its forward motion of desire and seems instead to linger in a moment of jouissance—where sucking and "being fucked" take precedence over the more obvious sequence from solicitation to tumescence to coitus to completion. Moreover, what the flea "enjoyes" seems identified as the specific pleasure of being able to suck both male and female bodies—and at least in part it is this, "alas," that is more than the male speaker will do. Thus through the knotting of one elaborate conceit, Donne manages to identify himself both with the female body and with a kind of "bisexualized" erotic pleasure.

The speaker of "The Good-Morrow" stakes a similar claim for a kind of sexuality that transcends the binarism of heterosexuality. The mood of wonder that opens the poem feels rich and tactile, and the stanza luxuriates in a polymorphous, sensual pleasure that is childlike and erotic at once:

I wonder by my troth, what thou, and I
Did, till we lov'd? were we not wean'd till then?
But suck'd on countrey pleasures, childishly?
Or snorted we in the seaven sleepers den?
'Twas so; But this, all pleasures fancies bee
If ever any beauty I did see,
Which I desir'd, and got, t'was but a dreame of thee.(Lines 1-7)

The speaker meets the morning with innocent fantasy and curiosity, as if paying a kind of marveling, rapt attention to the surprise of good feeling. What the speaker wonders about, of course, is what they "did," prior to a moment of loving that represents being "wean'd" from childish escapades. But the pleasure the stanza records is not the moment of adult sexuality that ostensibly inaugurates this "good morrow"; in fact, it is the pleasure of not being weaned. To be weaned is to be removed from and deprived of nursing at the breast; the speaker remembers—quite delightedly—having "suck'd on countrey pleasures, childishly" (line 3). (Crawford writes that since weaning was considered "a major change in the child's life," the appropriate age for it was the source of much discussion among physicians.) "Countrey pleasures" may be, as C. A. Patrides glosses in his edition, "rustic; hence unrefined," but the phrase also connotes something instinctual and unruled. The allusion to the seven sleepers' mythic two-hundred-year sleep heightens the atmosphere of snug satisfaction, because it implies not just a space in which danger may be escaped but also dragnet replenishment.

The speaker increases the sense of restful content with "den" and "snorted," which suggest a self so deeply comfortable that it can be unconscious of its surroundings. In these first few lines, pleasure is associated with deliberately and intensely "childish" behaviors—the greedy orality of suckling, the swaddled protectedness of sleep. Moreover, it is pleasure itself that the speaker sucks (rather than a breast or a body), as if it could be absorbed directly into the self—pure and undistilled.

The first is a stanza of affirmations, culminating in the speaker's unequivocal "'Twas so." The abundance of pleasure emerges through repetition ("countrey pleasures" and "all pleasures"), as well as by the fact that in both instances the word is pluralpleasures proliferate. Indeed, in the speaker's compacted phrasing, "all pleasures fancies bee" (line 5) suggests not so much that all those prior pleasures are mere fancies, but rather—and more emphatically—that all pleasures and fancies exist. But for this adult, complicated, divided love, he seems to hint, pleasure could actually be.

The ontological importance of the stanza lies in this metaphorical childhood, as a time of immediate gratification. In "The Good-Morrow," desiring means getting, with no intervening wait to survive"If ever any beauty I did see, / Which I desir'd, and got" (lines 6-7). It is also a time in which being emerges out of a bond between self and other defined by sucking and experienced not as a connection between two ultimately separable things but as undifferentiated pleasure itself. The "dreame"-like quality of this prior existence reinforces its evocation of early attachment between infant and caregiver and the infant's capacity to "create," through the illusion of omnipotence, what it needs. But the dreaminess also suggests a desire to do away with the barriers that make adult love so fraught with dangers. Here, difference itself is annulled"all pleasures fancies bee."

The fact that those prior pleasures are made meaningful

in "The Good-Morrow" by their relation to the speaker's current love affair reminds us that the explicit comparison also works to affirm the rapture of the "adult" present love over "childish" past dalliances. The poem has traditionally been read in just this way, as a statement of mature, "mutually successful love-making," to borrow David Daiches's phrase, in which younger flirtations are dismissed as insignificant. Yet the way in which the first stanza overlays a nostalgic fantasy of infant joy with those previous "fancies" complicates the idea that the poem charts a clear progression toward reciprocal, adult love. The first stanza of "The Good-Morrow" does not so much depict the activities of a literal childhood as it "wonders," through the relational vocabulary of play and potential spaces (not being "wean'd," "suck[ing]," sleeping, and seeing), about the possibility of an intersubjective eroticism free from anxiety and vigilance, physical "slaken[ing]" (line 21), or even actual death.

This is made apparent in the first lines of the second stanza—"And now good morrow to our waking soules, / Which watch not one another out of feare" (lines 8-9)—which usher in the spectre of doubt and surveillance. Where many critics take the speaker at his word, supporting his bid for the strength of the relationship ("we are not afraid of anything"), I would argue that these lines are haunted by distrust, by a surprising unease that deepens through the remainder of the poem. Why the insistence that their looking at each other is not done "out of feare"? Is it possible that fear prevents them from looking at each other? The hopeful myth, that love "controules" one's "sight" (and so might stop a woman from looking at other men), leads only to the poem's poignant, final conditional—"If our two loves be one" (line 20)—a sudden contingency which seems to undermine its own confident assertion of mutuality.

Wondering signals openness, but also wariness; the speaker begins the poem by working hard not to ask outright about his lover's prior loves. That the stanza then moves so quickly to a fantasy about childhood may point less to a kind of self-protective "regression" than, more provocatively, to a way of rearticulating the dynamics of intimacy. It is twoness that troubles the end of "The Good-Morrow," as if the very difference seemingly required to maintain what Stephen Orgel has called "the integrity of the perilously achieved male identity" ends up unraveling the pleasurable sameness captured by the repetition of "we" at the start of the poem.

If "The Good-Morrow" exalts the love of "thou and I" by rendering all else mere childish trifling, I would argue that it also inverts that trajectory, contrasting the intersubjective "weness" of potential space with doubt about the viability of intimacy in an era when conventional narratives about women make "sexuality itself... misogynistic."

The valediction poems tell similar stories of friction. As speakers prepare to depart across complicated thresholds, their ability to trust their lovers' faithfulness seems acutely stressed, and often some expression of the imminence of betrayal seeps into the frame of the poem. Nonetheless, Donne registers alongside the fretful worry an important recognition of women's separateness from the men who leave—an autonomy often indicated by speakers' suspicions that women have already "departed" long before the literal voyage that may occasion a valediction poem.

While Donne may experience separation as a kind of trauma, his fear does not prevent him from acknowledging a woman's independence from his efforts—literal or poetic—to hold onto her. Again and again, the poems locate in women the very sensation of centered wholeness male speakers wish they themselves could experience. And, recurringly, these poems contain nodal points of pleasurable exchange between male and female subjectivity.

In "A Valediction of My Name, In The Window," for instance, the speaker's concerns about what will take place in his absence—about who might take his place—both result from and give rise to a sense of his mistress's power over his emotional and bodily integrity. As the name in the window expands to represent the body of the absent lover, and as the boundaries between this name-body and the face-self of the mistress begin to merge, he comes to depend upon her eyes' ability to hold his body and self intact. Far from becoming dismembered by the gaze of a woman that reminds him of his inadequacy, and farther still from being able to strong-arm her vision, this speaker dismembers himself when he senses he is outside of a look that can restore and reconfigure him to wholeness. The power and importance of her look throughout the poem strongly counters such claims as Barbara Estrin's that "his vision controls." And it strongly evokes the power of the mother's look, in the mirroring exchange of gazes in which the infant arrives at its own subjectivity even as it learns to negotiate the separateness of the mother who "holds."

The "name engrav'd" (line 1) into the window, and by extension the self it represents, is rendered harder than glass, as hard even as the diamond that engraves it. In the first stanza, both the pane of glass and the self embodied there gain value by the lover's "eye," which gives "price enough" to the name-engraved window (line 6). She—the female "other"—does the looking. In Barbara Estrin's reading, this happens only because the speaker "limit[s]—by contraction—the woman's vision." Yet the imagined overlap of name and face within the window requires a specifically dialectical exchange of looks; she sees both herself and him when she looks into the window, as does he, looking back.

The complex visual dynamics of Donne's windowpane anticipate Winnicott's notion of a cohering maternal gaze which establishes a fundamental sense of self-integration even as it introduces the presence, and therefore the separateness, of the other. Winnicott describes mirroring as intersubjective and mutual, because what mother and infant see as they gaze into each other's faces is the simultaneity of their own and the other's desires. In Thomas Ogden's words, "this constitutes an interpersonal dialectic wherein 'I-ness' and otherness create one another and are preserved by the other." To look in this sense is thus once again to blur distinctions of subject and object. "Loves magique... undoe[s]" those "rules" (line 11) that demand separate bodies, separate consciousnesses, separate positions from which to "look"; to undo such rules is to transport oneself psychically, to confound the static linearity of gazer and gazed upon, so that the speaker becomes not "more himself" but rather her"Here you see mee, and I am you" (line 12).

Transparent, the window "confess[es]" (line 8) all that occurs on either side of it—glass will not conceal her actions once he has gone, but neither will it hide his watching. At the same time that glass is looked through, however, it can also superimpose their two "bodies"her face looking, his name being seen. The speaker's manipulation of the frame of the window to capture her gaze and superimpose them leads Estrin to claim that "the `I' binds the woman to him by imposing himself on her." "When the `I' says `I am you,'" Estrin writes, "he means`I want you to think I am you—and I want to make myself think you are I—so that I can be confident that your fidelity and love are what I propose them to beunfoundering.' But his `I am you' really is a way of saying `you are I.' The lady is urged to give up her identity for his." But the fact of being seen by her ("you see mee") leads less to a consolidation of his autonomous existence through appropriation of her (not "I am me") than to a collapse of their positions as separate selves ("I am you").

Rather than imprisoning the woman within its boundaries, the windowpane functions as a play space whose threshold both speaker and lover cross over, moving beyond their real, physical selves and thus also their divided, gendered identities. It is this blending together, I think, far more than any scopic pleasure produced by, or masculine power producing, the exchange of looks, that brings forth a sense of "intirenesse." The name engraved in the glass retains its shape because it manages to achieve the physical permanence that is otherwise elusive, denied by the kind of "departure" this valediction marks (the "plot" of parting provides a context for more psychological forms of separation). Its integrity cannot be "outwash[ed]" by the inundating fluidity of "showers and tempests" (line 15). But a certain kind of "intirenesse" (line 17)—to be so whole as to include each "point" and "dash," all the smallest "accessaries" of one's "name" (lines 13-14)—the speaker finds only within his lover. She contains the "patterne" of him within; he becomes her as she looks upon the overlay of their two "bodies" in the window. Thus while the engraved name may independently claim "firmnesse" and constancy "all times," he tells her, "[shall] finde mee the same" nevertheless he needs her to "better... fulfill" the "intirenesse" that will bridge the space between, salve the hurt of parting.

The speaker's experience of being attached to his mistress is not univocal in "A Valediction of My Name." If in one stanza he appears to celebrate their closeness so fully as to dissolve the distinction between them, in the next he reacts to the demands of that intimacy by losing hold of identity altogether, by breaking down into a variety of bones and body parts barely held together any longer by the name carved into the window. In stanza 3, the woman is filled with him in the way her face is "filled" with his name as she looks into the window, and somehow she brings the potential of his entirety into reality by containing the "patterne" of him within her.

But no sooner is this sense of being housed within her uttered than it defracts into the "ragged bony name" of the following stanza. It is as if the speaker's own expression of being so deeply embedded in the body of his lover (now figured explicitly as mother), so thickly entwined with her identity, overpowers the viability of the name that once withstood "showers and tempests." If, without her, there is nothing to hold him together, if he must depend on her for the blueprint of himself that will "repaire / And recompact" him, and if there is no fundamental "patterne" of him without her, then the leave-taking this poem commemorates must bring forth fears of chaotic unraveling, a dismembering that leaves his body-self "scattered". Simultaneously, though, intimacy is itself a danger precisely because his lover becomes too large—or too constricting. What independent existence can his "self" attain if its very architecture relies, in order to be built, on a pattern she controls?

Thus the "scratch'd name" burgeons into a "deaths head," ominously warning her of "lovers mortalitie". The name that could not be "outwashed" just the stanza before now signifies the awful temporality of a love unguaranteed and unguarantee-able, no longer impervious to the effects of tempests both external/poetic and internal/psychic. The glass that was both charmed and "grav'd" (i.e., made serious? legitimized?) by the name it held now shows not a gracefully "accessorized" name that sloughs off rain but a "ragged bony name," a "ruinous Anatomie" (line 24) that itself seems to "ruin" the glass and the love it is meant to solidify. His fantasy of a window that places them one upon the other seems both to manifest an awareness of and to display back to him the extent to which his identity (signed by his name) is contained within her face, the sign of her personhood.

To be her ("I am you") is specifically to experience himself as within her, to want to be and to feel himself as contained. But this connectedness then evokes fears of being frighteningly loosened and dissolved. No small feat, then, that in the fifth stanza the speaker rebuilds himself. Declaring to his lover that "all my soules bee / Emparadis'd in you" (lines 25-26), he is newly confident that this core of connection between them will refashion again the "house" (line 30) of "Muscle, Sinew, and Veine" (line 29), literally fleshing out the skeletal "rafters" (line 28) that remain following the self-annihilation of the previous lines. In his absence, she will "repaire / And recompact" his "body" within her (lines 31-32).

The casement that contains the name works as a barrier and a passageway between the room within and the world beyond. When he imagined her face reflected in the window surrounding his name, the window became a limit; both her image and the name would look back at her (he would look back at her), inverting and turning inward her act of looking outward. Now, as he imagines her receiving and greeting a new lover, the window once again opens outward—literally, symbolically—to the world the speaker has himself entered, but from which he cannot help looking back, over his shoulder. These shifting attempts to manipulate and respond to space suggest forms of attachment that are liberating and threatening at once. Framing himself in the casement—to be "encased"—provides some firm sense of embodiment. To be embodied within the "face" of his lover is also to feel whole and integrated. But the window that performs the superimposition also measures the limits of security, for there is a world beyond, one that seems excitingly full of possibilities and disturbingly populated by potential rivals for his lover's attentions. What happens to his name, his body and identity, if her face no longer looks through it in the window—if, indeed, the window is thrown aside to allow her clear view to another man's "name"?

More central an image, perhaps, than even the name itself, the window is defined by a transparency evocative of a desire to "see-through," to know but also to be known. Glass can be looked through as well as "look back," like the eyes of a lover. The fantasy of experiencing himself contained seems to allow the speaker to stop a motion that is both inevitable (the poem "bids farewell") and feared.

He is like a child looking in at a doorway to remind himself that the mother is there, reacquainting himself with her by her reassuring glance. Since he cannot look through the window in fact (and there is perhaps a voyeuristic wish here as well), he leaves something behind in fantasy and in the poema body scattered; a ruined anatomy; his bones, sinews, veins, and muscles—in short, himself, barely held together. In this context the phrase "being still with you" (line 29) takes on multiple meanings. The parts of him are still with her, with her as yet and always, waiting to be "bodied" again at his return. But there is also, I think, a wish to be in a kind of motionless overlap with her. This is what makes engraving so important; it grants a motionlessness to the speaker's body (and emotions, devotions?) that is itself an expression of her movement away from him and toward other lovers. Estrin suggests that the speaker, by pinioning the face of his mistress against his name in the window, denies the possibility of an "other" capable of moving out of the frame he has created. But the very engraving of the name in the window suggests how far the poem goes to acknowledge her separateness from him. The engraved name will never move as his real body and her real face so emphatically do. The repetition of "Till my returne," "till I returne" (lines 31, 41) signals visions of the blank space of his absence, which is also her absence from him, conveying both his anxiety about these absences and his determination to return. If there is a subtle warning here, he is also assuring her, and himself as well.

Like the windowpane, the teardrop is one of Donne's most evocative representations of the delicate boundaries that separate as well as connect the self and the external world. Fragile, rarely solitary, of a shape so distinctively recognizable and yet so easily ruptured, the teardrop's thin membrane perfectly imitates the edges between people that Donne is always testing. The teardrop itself, though knowable, meaningful, and extant only on the outside surface of the skin, is also somehow always "looking" inward, because it is so much of the body's interior, always representing some internal state. Winnicott writes that "there comes into existence what might be called a limiting membrane, which to some extent (in health) is equated with the surface of the skin, and has a position between the infant's 'me' and his 'not-me.' Accordingly, it is through images of teardrops that Donne articulates his sense that boundaries can be so easily defocused in ways both pleasurable and threatening. The tear—like an eye or window—behaves like a tiny mirror, reflecting the face of the lover looking toward it; at the same time, the exquisitely delicate surface of a teardrop gives it its paradoxical quality, vulnerable to dissolution, but also, thrillingly open to exchange.

The dynamics of looking become ever more taut on the threshold of parting in "A ValedictionOf Weeping." The implied face-to-face positioning of "Let me powre forth / My tears before thy face" (lines 1-2; he specifies her face, rather than her eyes) suggests that looks are being exchanged, that he looks into her face in search of her whole expression, which he then encapsulates in his tears. His tears, not her eyes, accomplish the reflectinghe is the reflecting surface; he looks at her to capture what she looks like and then integrates that look into himself, reproducing her in his tears while she faces him with her own face and being. It seems vitally important to this Donnean speaker that there is another body there, a face that looks back in a mutually created experience.Produced from within himself but reflective of her, his tears are now of self and other simultaneously; he seems to experience her as something that both originates from within himself and is superimposed onto his tears and then looked at through the commingling medium of his fluidity.

With her image contained in the tears that course across his face, the speaker can "stay" (line 2) and be still; it is as if her face "stays" him from the imminent leave-taking. "Here" (line 2) suggests, therefore, "with you" (and thus not "out there"), but also "over here, where I am, on my side of the boundary between us." With her image imprinted upon them, but shed only in the "absence" of her as one lover faces another, tears measure an irreducible distance between them. At the same time, however, they contain an impression as vital as the seed of her, as if they could give birth to her. Such fullness is intensely pleasurable—he can contain her within himself, if only on the outskirts of his body, within the fragile membrane of the tear. (The metaphor of pregnancy is prefigured in line 3 by "beare"; they are "something worth" [line 4] for containing her in this way.)

But the fantasy of being pregnant with her—of needing, as it were, to give birth to her—implies that he does not already have a connection to her that fulfills him the way her image "fulfills" the tear. Those tears are, as he quickly remembers, produced by "much griefe" (line 7), and while the ostensible meaning is clear (he is leaving), the phrase connotes as well something far more interior, as if "griefe" has been accumulating within him over countless unspoken betrayals. Indeed, the rest of the line—"emblemes of more..." (line 7)—trails off vaguely, as if he cannot find adequate words with which to articulate the many reasons for these tears. His own descriptive metaphors work to belie what might seem important here to disguisethe progression from tears coined by her image to tears "pregnant" (line 6) with the "seed" of her leads him to the paradox of "fruits" (line 7), a word which carries suggestions of transgression and delight at once, as if the very objects by which he tries to hold her to him (in place?)

become symbols of the kind of act that could breach that connection. The tears perform the transgressiveness, in fact, by "fall[ing]" (line 8) as he cries them.

The parts of him that successfully "contain" her—those tears—are always already on the move away from him as soon as they achieve shape and meaning outside of his eyes (he, his body and "self," can never really hold her as his tears do). Tears always fall; they can never go back in, never return to connect with the body that forms them. It is this incessant "falling" that triggers the shift in tone and emotion in the second part of the first stanza. It is as if his own image of pregnant tears, seeming to grant a wonderful wholeness, requires that he track back to the dangerous sexuality of which pregnancy is a literal fruit and which causes even further pregnant tears. The tears that "bore" (line 8) her detach from his eyes and give birth to a "fallen" her. His desire, and attempt, to retain a sense of her in his tears ends up "falling," measuring as it does so how little he can ensure that she will not "fall" after he departs (or, perhaps more acutely, even prior to this moment). Nor can he guarantee in her the stasis that is so important to him; as if to counter his own assurance that "I stay here", he seems to accuse her, "thou falst".

Nevertheless, the tear maintains its transformative powers, as the speaker redoubles his efforts to locate spaces in which their two subjectivities can experience a pleasurable melding. As the empty "round ball" (line 11) devoid of meaning becomes an identifiable, navigable "All" with maps of the world pasted upon it (line 14), so the value of a tear increases with her reflection "worn" within it; the "impression" (line 16) of her face makes the tear an all, the way she—if she could also be contained within him—might grant him the completeness of a world. It is as if she covers him like the overlain "copies" (line 11) of the continents and fills him from within like tears "pregnant of" (line 6) her, until the space they share "overflow[s]" (line 17) with tiny crystalline worlds of which both have been the creators—she with her face and looks and presence, he as the "workeman" (line 11) who cries the englobing tears. And while it seems that she too has begun to cry—"Till thy teares mixt with mine doe overflow / This world, by water sent from thee, my heaven dissolved so" (lines 17-18)—"thy teares" may also refer, in a way that underscores the spatial and psychic entanglements the poem depicts, to his own tears, which "belong" to her because her face gives them meaning and worth, because it is her relation to the speaker that elicits them, and, too, because they wet her face as he weeps. In the dissolution of tears, then, what is "hers" becomes indistinguishable from what is "his."

The penetrability of the teardrop further demonstrates the exciting experience of exceeding the limits of one's boundaries. When lovers cry together, their tears intermingle, blurring distinctions by combining the positions of mourned-mourner, performer-spectator, self-other. The act of crying itself here repeats the reorientation of the gaze enacted by "A Valediction of My Name"initially, it is the man's tears that are "pregnant" and pour forth uncontrollably, the man who is uncontained, flowing, fluid, while the woman watches. The many distortions of space (the proportions of the cosmos are stretched from micro to macrocosmic, with teardrops reflecting faces and encapsulating worlds and a woman expanding to become the moon) exaggerates the poem's willingness to ignore outline and limitation, its eagerness to experience a comfortable at-one-ness. While it seems clear that, as Mark Breitenberg points out, water imagery symbolizes a constellation of anxieties in early modern texts—from maternal engulfment to the frightening fluidity of a humoural body to the real danger of shipwreck—Donne's use of the tear also unthinks anxiety, measuring a sensitivity to edges and to various ways of crossing or even dispensing entirely with boundaries—of the body, while crying; of tears, which dissolve; of the self, in love with another. Of course, these suggestions are not intended to supersede entirely the poem's culminating tone of despair. "More than Moone" (line 19), the woman here is an omnipotent woman who can house or fragment the body of her lover, look back in a mutual gaze, or look away with murderous unconcern. The woman who is more commands his very life; to be close to her is to experience his self as dangerously loosened, so unpredictable is her "spheare". She can, and might, "draw up seas" to drown him. And the imagined mourning seems to record what is coursing beneath this poemthat once he is gone, she is free ("dissolved"? [line 18]) to pursue other lovers. Indeed, his pleas to her to "forbeare / To teach the sea, what it may doe too soone", to "Let not the winde / Example finde" (lines 23-24), disclose the worry that sadness and separation may happen "too soone" (which sounds like "soon enough" and suggests an inevitability); that whatever actual danger exists in the literal plot of the poem is outweighed by the increase in harm she could cause (she sets an "example" that is more than the moon, the sea, and the wind together). Even the personified "winde"—already perceived as a malevolent force that "purposeth" to do him some degree of "harme" might be impelled toward "more harme" by her example.

So much danger may be offset by the possibility of them "holding" each other and of being held in a space that staves off unstoppable floods. The intermingling of breaths—her body contains his, his body her breath—works to control their lives and deaths. He wants them to "hold" each others' breaths by not sighing, and so maintain a feeling of keeping-in, of repletion and completion. But of course they cannot hold their breaths forever, and the inevitable breathing out (which he seems to watch and wait for in an agony of anticipation) is thus an unfathomable cruelty that "hastes the others death". Yet the very imagery that conveys grief and doubt in "A Valediction of Weeping" serves also to modify, on a perhaps more subterranean level, the poem's tendency toward such expressions. Tears, coins, fruit, globes, maps, tides, sighs—each of these suggests overlap and exchange within liminal spaces that allow the speaker to play with the indeterminacy of selfhood and the undulating limits of relationality.

"A Valediction Forbidding Mourning," in a similar way, complicates our sense of which subject position (self-other, male-female, traveller-left-behind) the speaker identifies with most emphatically. The opening analogy between parting lovers and dying men who "passe mildly away" and "whisper to their soules, to goe" (lines 1-2) makes the separation as natural—and the reunion as inevitable—as that of "virtuous" (line 1) bodies and souls. It may be the certitude of rejoining that renders death a mild passing (so subtle is this parting, in fact, that it is nearly imperceptible to others; as Geoffrey Hartman points out, "the evidence of life [hangs] on a word, on less than a word, on a vocal inflection or quantity, the difference between `now' and `no'"); on the other hand, the stanza confuses one's sense of which—body or soul—is figured as leaving. It is as if they both "leave"the one "passe [s]," the other is whispered at "to goe," they move away from each other as if simultaneously, and neither "stays."

Saying good-bye, the speaker suggests, might be just as internal an event as this parting of body and breath—so private, others can't perceive it; so "mild," it feels less like a wrenching breakage than like melting. Let us part, he seems to say, as if only gradually dissolving, separating out of oneness and into twoness in a way that is simultaneously a melding; and let us do this so quietly that no one else will notice. If the parting of body and soul will look like just one more exhalation of breath, so their parting should feel like just another normal parting.

Despite the speaker's confirmation that it is he who physically leaves ("I must goe" [line 22]), the poem expresses a familiar ambiguitynotice that it is the breath that leaves, not the men who hold the breath; and the soul that goes, not the male body that houses the soul. And if the instruction to "make no noise" (line 5) stems from a wish to protect "our joyes" from the misunderstanding of others, it also serves to soften the distress of separation, to allow each individual to "melt" (line 5). Such blending together seems delicious, rather than inundating. Mere earthly lovers, dependent on the body with its simple sensuality and reliance on the senses, cannot tolerate physical absence. But a love that can withstand "motion" is one independent of physical connection. Not having to rely on sight, touch, even the sound of each other's voices, their love is of the spheres, "innocent" (line 12) of the requirement of constant contact. So "refin'd" (line 17) is that love, they are made pure by it—made so subtle and precise, that they cannot even define what it is that they experience together, though they nonetheless escape the dull interpretation already belittled in the third stanza.

The speaker makes explicit the terms of so fine a fitto withstand physical separation, lovers must have internalized each other as sustaining imagos, carried within and related to as vividly as their physical selves. To be "inter-assured of the mind" (line 19) is to experience reciprocity and understanding as guaranteed—and "inter-assured" seems just the right phrase, since it conveys the mutuality and exchange that are so vital, along with the sense of being reassured of a continued affection. Separation means destruction to an infant; it feels annihilating, as if both object and self might never return. But when (or more specifically here, because) there is such psychical connection, the lovers' physical disconnection feels neither obliterating nor even disruptive of love itselfthey can "care less" (line 20) about the absence of lips, eyes, and hands. In turn, the speaker can be "careless" about togethernesshe seems jaunty, playful, and confident.

Not to know "what [love] is" (line 18)—to be beyond (even prior to) explanations and definitions that would require observation of oneself and consideration of the self's interaction with another—suggests a doubled state of simultaneous union and exchange in which conceptions of "twoness" have no meaning. The "inter-assurance" of their minds creates an experience of oneness that, far from presupposing knowledge and experience of dualities, smudges all delimiting outline between their separate selves. So their "two souls therefore,... are one" (line 21) and, equally paradoxically, the space that keeps them apart is but a continuation of themselves and thus of their bond, just as the ends of a sheet of gold hammered to thinness stand apart, yet uninterruptedly attached:

Our two soules therefore, which are one,
Though I must goe, endure not yet
A breach, but an expansion,
Like gold to ayery thinnesse beate. (Lines 21-24)

This last image of "gold to ayery thinnesse beate" is an index of the speaker's willingness to tolerate distance, and it sounds less like a buttressing of a vulnerable self (increasing its sense of identity, in effect, by adding her identity) than like a liberating continuum of connectedness in which confident selves expand toward the other and lose rigid definition in that intimacy. Whatever disappointment might be felt by the loss, even abandonment, that parting entails is assuaged by the ability to remember good feelings and to remain "in contact," as it were, intrapsychically.

The compass metaphor complicates this fantasy, if only because the physical reality of the device necessitates that the two souls previously figured as one are suddenly returned to a condition of divided twoness. Like one leg of a compass joined to the other, each lover's motion is now contingent upon the others. She is "the fixt foot," which "makes no show / To move, but doth, if the other doe" (lines 27-28); he, "the other," which "far doth rome" (line 30). She is "the centre" (line 29), still and sure, that marks the home base of the circle circumscribed around her by the speaker's roaming. This would seem to substantiate some critics' belief that the compass is used here as an emblem of constancy and that the speaker means to express his belief in (or anxious wish for) his lover's fidelity. But the image also, once more, works to destabilize what the solidity of the compass would seem concerned to assure. That the "fixt foot" "makes no show" to move implies that it might at any moment, unpredictably, or perhaps that she moves internally, imperceptibly, emotionally—in short, in some way that cannot be measured by outward show. Her immobility is hardly guaranteed. The apparent readiness to follow after the "the other" foot, then, along with the joint that holds the two legs of the compass together, are both undone by doubts only the grammar works to evidence.

The speaker allows that "though [the fixt foot] in the centre sit / Yet when the other far doth rome, / It leanes, and hearkens after it, / And growes erect" (lines 29-32). In a poem that has already subverted its own fiction through implications that it is the female other that "goe[s]" (line 22), and in which issues of selfhood and subjectivity are very much at play, the phrase "the other" seems suddenly to reverse the positions man and woman occupy in the terms of the compass analogy. Imagistically, "the other" defines the roaming man, but rhetorically it hints, once again, that the "self" of this poem—its male speaker—is aware of the potential roaming of his mistress. At the same time, he fashions himself as a wandering, transgress other in terms of a stable "centre" meant to establish origin and to contain his motion around her.

Donne maximizes such "misidentifications" by relying on ambiguous pronounsin four lines, three instances of "it" and one of "that," detached from their referents, inhibit firm assignment of self and object (indeed, at line 31, "it" applies both to the man and to the woman). Furthermore, the fixed foot moves (already a paradox) not simply in a barely measurable circle controlled by the movement of "the other"; it actually "hearkens after" the other and "growes erect, as that comes home."

In the "hardly gendered bodies" of the seventeenth century, sexual arousal was not imagined in clearly differentiated terms; a woman's genitals were thought to "swell" and her "seed" to be ejaculated much like a man's. Thus the "firmness" of the centre foot of the compass, its excitement at the return of the wandering leg, may emphasize the speaker's need to ensure his lover's continued desire for him. At the same time, however (and granting that the fixed leg of a widened compass would, literally, straighten as the other moved inward), the overtly masculine image reverses conventional expectations about constancy, furthering the hint that it is the man who perceives himself as stationary. As she roams in a circle around him—a circle that will be narrowed only by her moving toward him—he wonders after her and grows erect at her return.

"Such," then, "wilt thou be to mee, who must / Like th'other foot, obliquely runne" (lines 34-35). "Such" here sets up a comparison whose elements are already deeply conflicted and unclear. On the surface, the word recovers the terms of the analogy from whatever may have problematized them in the previous stanza, and seems to confirm that she will be the one to lean and hearken after him. The syntactical progression of these lines, however, pulls out of shape what the simile at first tries to render. "Such" seems to work backward to the immediately preceding phrase—as if to say, "you will be to me `as [the one] that comes home'"; to the degree that the penultimate stanza has already confused one's sense of who stays, who leaves to roam, such a succession reinforces the subtexthe experiences himself as left behind by her.

Thus "who" (in "Such wilt thou be to mee, who must... obliquely runne") also seems detached, applicable to either of them grammatically as well as thematically. And which of them is "like th'other foot"? Must she, too, run? Do they both move, both grow erect at the prospect of reunion? Tellingly, the trope that is meant to show the two lovers in relation to each other in fact doubles them at firstthey are "twin compasses" (line 26), identical.

The effect of so much layering of language and subjectivity (which may also be its point) is to call radically into question both the nature of the mourning the poem seems to prohibit as well as the identity of the individuals involved. The poem piles up images of attachment and motion, only to deny the fixity of meaning those very images seem to strive so much to assure. In the highly determined, seemingly stabilized space inside of which the poem comes to a close—the circle drawn by the compass in which, the speaker says, "Thy firmness... makes me end, where I begunne" (line 36)—a kaleidoscopic interplay of position and movement threatens to bulge the outline of that perfect circularity (the course of "th'other foot" is "oblique"; the poem ends by being "begunne").

Thus the other must be invested with "firmnes" to make things "just," to make him stop "running." She must stand firm, straighten up, perhaps, even get excited for him, in order for him to return. He depends on that reliable durability to counter his own ambivalent roaming, to reassure him that his own wanderings are "just," right, and safe, and to bring him around again to himself. And yet, simultaneously, she is the one moving, circling, and wandering. The poem's figurative language allows two stories to be told at once.

I will conclude with a brief reading of "The Sunne Rising" as one of Donne's most singular poetic acts of playing with space. Thomas Docherty writes of the poem that the "fundamental point at issue is that the space is relativized and made mutable." The world beyond the bed that contains the intertwined lovers is controlled by the speaker, first by a gesture of audacious dismissal, then by an act of encompassing inclusion. The window through which the voyeuristic sun intrudes is both barrier and passageway between two realms (as in "A Valediction of My Name"); the pair luxuriates in a loving "wee"-ness (line 25)—reinforced by the repetitions of "us" (lines 3, 23, 28), of "bed" (lines 20, 30), of "warme" (line 28), of "all" (lines 20, 21, 24)—that is distinguished from the particulated world of "boyes," "ants," and "the rags of time" (lines 6, 8, 10).

It is just this sense of a union so solid as to be condensed into the solemnity of "Nothing else is" (line 22), that infuses the speaker with an illusion of magical control over the objects of the world. Secure in his bond with his lover/other, the speaker can make the "out-there" accord with his own expectations and desires—he can define not only the movement and proportion of the world (e.g., "the King will ride" [line 7], and "both the' India's of spice and Myne... lie here with mee" [lines 17-18]), but also the very configuration of the cosmos as well ("This bed thy centre is, these walls, thy spheare" [line 30]). The bed and then the room the lovers inhabit in "The Sunne Rising" are first isolated from the bother of kings and suns and "ants," then expand to encompass all of that, to become the whole world. In Robert Wiltenburg's words, "The Sunne Rising" strikes us with its "imperative nood, gigantic, engorged with the physical and emotional immediacy and sufficiency of its experience of love," an experience through which the self discovers "the power not only to shape itself... but to shape the world to itself."

But there is something else at work in the poem, too, other than a childlike belief in magical omnipotence. Rather than representing separation, with disturbing implications of unknowability and loneliness, the window in "The Sunne Rising" takes on the intermediate nature of potential space, allowing the speaker imaginatively, and pleasurably, to push away ("goe chide," "goe," "tell" [lines 5-8], "call," "looke" [line 16]) or pull in ("shine here to us" [line 29]) what lies beyond. The speaker mediates his perception of what lies beyond the threshold of the window through his trust in the depth and durability of his relatedness to his lover.

The intensity of the poem's articulation of potential space (neither "all-me" nor objects beyond the self's control) renders the "contract[ion]" (line 26) of the final stanza more an experience of "holding"—in which "wee" are "happy" (line 25) and "warme" (line 28) and the "centre" of "every where" (line 29)—than the oppressive space of "The Good-Morrow's "one little roome." In that in-between area, the speaker articulates not so much a fantasy of self-centered omnipotence as an absenting of self in deference to his mistress. Thus the line that critics so frequently seize upon as proof of Donne's colonizing stance toward women might be more provocatively read as a profound acknowledgment of one woman's utter completenessless a strident "she is all the states, and I am all the princes" than a loving She is all states and all princes. Aye.

The cumulative evidence of the readings I have presented here suggests that the genderedness of Donne's poetic imagination is not as emphatically, certainly not as consistently, "masculine," or masculinity, as has so often been claimed. In a recent study of Donne's "articulations of the feminine," H. L. Meakin juxtaposes "Donne's attempts to 'emprison' the various figures of the feminine" with "the 'excess' which is woman beyond the margins of patriarchal discourse." In the threshold spaces mapped out by images of liminality, however, it is just this sort of hierarchical schema that Donne reconfigures, repositioning male self and female other in ways that elude stock oppositions of "centre" and "margin." If certain poems in Songs and Sonnets point up the limitations of identifying Donne as consistently evacuating or appropriative of women, so, too, do they suggest that

Donne's recognition of women extends beyond simple tributes paid from uncomplicatedly conventional, gendered positions.

While there can be no intermediate space without eventual separation, no recognition of separate subjectivity without acknowledging the difference-between, the question of what Donne does with difference remains an intricate one. The very breadth and richness of recent Donne scholarship points to the impossibility of confining Donne to a unified style of relating to female others (there may be no poet so capable of rhetorical escape as Donne), yet I would argue that it is equally untenable to maintain that Donne's identifications with women serve unequivocally, or univocally, to suppress them and to reassert the primacy of his own masculine identity.

Through the conceptual metaphors of play and liminal space, Donne liberates his speakers from anxieties about gender by exploiting the very notions that tend to produce anxiety in the first place, maximizing rather than reductively denying the ambiguity of gendered identity. In the kinds of moments explored in this article, acts of identification become ways of questioning—transgressing—the very terms of being male, being a self, and loving each other.

Bibliography

John Carey, John Donne: Life, Mind and Art, (London 1981)

A. L. Clements John Donne's Poetry (New York and London, 1966)

Stevie Davies, John Donne (Northcote House, Plymouth, 1994)

T. S. Eliot, "The Metaphysical Poets", Selected Essays, (London 1969)

G. Hammond The Metaphysical Poets: A Casebook, (London 1986)

Sir Geoffrey Keynes, Bibliography of Donne, (Cambridge, 1958)

George Klawitter, The Enigmatic Narrator: The Voicing of Same-Sex Love in the Poetry of John Donne (Peter Lang, 1994)

Arthur F. Marotti, John Donne, Coterie Poet, (Madison: University of Wisconson Press, 1986)

H. L. Meakin, John Donne's Articulations of the Feminine, (Oxford, 1999)

Joe Nutt, John Donne: The Poems, (New York and London 1999)

E.M. Simpson, A Study of the Prose Works of John Donne, (Oxford, 1962)

C. L. Summers and *T. L. Pebworth* (eds.) The Eagle and the Dove: Reassessing John Donne (Columbia: University of Missouri Press, 1986)

John Stachniewski, The Persecutory Imagination, (Oxford, 1991)

James Winny, A Preface to Donne (New York, 1981)

Bald, *R. C. John Donne*: A Life., Oxford, 1970

Le Comte, Edward. Grace to a Witty Sinner: A Life of Donne, (Walker, 1965)

Stubbs, John. Donne: The Reformed Soul, Viking, 2006. ISBN 0670915106

Warnke, Frank J. John Donne, (U of Mass., Amherst 1987)

Wilson, F. P. (July 1927). "Notes on the Early Life of John Donne". The Review of English Studies 3 : 272–279.